Corporate Governance in Tanzania

Increasingly the importance of corporate governance for economic development in developing economies like Tanzania is indisputable. This book explores the effectiveness of corporate governance in Tanzania and asks how it can be further developed and improved so as to make a difference in the contribution of state-owned enterprises to the economy. The book tries as fairly as possible to probe further into effective corporate governance, using cases of public entities, highlighting shortfalls in their governance and the consequent multiplier effects on socio-economic life. On the other hand, the book also aims to present examples of good governance in multi-layered ways, to show that there is room for creativity and innovation in applying principles of good corporate governance.

Recognising that context is crucial, the book starts by assessing Tanzania's socio-historical and economic context, and gauging various applicable metrics. Using historical and theoretical lenses, including the ethics-accountability relationship, the author aims to improve our understanding of corporate failures and consequent waste in Tanzania. Explaining failures in governance is far from straightforward, as by definition they operate beyond rules and regulations, systems and processes, yet the author draws from decades of local experience and expertise in order to assess the real situation on the ground.

The Tanzania case will be of considerable interest to researchers looking at questions of corporate governance and economic development both within the country itself, and across Africa.

Peter C. Mhando is an Associate Teaching Professor in the Risk Management Department at Smeal College of Business, The Pennsylvania State University, USA. An economics graduate of the University of Dar es Salaam, he received his Masters in Economics and Finance from Binghamton University and earned a PhD from Penn State University. Peter is a native of Tanzania, where he is also a partner at the Centre for Business Excellence (CfBE) and INTERFINi Consultants. He is an accomplished economics, finance and management professional with over 25 years of international consulting experience.

Routledge Studies in African Development

National Liberation Movements as Government in Africa
Edited by Redie Bereketeab

Hunger and Poverty in South Africa
The Hidden Faces of Food Insecurity
Jacqueline Hanoman

Extractive Industries and Changing State Dynamics in Africa
Beyond the Resource Curse
Edited by Jon Schubert, Ulf Engel and Elísio Macamo

Peacebuilding in Contemporary Africa
In Search of Alternative Strategies
Edited by Kenneth Omeje

The Challenge of Governance in South Sudan
Corruption, Peacebuilding, and Foreign Intervention
Edited by Steven C. Roach and Derrick K. Hudson

African Peacekeeping Training Centres
Socialisation as a Tool for Peace?
Anne Flaspöler

Corporate Governance in Tanzania
Ethics and Accountability at the Crossroads
Peter C. Mhando

Economic Dualism in Zimbabwe
From Colonial Rhodesia to Post-Independence
Daniel B. Ndlela

For more information about this series, please visit: www.routledge.com/Contemporary-Geographies-of-Leisure-Tourism-and-Mobility/book-series/SE0522

Corporate Governance in Tanzania

Ethics and Accountability at the Crossroads

Peter C. Mhando

LONDON AND NEW YORK

First published 2019
by Routledge
4 Park Square, Milton Park, Abingdon, Oxon OX14 4RN
605 Third Avenue, New York, NY 10017

First issued in paperback 2023

Routledge is an imprint of the Taylor & Francis Group, an informa business

© 2019 Peter C. Mhando

The right of Peter C. Mhando to be identified as author of this work has been asserted by him in accordance with sections 77 and 78 of the Copyright, Designs and Patents Act 1988.

All rights reserved. No part of this book may be reprinted or reproduced or utilised in any form or by any electronic, mechanical, or other means, now known or hereafter invented, including photocopying and recording, or in any information storage or retrieval system, without permission in writing from the publishers.

Trademark notice: Product or corporate names may be trademarks or registered trademarks, and are used only for identification and explanation without intent to infringe.

British Library Cataloguing-in-Publication Data
A catalogue record for this book is available from the British Library

Library of Congress Cataloging-in-Publication Data
Names: Mhando, Peter C., author.
Title: Corporate governance in Tanzania : ethics and accountability at the crossroads / Peter C. Mhando.
Description: Abingdon, Oxon ; New York, NY : Routledge, 2019. | Series: Routledge studies in African development | Includes index.
Identifiers: LCCN 2018060192 | ISBN 9780367150853 (hardback) | ISBN 9780429054907 (ebook)
Subjects: LCSH: Corporate governance—Tanzania. | Corporations—Moral and ethical aspects—Tanzania.
Classification: LCC HD2921.3 .M43 2019 | DDC 658.4009678—dc23
LC record available at https://lccn.loc.gov/2018060192

ISBN: 978-1-03-257066-2 (pbk)
ISBN: 978-0-367-15085-3 (hbk)
ISBN: 978-0-429-05490-7 (ebk)

DOI: 10.4324/9780429054907

Typeset in Times New Roman
by Apex CoVantage, LLC

Publisher's Note
The publisher has gone to great lengths to ensure the quality of this reprint but points out that some imperfections in the original copies may be apparent.

Contents

List of tables		vi
Acknowledgements		vii
List of abbreviations and acronyms		ix
	Introduction	1
1	Background of the corporate environment in Tanzania	6
2	Ethics, accountability and governance	15
3	The public sector code of ethics	30
4	Corporate evolution and challenges	44
5	Governance failure and corporate waste cases analysis	66
6	Reflections and recommendations	122
	Index	144

Tables

2.1	The seven principles of public life	22
5.1	Chronology of events – ATCL aircraft lease	70
5.2	ATCL human capital	71
5.3	Challenges facing TPA	107
5.4	National benchmark vs TPA dar performance	109

Acknowledgements

The idea for this book came during one of the regular '*chai*' times at the café called A Tea Shop in Dar es Salaam city centre, with a great friend, Mr. Andulile Mwakalyelye. From that day forward, the book was conceived to link corporate governance to sustained development, and eventually climaxed to a discussion of public corporate resource waste in Tanzania, from a governance perspective. I however, am not taking all the credit. This book could not have come to fruition without the intellectual provocation, hard work and insistence from several friends and professional associates, over and above the never-ending debates between me and Andulile, a seasoned governance expert.

Andulile like me, is from the school of thought which believes that corporate governance is an important and developing field of study, especially in developing economies. That being the case, the analysis of the relationship between ethics and accountability and how that relationship is of relevance to an economy in transition such as Tanzania, remains crucial. How the two elements in corporate governance relate to each other in an economy that is in transition is of importance to understanding public policy in general. Governance is at the heart of managing corporate risk.

To several other colleagues and friends, thank you for accepting to not only assist in a great endeavour, but also giving it your all. I appreciate the inspiration that came from hordes of professionals across the board. Discussions with former and current corporate directors and board members, as well as the many managers, and management teams provided the motivation an insight into, not only the perception of governance, but also how governance and accountability in general have fared across sectors in corporate Tanzania.

Amongst professional organizations, many thanks to the National Audit Office (NAOT), Office of the Controller and Auditor General, whose expert comprehensive reports I utilized extensively, and have been especially helpful in providing the yardstick for the cases used in this book.

Thanks to the Dean and the Risk Management Department, Smeal College of Business as well as the Africana Research Center at Penn State University. They provided additional support that enabled me to travel to and interact with key people in Tanzania for the purpose, as well as additional time off to work on the manuscript.

The Center for Business Excellence (CfBE) and INTERFINi Consultants, my home bases in Tanzania provided the space, administrative support and conducive operational backbone. Thank you so much.

Calvary Baptist Church, my home church community in State College, Pennsylvania. Thank you for the prayers.

I am lucky to have had three members of my immediate family serve, and they shared their respective rich experiences as public parastatals' heads in corporate Tanzania. To them all, I say thank you. My family endured some of the loneliest times, as I often tuned them out to concentrate on the manuscript. To my better half Lindah and my children, I promise that I will do my best to make up to each of you.

While the principles of good governance may be the same for all corporate bodies, there is great scope for creativity and innovation in applying such principles to the specific circumstances facing individual institutions. In this book, I have tried to be as fair as possible in questioning issues pertaining to ethics and accountability. I provoke corporate and other leaders to probe further into effective corporate governance for the Tanzania envisaged to be built. In the final analysis, the question of good corporate governance is often tangled with resource management. The challenge is to thus find the path and solutions that fit the circumstances. Much as I have used public entities to bring forth the arguments by looking back to be able to move forward, shortfalls in governance touch all aspects of the Tanzanian corporate life; the private sector is not spared.

In these cynical times flooded with constant reminders of mistakes made, it is important to remember that there is still room for greatness. It is my hope that this small contribution of mine will spur more thought-provoking discussions about different aspects of good governance, for the better. I sincerely believe that leaders enable change, for they make decisions big and small that are catalysts for necessary and needed transformations. It is time we groom such leaders.

To me, writing this book was a labour of love. It is something I dreamt about for quite sometime – since my college days and onward into my professional life – as a token contribution to my fatherland. None of the abovementioned people and institutions bear any responsibility for the assumptions, errors, exaggerations, incendiary statements and at times passionate arguments expressed throughout the book. I alone am responsible.

Peter Mhando
State College, Pennsylvania

Abbreviations and acronyms

ARMS	Airtime (Automated) Revenue Monitoring Solution
ATCL	Air Tanzania Corporation Limited
ATIP	Accountability, Transparency and Integrity Programme
BoT	Bank of Tanzania
CAG	Controller and Auditor General
CHRAGG	Commission for Human Rights and Good Governance
CMSA	Capital Markets and Securities Authority
CSO	Civil Society Organizations
CSR	Corporate Social Responsibility
EPP	Emergency Power Projects
EWURA	Energy and Water Regulatory Authority
GDP	Gross Domestic Product
GNP	Gross National Product
IATA	International Air Transport Association
ICSID	International Center for Settlement of Investment Disputes
IOSA	IATA Operational Safety Audit
IPP	Independent Power Producer
IPTL	Independent Power Tanzania Limited
KPI	Key Performance Indicators
NACSAP	National Anti-Corruption Strategy Action Plan
NDC	National Development Corporation (NDC)
NFGG	National Framework on Good Governance
NGO	Non-Governmental Organization
OECD	Organization for Economic Cooperation and Development
OGP	Open Government Partnership
PCCB	Prevention and Combating of Corruption Bureau
PLCE	Public Leadership Code of Ethics
PMP	Ports Master Plan
POAC	Parliamentary Parastatal Organisation Accounts Committee
PPA	Power Purchase Agreement
PPRA	Public Procurement Regulatory Authority
PSRP	Parastatal Sector Reform Programme
SCOPO	Standing Committee on Parastatal Organisations

SOE	State-Owned Enterprises
SUMATRA	Surface and Marine Transport Regulatory Authority
TANESCO	Tanzania Electric Supply Company
TCRA	Tanzania Communications Regulatory Authority
TICTS	Tanzania International Container Terminal Services
TILT	Tanzania Institute of Leather Technology
TLAI	Tanzania Leather Associated Industry
TPA	Tanzania Ports Authority
TRA	Tanzania Revenue Authority
TTMS	Telecommunication Traffic Monitoring System
UNIDO	United Nations Industrial Development Organization
URT	United Republic of Tanzania
USD	United State Dollar
WMA	Weights and Measures Agency

Introduction

Tanzania's socio-economic history and development are some of the significant factors that determine the level of and the importance that highlight as well as give credibility to the case for good governance. Indeed, via the Public Leadership Code of Ethics, a case had long been made within Tanzania's constitutional framework for clear ethical standards and conduct (Kiwale, 2007). In addition to the code of ethics, numerous reform programmes have been put in place to strengthen public accountability and governance. Ethics, "a system of moral principles or rules of behavior, or moral principles that influence a person's behavior," according to the *Oxford Advanced Learner's Dictionary*, can thus be seen as a set of shared societal values that are experienced individually.

The long history of corporate governance, ethics and accountability in Tanzania cannot be retold without looking into numerous pertinent factors. First and foremost is the spirit of *Ujamaa*, i.e. the Arusha Declaration (and its subsequent demise); governance and economic management, i.e. the apparent collapse of corporate ethics and the economic impact; the role of the Parastatal sector (and entrepreneurial ethics); and new expectations in business ethics, i.e. renewed efforts at corporate accountability.

It has long been established that there is an unmistakable correlation between ethics and accountability. It is this relationship that good governance relies upon over and above the strength of any set of rules and regulations laid down, as well as such issues enshrined in societal norms (Arjoon, 2005). Weak accountability may be traced back to ill-defined ethical standards. As such, the importance of ethics as the cornerstone of accountability deems necessary clear ethical standards. The standards are required not only to gauge good governance, but also as a critical metric in maintaining and enhancing public confidence (Carlos, Guerrero, & Lera, 2014).

The problem statement

Increasingly, the importance of corporate governance for economic development in Tanzania is recognized by policymakers and regulators alike. A reflection of this recognition can be seen, for instance, in the ensued transfer of corporations from state to private ownership following economic liberalization. In a market economy, private shareholding is considered more effective in controlling management than is government shareholding under a centralized system (Bagachwa et al., 1992), which Tanzania had for a long time. The expectation is in the efficient allocation of the society's meagre resources (URT, 2001). The introduction, by the Steering Committee on Corporate Governance in Tanzania, of guidelines for corporate governance for Tanzania and the development and recommendation of principles for effective corporate governance by the Capital Markets and Securities Authority (CMSA) are further indications that corporate governance has received increased attention. Policymakers and regulators view the adoption of the recommended practices as an important step in influencing the behaviour of managers and directors regarding effective discharge of their respective roles (Kiwale, 2007).

The transmission of effective governance values requires providing a basis for decision-making and implementing appropriate steps (OECD, 2014a). It is unfortunate that the understanding of the determinants of effective corporate governance in Tanzania is still limited.

Kiure, among others, ascertained that corporate governance practices do influence investment decisions (Kiure, 2002), and finding out the effectiveness of these practices in a Tanzanian context is certainly important as the country strives to become a middle-income economy. Given the relevance of this issue for business development, the central question being addressed is, *What are the determinants of effective corporate governance in Tanzania?*

The central question thus reflects two aspects: the need to understand the context of Tanzania and the prevailing corporate governance practices, and the functional objectives of corporate governance within the relevant perspective. Indeed, in addressing the central question, the effectiveness of corporate governance is assessed in relation to its functional objective in the Tanzanian socio-historical and economic context, using the public corporation (state-owned enterprises) to gauge various applicable metrics.

Key questions

To address the central question, several sub-questions have been brought forth:

1. What is the current situation with respect to the effectiveness of corporate governance in Tanzania?
2. What are the factors crucial for assessing and determining the effectiveness of corporate governance in Tanzania?
3. What are the relevant issues for further development of corporate governance in Tanzania?

Firstly, this book is an exploration of the historic and economic context to obtain insights into and be current in the subject at hand, i.e. corporate governance in Tanzania. The review will provide the springboard to reconnoitre policies, practices and challenges in corporate governance. Secondly, with respect to the issue of the effectiveness of corporate governance in Tanzania, this volume seeks to share experiences as evidenced by governance failure and corporate waste emanating from corporate governance practices in Tanzania; to learn from the rich experience and be more informed moving forward. If anything, it was expected that at the time of establishing the public body corporate in Tanzania, as Keynes argued, what was important for the government to do were not things that individuals were already doing and do them a little better or a little worse, but to do those things which were not done at all (Keynes, 1926).

By so doing, this volume would be able to raise issues that need to be addressed to further improve governance practices in Tanzania and to advance the debate by highlighting issues of significance with respect to the development of corporate governance in Tanzania, and the developing world in general. How successful or otherwise corporate governance has been is at the core of this effort.

Relevance

In this introduction, we strived to view corporate governance failures in Tanzania through historical and related theoretical lenses. In the ensuing chapters, we follow up with an elaborate discussion of related items in the context of Tanzania, including ethics-accountability relationship; a historical background to the code of ethics and Tanzania's ethics and economic blueprint, the Arusha Declaration; the corporate setting elucidating ethics and accountability; case studies evidencing corporate governance failures; and finally recommendations for the way forward. We cannot agree more with management guru Peter Drucker's argument that "It can be said without too much oversimplification that there are no 'underdeveloped countries.' There are only 'undermanaged ones' . . . this means management *and therefore governance* is the prime mover and that development is a consequence" (Drucker & Nakamuchi, 1997, emphasis added).

Structure of the book

Chapter 1 provides the background to the work. It addresses the rise of corporate governance via the corporate environment in Tanzania between 1967 and 2015. It also highlights the early as well as recent experiences of corporate governance and addresses the central question via discussions of ethics and corporate responsibility, corporate failures as well as governance and economic management.

Chapter 2 addresses ethics, accountability and governance via an analysis of the context in which companies operate in Tanzania. Here, the theoretical basis of ethics and accountability as well as the implications for corporate governance are highlighted. Public sector governance in the context of Tanzania is discussed and the chapter ends by revealing the big picture.

Chapter 3 addresses the public sector code of ethics, given its prominence, and thus acknowledging the importance of governance as enshrined in the constitution. That beginning provides the basis to discuss the evolution of the code of ethics and its applicability throughout history. The detours via critical incidents such as the Arusha Declaration and the Zanzibar Resolution are discussed in detail alongside their implications in relation to business ethics and the governance of state-owned enterprises (SOEs). The discussion dwells in both the Ujamaa era and the period after economic liberalization, before looking at the future of Tanzania in relation to corporate governance.

Chapter 4 discusses corporate evolution and governance-related challenges faced by SOEs. From the discussion of the evolution of the public corporation (parastatal) to its role across the different sectors of the economy (as the dominant player), the chapter takes us through the governance system, resource management and managerial capabilities as elements for a national framework for good governance. The inadequacies in legal frameworks, enforcement and performance, as well as twisted accountability leading to resource waste, are discussed prior to that of the current corporate setting.

In Chapter 5, the individual corporate governance failures and waste case studies are described and analysed. The analysis entails verification of the propositions and discussions. This is in line with the objective to enhance corporate governance as recommended by the Steering Committee on Corporate Governance in Tanzania and the Capital Markets and Securities Authority (Bank of Tanzania, 2008).

The case selection was guided by a multiplicity of factors but are basically, as Stake (1995) contends, two types of cases, namely, intrinsic and instrumental. An intrinsic case is preselected and represents a situation of having no choice. This implies that in order to understand the phenomenon of interest, only one particular case can be studied: the cases of ATCL, TANESCO and TLAI are great examples. An instrumental case, on the other hand, is selected to deal with intriguing questions, puzzlement, beyond a need for general understanding, and a feeling that one may gain insights into the question by studying a specific case. The instrumental argument encourages studying a case if that case provides the possibility of understanding a specific phenomenon. This is also described by Patton and Appelbaum (2003) as strategic case selection. The cases of TCRA and TPA fit particularly well under this banner.

Overall, these descriptive cases are an attempt to paint a picture of what a phenomenon looks like or how it occurs. Many argue against describing these cases, in that such choices are guided by paradigms, access and prior knowledge (Gummesson, 2000). This, they observe, accords the methodology low status and views it as ancillary to other methods. A source of this criticism is the frame of reference. Those who subscribe to an objective reality, a determinist perspective aiming for generalization, are likely to view case studies with scepticism. On the other hand, those who subscribe to an interpretive view of the world and wish to gain deep insight into a phenomenon favour the case study approach as a research tool. The data and information have been obtained from publicly available sources.

Chapter 6 encompasses conclusions, reflections and recommendations for further development of corporate governance in Tanzania as well as suggestions for additional areas that need to be addressed. It highlights corporate good governance from the perspective of ethical conduct in business, which navigates beyond the jurisdiction of the law. The contextual topical reflections are meant to provide more contemporary relational attributes. The chapter is a reflection of the authors take and wish for corporate governance in Tanzania into the future. Indeed, in our humble recommendations, we set out to respond to the question: So what needs to be done at this juncture? The recommendations we offer do not encompass everything that is out there. We are aware of the different levels that are involved, i.e. public enterprise, leadership, industry/sector, societal levels etc. Nonetheless, we restrict our recommendations to the former two.

Bibliography

Arjoon, S. (2005, November). Corporate governance: An ethical perspective. *Journal of Business Ethics*, *61*(4), 343–352.

Bagachwa, M. S. D. (1992). Background, evolution, essence and prospects of the current economic reforms in Tanzania. In M. S. D. Bagachwa, A. V. Y. Mbele, & B. Van Arkadie (Eds.), *Market reforms and parastatal restructuring in Tanzania*. Dar es Salaam: Economic Research Bureau (pp. 19–43).

Bank of Tanzania (2008). *Guideline of boards of directors of banks and financial institutions in Tanzania*. Dar es Salaam & Tanzania: Government Printers.

Carlos, J., Guerrero, C., & Lera, I. (2014). Implementing good governance principles for the public sector in information technology governance frameworks. *Open Journal of Accounting*, *3*(1). Article ID: 41979, 19. doi:10.4236/ojacct.2014.31003

Drucker, P., & Nakamuchi, I. (1997). *Drucker on Asia: A dialogue between Peter Drucker and Isato Nakamuchi*. London and New York: Routledge.

Gummesson, E. (2000). *Qualitative methods in management research* (2nd revised ed.). Newbury Park, CA: Sage.

Keynes, J. (1926). *The end of laissez-faire*. Retrieved May 15, 2016, from www.panarchy.org/keynes/laissezfaire.1926.html

Kiure, N. J. (2002). *Corporate governance practices in Tanzania: An exploratory study* (Unpublished MBA dissertation), University of Dar es Salaam.

Kiwale, C. (2007). Strengthening public accountability and governance in controlling corruption in Tanzania: The role of the Ethics Secretariat. In S. Tindifa (Ed.), *Public accountability and good governance in East Africa* (pp. 19–23). Kampala: Fountain Publishers.

Msekwa (2016, May 12). Ethics is the heart of leadership: Appreciating President Magufuli's refreshing stance on leadership ethics. *The Daily News*, Tanzania.

OECD (2014a). *Risk management and corporate governance, corporate governance*. OECD Publishing. Retrieved from http://dx.doi.org/10.1787/9789264208636-en

Patton, E., & Applebaum, S. (2003). The case for case studies in management research. *Management Research News*, *26*(5), 60–71. Retrieved from https://doi.org/10.1108/01409170310783484

Stake, R. E. (1995). *The art of case study research*. Thousand Oaks, CA: Sage.

URT (2001). *The Surface and Marine Transport Regulatory Authority Act 2001*. Dar es Salam: Government Printer.

1 Background of the corporate environment in Tanzania

Tanzania's socio-economic history is informed by the demands of the economic environment, which in turn informs the operating environment for both public and private enterprises. When it comes to state-owned (public) enterprises (SOEs), history reveals the arduous and interesting journey travelled since independence, during the Arusha Declaration era and the post-Arusha economic liberalization and privatization periods.

It is important that when the public sets out to evaluate the performance of SOEs today, it is aware of the history and the performance benchmarks that formed the basis for their existence. This is not to say that SOEs deserve empathy from the public, but the public should understand that they have little choice but to leverage their performance and earn the trust of the tax-paying public (Mwapachu, 2013). The foregoing highlights why it is important to understand the corporate governance challenges that SOEs faced and continue to face in the evolving policy environments characterized by, among other things, rampant undercapitalization, blurred separation of power, limited powers of boards, limited enforceability of agreements and ineffective oversight functions.

Corporate environment 1967–2015

The 1995 constitutional amendment facilitated the establishment of the Public Leadership Code of Ethics Act and its operationalization through the Ethics Secretariat under the Office of the President. The basic principles that underlie the code range from incontestable integrity among public leaders, decision-making in accordance with the law and public interest and avoiding conflict of interest, to the refusal to solicit or accept gifts and benefits. It also extends to confidentiality with respect to public information, misuse of government property for private benefit and declaration of wealth and liabilities. In a two-way transparent approach, in addition to receiving declarations of wealth by public leaders, the Ethics Secretariat is also mandated to receive complaints from the public on breach of the code and inquire into allegations of breaches of the code by public leaders. Public leaders include members of the executive, legislature and judiciary branches, state enterprises executives, the police and the military.

By his recent actions, the current head of state, President John Pombe Magufuli, highlights his government's ethics-related priority areas. They include combating impunity in public service delivery, eliminating wasteful and unnecessary public expenditure and confronting corruption, which have long overwhelmed the nation.

The areas mentioned above are a clear indication of the serious lack of the requisite leadership ethics in Tanzania's governance system. The president's actions are therefore aimed not only at ensuring strict compliance to the requirements of revered leadership ethics, for ethics are at the heart of leadership, but also at having leaders that walk the talk. In other words, ethics is the *sine qua non* of a good leader (Msekwa, 2016).

Business ethics and corporate responsibility

It is important at the outset to highlight the close relationship between business ethics and corporate responsibility. These two intriguing terms go hand in hand as far as business is concerned. Ethics guru Kenneth Andrews identified three main characteristics to the problem of corporate ethics, namely the development of the executive as a moral person, the influence of the business enterprise as a moral environment and the actions needed to map a high road to economic and ethical performance (Andrews, 1989).

The development of the executive as a moral person starts from the standpoint that unethical conduct or behaviour in business is often regarded as individual failure. Morality and ethical behaviour in real life, however, are influenced by factors beyond an individual's upbringing. For example, we often witness what has come to be regarded as bi-polar personality in professional executives' and entrepreneurs' conduct in corporate settings (Mwapachu, 2005).

Indeed, it is true that there are challenges that confront business as a moral environment. In effect, there is a school of thought in Tanzania that believes that the onset of the free market system is what invoked unethical business practices. The free market system and its constituent economic liberalization became indicative of unethical business behaviour. This justifies the argument that societies which embrace the free market often forget that the free market can only thrive where morality and social values predominate (Velshi, 2013). True to form, in Tanzania it reached a point where unethical corporate conduct undermined and subverted economic and social well-being. If business fails to become ethical, the market will lose its legitimacy and credibility, and private enterprise will be despised (Mwapachu, 2005).

Over time, the conduct of business moved from the logic of business competition which broils in ethical business (fair trade practices) to subverting such logic. This rendered a bad name and image to business, as the erosion of business ethics continued across the different strata. A belief that success in business went hand in hand with circumventing procedures and cutting corners grew within various categories of stakeholders including regulators and consumers. Diluted was the premise that business ethics hinge on ethical governance. Moreover, ethics are about values. Ethics and ethical conduct cannot blossom in absence of clear preference for what is right over what is wrong.

Corporate governance

Monks and Minow (2004) assert that corporate governance has emerged more and more as an integral and critical part of modern management. Whereas corporate governance may be viewed as a system utilized to shield investors' interests, Shleifer and Vishny (1997) defined corporate governance as the ways in which suppliers of finance to companies assure themselves of getting a return on their investment. Likewise, La Porta, Lopez-de-Silanes, Shleifer and Vishny (2000) refer to corporate governance as "a set of mechanisms through which outside investors protect themselves against expropriation by [managers and controlling shareholders]."

Corporate governance guidelines as mechanisms can help a company reduce agency costs and better align the interests of the boards and investors (Picou & Rubach, 2006). To maximize shareholders' return on investment, corporate governance mechanisms exist to provide accurate information to investors and shareholders, important in terms of investment and resource allocation decision-making.

Corporate governance is also regarded as "a set of relationships between a company's management, its board, and other stakeholders" (OECD, 2004). This approach looks into a broader network of relationships including other stakeholders, way beyond the relationship between shareholder and director.

The myriad definitions address stakeholders' roles along the company value chain, in the context of corporate governance. Furthermore, the definitions look at corporate governance both mechanistically, as ways or mechanisms, and as relationships among stakeholders, reflecting ethics in many shades.

Defining corporate governance as "the exercise of power over and responsibility for corporate entities," Mallin (2002) places responsibility as an element of ethics, beyond the control mechanisms of laws, rules and regulations. Gillan and Starks (1998), for instance, view corporate governance as the system of laws, rules and factors that control operations at a company. The famous *Cadbury Report* depicted corporate governance as "the system by which companies are directed and controlled" (Cadbury, 1992). The report was certainly concerned with the control mechanism alongside the leadership required for that mechanism.

From a stakeholder's perspective, researchers are known to categorize corporate governance mechanisms into two typologies, namely, those internal to companies and those external to companies. The typologies paved the way for the two models of corporate governance, viz. the "shareholder" model ("external" control exerted by shareholders) and the "stakeholder" model ("internal" control exerted by diverse parties having a stake or an interest in the company's operations). The model of corporate governance built on agency theory is also popular. In this model, shareholders (as principals) delegate to managers (as agents), sharing risk between the two as well as underlying conflict of interest (Eisenhardt, 1989). Agency theory, however, falls short in elucidating how managers address interests represented by non-shareholders, including political pressures and communal expectations (Nwabueze & Mileski, 2008).

The Arusha Declaration

The 1967 Arusha Declaration encompassed the essence of the ideology of socialism and self-reliance (*Ujamaa na Kujitegemea*) as the cornerstone of Tanzania's socio-political and economic blueprint (Kiondo, 1993). In part, the move emanated from the pressure to adopt a system of coordination of economic opportunities that would provide equal access to resources and benefits, congruent with the aspirations of building Ujamaa (Melyoki, 2007). The declaration represented a formal rejection of the classical liberal market system of coordination and provided a vision of an egalitarian nation. To that effect, it expounded the role of the leadership and expectations toward building the envisaged society. The Arusha Declaration was, in effect, the first national ethics creed, although it embraced the party's ideology under what came to be known as the leadership code.

As far as leadership is concerned, it was resolved under the Arusha Declaration that:

i   Every TANU[1] member and government leader must be either a peasant or a worker and should not be associated with the practices of capitalism or feudalism;
ii No TANU or government leader should hold shares in any company;
iii No TANU or government leader should hold directorships in any privately owned enterprise;
iv No TANU or government leader should receive two or more salaries;
v   No TANU or government leader should own houses which he rents to others.

The declaration ushered in the emergence of state-owned enterprises (the parastatals), then a relatively new phenomenon, as part of the people's ownership of the means of production it elucidated. Implementation of the objectives of the Arusha Declaration involved the nationalization of private entities under the public ownership policy. The policy outlined strategic areas reserved for the government and attempted to encourage private investments into other areas (Nyerere, 1968).

In a turn of events, the leadership code introduced under the Arusha Declaration was reversed in 1992 through what has come to be called the Zanzibar Resolution.

The Zanzibar Resolution

To many across the country, the 1992 Zanzibar Resolution represented a critical turning point in ethics and governance in Tanzania as a society. It revisited the tenets of the Arusha Declaration as it related to governance, the leadership code. The crux of the Zanzibar Resolution was that with the new economic and political realities, the Arusha Declaration's leadership code was outdated. The subsequent adoption of the Zanzibar Resolution reflected a major shift from the fundamentals of the Arusha Declaration. As it turns out (in hindsight), it was at this point that the erosion of the socialist ethics was revealed via unethical behaviour in governance, corruption and the disintegration of the social fabric (Mwapachu, 2005). This was also the time that Tanzania adopted market-driven policies and political pluralism.

It was at this juncture that we witnessed deteriorated social service delivery, the collapse of parastatal sector public ownership and cracks in the national fabric. Wanton privatization cut across the economy, not sparing either unprofitable or profitable and strategic productive entities in the parastatal sector. For instance, to date, multiple Controller and Auditor General (CAG) reports reveal that proceeds of public entities under liquidation recorded in audited financial statements of the principal do not correspond to the realized amounts reflected in the statement of affairs of the entities under liquidation (CAG, 2016).

Unfortunate as it is, there is no proof that the adopted privatization measures, for instance, took into consideration the bearing that ethics and governance have. Overall, the objective fell short. The reason behind the below-expectation performance is largely attributed to ineffective governance. This period started to witness every form of ineffectiveness through ineptitude. It extended from wilful tax evasion to poor expenditure controls, and from ineffective governance and reckless implementation to wastefulness (Mwapachu, 2005).

What the nation witnessed was a period of what some have termed as poor ethics in governance (Mwapachu, 2005). As evidenced by multiple CAG periodic reports year in and year out, there has been massive resource wastefulness across the sectors of the economy. Poor ethics were entrenched in the failure to embrace new ideas by leaders and revealed in the numerous ills that became the way of doing business in Tanzania – a further deficit in entrepreneurial ethics.

Given the public's concern on increased need for accountability, transparency and good governance, informed decisions are vital. CAG annual reports cover all significant issues pertaining to the audit of public entities and include recommendations to entities to ensure that all the weaknesses are addressed. The reports also reviewed the strategic and governance issues with the aim of responding to fundamental policy questions or critical challenges and business risks affecting mandates, strategies, business processes and productivity of public entities (CAG, 2015).

The deficit in entrepreneurial ethics is revealed in three problems that stand out, namely the application of outdated ideas, the inappropriateness of a problem-solving culture and the negative orientation of cultural ethos. Nowhere else in Tanzania's economic history can one get a better understanding of entrepreneurial ethics than public entities, the parastatals, which embody all the three.

Governance and Tanzania's Development Vision

Tanzania's Development Vision 2025 (TDV 2025) brings to the fore the issue of good governance at a national level as one of its principal objectives. It states the following:

Tanzania cherishes good governance and the rule of law in the process of creating wealth and sharing benefits in society and seeks to ensure that its people are empowered with the capacity to make their leaders and public servants accountable. By 2025, good governance should have permeated the national socio-economic structure thereby ensuring a culture of accountability, rewarding good performance and effectively curbing corruption and other vices in society.

(Tanzania Development Vision 2025; URT 1999a)

The vision also registers failures in good governance (and in the organization of production) as one of the four major impediments toward Tanzania's socio-economic progress, and targets attaining good governance through the rule of law. The relationship between good governance and the rule of law, as elucidated in the vision, foresees it permeating all modalities of social organization, promoting a culture of accountability and specifying rewards and sanctions. It asserts that synonymous to the aspirations of the Arusha Declaration, good governance is an essential component to the attainment of development endeavours (URT, 1999a).

Despite the vision being a good starting point, it is important to highlight that corporate governance practices in Tanzania, until recently, have been narrowly debated (Melyoki, 2007). If anything, the debate has remained in the context of state-owned enterprises, in which unethical practices (corruption, embezzlement, ineptitude, nepotism etc.), managerial incompetence, political interference and continuous government bailout of failing enterprises remained the central features (Bagachwa, 1992; Kihiyo, 2002). Recently, through policy pronouncements and enactments, there have been efforts at addressing the numerous corporate governance challenges in Tanzania. Such measures as the privatization policy, the executive agencies legislation, and the Banking and Financial Institutions Act (1991) are some of the important developments around governance. The Capital Markets and Securities Authority and the Steering Committee on Corporate Governance in Tanzania in 2002 introduced separate but related sets of principles for effective corporate governance, which companies are encouraged to adopt for implementation (Melyoki, 2007).

The issue of context, in terms of the system for coordinating economic activities, is an important influence on corporate governance (Melyoki, 2007). Indeed, systems of corporate governance worldwide reflect differences in not only societal history but also cultures and institutions (Weimer & Pape, 2000) over the long haul. To analyse Tanzania's corporate governance context calls for a special contextual framework as well.

Corporate failures

After three (or four) tumultuous decades in terms of economic performance, what did Tanzania have to show? Not much. In fact, the policy decisions via reforms enshrined in privatization, restructuring and overall public sector review, in essence, was an admission of failure; in our case corporate failure. Indeed, there are several examples to highlight some of the indicators of failure.

Several reasons have been brought forth to explain the causes behind the failures but the truth of the matter remains that leadership failure in governance cannot be ruled out. As such, we regard the period as 'wasted decades,' for instance, because of the failures reflected in not only the economy but also value for money, service delivery and overall performance of public entities entrusted with efficient and effective delivery of goods and services to the public.

Since then, the role of parastatals has diminished except for in strategic areas. Public Private Partnership has taken root alongside an emerging development paradigm that requires and expects the private sector, albeit weak, to play a more active role (Mwapachu, 2005). At the same time, the remaining public sector entities are put under scrutiny to ensure efficient delivery of public service and value for money across the board.

After nearly three decades since abdicating socialist economic management through economic reforms, privatization, the establishment of sectoral regulatory entities to promote fair, ethical and competitive level playing fields, not much could be shown from the public corporation, the state-owned enterprises. This gave the private sector the nod as the prime driver of social and economic transformation, much as the Tanzanian corporate governance environment still leaves a lot to be desired.

Wasted decades – governance and economic management

Many in Tanzania believe that there is an indirect association between good governance and economic issues. It remains a fact nonetheless that as far as economic pursuits are concerned, good governance is paramount at all levels to a developing country like Tanzania. Good governance is both a necessary and sufficient condition to economic development endeavours, alongside stable and predictable economic policies (Mwapachu, 2005). If anything, what good governance reaps goes beyond the classical interpretation of the growth statistics in an economic perspective, to rather what the numbers amount to. The translation or true meaning is a product of good governance and is evidenced in the populations' economic and social well-being.

It is justifiable, therefore, to say that good governance is neither simply a buzzword nor a mere trend on social media and in corridors of power; be they at Davos, the G8 or the United Nations. It is the necessary and sufficient condition toward the attainment of meaningful development, more than merely economic management. Well-balanced and focussed governance calls for the harmonious interaction of all stakeholders, the private sector, NGOs and CSOs, and not limited to the government only (Mwapachu, 2005).

Both the absence of adherence to due diligence and arrogance are found to be the root cause of many business failures (Chorafas, 2004), as is mismanagement which leads to waste of the meagre resources that should have been preserved and used to create new wealth. Poor corporate governance and failures of ethics are the most widespread reasons why businesses get into trouble. Substandard management to obsolescence in know-how, inadequate internal controls, non-compliance to regulations, and tarnished reputation are all indications of failures in governance.

Economists believe in the assumption of rational self-interest. Yet it is this principle that reduces ethical conduct across the board. In the corporate world, there have always been calls for more ethical business practices. A good number of people and organizations in the same arena have been long dedicated to doing things differently. We must also acknowledge that, lately, there has emerged a momentum toward bridging the gap between what have been considered as two opposing forces, business and ethics. Indeed, Milton Friedman's (1962) often-quoted statement, "There is one and only one social responsibility of business – to use its resources and engage in activities designed to increase its profits so long as it stays within the rules of the game, which is to say, engages in open and free competition without deception or fraud," sums up what some consider to be the dilemma and others the virtue of ethics in business.

Note

1 Tanganyika African National Union (TANU), the ruling party under the old one-party system.

Bibliography

Andrews, K. (1989, September/October). Ethics in practice. *Harvard Business Review*, *67*(5), 99–104.

Bagachwa, M. S. D. (1992). Background, evolution, essence and prospects of the current economic reforms in Tanzania. In M. S. D. Bagachwa, A. V. Y. Mbele, & B. Van Arkadie (Eds.), *Market reforms and parastatal restructuring in Tanzania*. Dar es Salaam: Economic Research Bureau.

Cadbury, A. (1992). *Cadbury report – Report of the committee on the financial aspects of corporate governance*. London: Gee & Co. Ltd.

CAG (2015). *The annual general report of the controller and auditor general on the audit of public authorities and other bodies for the financial year 2013/2014*. Dar es Salaam: Office of the Controller and Auditor General, National Audit Office.

CAG. (2016). *The annual general report of the controller and auditor general on the audit of public authorities and other bodies for the financial year 2014/2015*. Dar es Salaam: Office of the Controller and Auditor General, National Audit Office.

Chorafas, D. (2004). *Corporate accountability: With case studies in pension funds and the banking industry*. New York, NY: Palgrave Macmillan.

Eisenhardt, K. (1989, January). Agency theory: An assessment and review. *The Academy of Management Review*, *14*(1), 57–74.

Friedman, M. (1962). *Capitalism and freedom*. Chicago, IL: University of Chicago Press.

Gillan, S., & Starks, L. T. (1998). *A survey of shareholder activism: Motivation and empirical evidence*. Retrieved from SSRN https://ssrn.com/abstract=663523 or http://dx.doi.org/10.2139/ssrn.663523

Kihiyo, H. (2002). *Corporate governance and corruption- the case of Tanzania, governance and corruption in parastatals.* Paper presented at the International Seminar on: Corporate Governance and Development of Appropriate National Codes Programme, Dar es Salaam.

Kiondo, A. (1993). *Political implications of Tanzania's economic reforms: 1982–1992.* Paper presented at a conference on: On the Road to a Market-based Economy in Tanzania, Dar es Salaam.

LaPorta, R., Lopez-de-Silanes, F., Shleifer, A., & Vishny, R. W. (2000). Agency problems and dividend policies around the world. *Journal of Finance, 55*(1), 1–33.

Mallin, C. (2002). The relationship between corporate governance, transparency and financial disclosure. *Corporate Governance – An International Review, 10*(4), 253–255.

Melyoki 2007 (2005). *Determinants of effective corporate governance in Tanzania* (Doctoral Dissertation), University of Twente. ISBN 90-365-2160-2.

Monks, R. A. G., & Minow, N. 2004 (2002). *Corporate governance* (2nd ed. (reprint)). Oxford: Blackwell Publishing Ltd.

Msekwa (2016, May 12). Ethics is the heart of leadership: Appreciating President Magufuli's refreshing stance on leadership ethics. *The Daily News*, Tanzania.

Mwapachu, J. V. (2005). *Confronting new realities: Reflections on Tanzania's radical transformation.* Dar es Salaam: E&D Ltd.

Mwapachu, J. V. (2013). *Parastatals: Architecture of corporate governance.* Tanzania: The Citizen.

Nwabueze, U., & Mileski, J. (2008). The challenge of effective governance: The case of Swiss Air, corporate governance. *The International Journal of Business in Society, 8*(5), 583–594. Retrieved from https://doi.org/10.1108/14720700810913250

Nyerere, J. K. (1968). *Freedom and socialism.* Arusha: Oxford University Press.

OECD (2004). The OECD *principles of corporate governance.* Retrieved June 2004 from http://www.oecd.org.

Picou, A., & Rubach, M. (2006). Does good governance matter to institutional investors? Evidence from the enactment of corporate governance guidelines. *Journal of Business Ethics, 65*(1), 55–67.

Shleifer, A., & Vishny, R. W. (1997). A survey of corporate governance. *Journal of Finance, 52*(2), 737–783.

URT (1999a). *Development Vision, 2025.* Dar es Salaam: President's Office, Planning and Privatisation Commission, Government Printer.

URT (1999b). *The national framework on good governance.* Dar es Salaam, Tanzania: United Republic of Tanzania, Steering Committee on Good Governance. President's Office, Planning Commission.

Velshi, A. (2013). *Is it possible to have morality in a free market?* Speech delivered at the Chautauqua Institution in Chautauqua, NY. Retrieved July 17, 2015, from https://qz.com/105311/is-it-possible-to-have-morality-in-a-free-market/

Weimer, J., & Pape, J. C. (2000). Inside western systems of corporate governance. *Executive Talent, 1*(3), 54–61.

2 Ethics, accountability and governance

In today's world, it is certainly true that conducting business in an ethical way is a significant contributor to business success for both private and public enterprises. But what constitutes an ethical way and what does not? Do all economic agents that operate on the same platform have the same understanding of what is and what is not ethical? Do all nations and economies subscribe to the same meaning of the term 'ethics'? Maybe they do literally, but not by their deeds and policy actions

According to the *Merriam-Webster Dictionary*, accountability is the "quality or state of being accountable; especially an obligation or willingness to accept responsibility or to account for one's actions." (Merriam-Webster, Inc., 2014)

It is important to note how the definition highlights "an obligation," implying little room for choice. The somewhat powerless definition is indicative of the feeling amongst some circles that accountability is viewed as consequential – accounting ill-performance, short of expectation, thus agreeing to heed to obligatory stipulations etc. In other words, public accountability rests both on giving an account and on being held to account.

That has led others, like the authors of *The Oz Principle* to come up with alternative definitions of accountability, including "A personal choice to rise above one's circumstances and demonstrate the ownership necessary for achieving desired results – to See It, Own It, Solve It, and Do It." (Connors, Smith, & Hickman, 2010, p. 44). Such a definition comes from the perspective of a s or attitude of mind riding on the premise of consistently querying, "What else can I do to rise above my circumstances and achieve the results I desire?" (ASME, 2011). In this case, a level of ownership is obvious and includes making, keeping and answering for personal commitments. It is a perspective that embraces not only the present but also future efforts. With this definition of accountability on hand, one can facilitate culpability for oneself and others as well as overcome difficult circumstances and attain desired results. (ASME, 2011)

Several scholars writing on ethics and accountability have advanced various reasons to explain the causes of the deterioration of ethical standards and accountability in public services delivery in Africa (Rasheed & Olowu, 1993; UNDESA, 2001). Ayee (1998) further maintained that notions of ethics and accountability have become critical because of the continued public sector institutional shortfalls due to the moral failings of public servants. The failings are linked to weak values and weak systems.

When it comes to public service ethics, expectations and realities, the beginning point is the realization that, in terms of public service, ethics in public office is public trust, i.e. public officials act on behalf of all citizens. Since public officials are given the powers to make decisions and allocate resources, the citizenry expect the officials to be transparent, fair and equitable, much as there are pertinent complex issues related to legal and political attributes that come with the respective public office (Painter, 2000; Chapman, 1993).

By implication, holding public office comes with expectations of the highest standards upon which officials develop, uphold and maintain public interest. This encapsulates the essence of public service. Couzens (1985) noted that people enter public service aware that in addition to earning a living, they embark on public service delivery, first and foremost. Assuming a position in public service, be it as an employee or an employer, comes with acknowledging and accepting certain obligations.

Indeed, the concern over the need for corporate bodies to enhance ethics, integrity, transparency and accountability is real. The belief is that this would facilitate not only the optimal use, protection and preservation of resources, but also public sector performance, which has been lacking. Moreover, a subculture in Tanzania emerged, which encompassed an ironic situation where public officials did not need to be accountable for their actions and the citizens could not demand accountability. A recurrent theme in the continual exposition of poor service delivery is lack of accountability in governance and poor performance of public sector entities.

What ethics – what are ethics?

Much as it has been contended elsewhere that there is no universal definition of the term "ethics" (Ayee, 1998), the question of ethics can be linked and traced back to the history of humankind. As such, ethics is said to deal with the character, conduct and morals of human beings. It addresses behaviour good and bad, right and wrong; it evaluates conduct vis-à-vis set absolute values (Hanekon, 1984). Along the same lines, Chapman (1993) defines ethics as the basic principles of the right action and rules of conduct.

The term ethics deals with moral issues and the determination of what is right and wrong behaviour in a society or workplace. *Encyclopedia Britannica* defines ethics as follows:

> Ethics, also called moral philosophy, the discipline concerned with what is morally good and bad, right and wrong. The term is also applied to any system or theory of moral values or principles.
>
> (Britannica.com)

According to the *Oxford Advanced Learner's Dictionary*, "Ethics is a system of moral principles or rules of behavior, or moral principles that influence a person's behavior." It is societal but experienced at an individual level.

On the other hand, most dictionaries define the adjective 'moral' as relating to the principles of *right and wrong behaviour* and the *goodness or badness of human character*. To put it into an even better context, anything moral would be *considered right and good by most people or conforming with a standard of right behaviour*. So, the setting must have a society and then a standard of what that society considers the right behaviour. In this regard, a moral or immoral act or deed cannot be defined by an individual's own standards.

Ethics inform us about our moral duties and obligations to respective societies so that our behaviour at work or at home is right, truthful and just. Ethics, as a set of standards and rules, relate to both family and professional or business lives.

We observe ethical behaviour through several habits. Some of the general habits that determine ethics include sincerity and honesty, truthfulness and respect for others, respect for time and respect for work.

Besides the above in our everyday social lives, our workplaces may demand certain general behaviours to gauge one's ethics, such as:

- regularity and punctuality;
- confidentiality;
- loyalty; and
- respect for and cordial relations with co-workers, clients and suppliers.

In today's world, and particularly in the developed economies, a fundamental aspect of ethical behaviour now also comprises *caring and respect for the environment; sustainability*.

Why do we need to be ethical?

The question to ask ourselves is why do we need to be ethical? Maybe the best way to confront this question is to find out how ethics affect our work performance and interpersonal relationships.

Work situations have a number of components, key among them are the work or the tasks to be performed, the employees or workers who perform the tasks, and the work environment – consisting of premises, tools, equipment, processes etc. The components cannot be disconnected if the objectives are to be attained. Depending on the cultural and economic setting of the enterprise, the employee is often considered the most critical or important component of the work environment. This is the human component of the environment, with the ability to visualize, think, analyse and manipulate all that is around the workspace.

How an employee or employees behave and interact, first among themselves and then with the tools and equipment or processes, is a choice. They may choose to be effective and productive or exhibit behaviours that retard or even ruin the enterprise.

To achieve the enterprise objectives and goals, resources (financial, human, time, environmental) must be efficiently employed and utilized under a clear order and discipline. This order and discipline is the core of what we have referred to as

18 *Ethics, accountability and governance*

ethics; in this regard *work ethics*. For it to be meaningful, it must be known to all involved, because it will have clearly defined how each will interact with another and how each will employ the tools, equipment and processes in the workspace.

Work ethics influence the employees' choice of whether to stay and perform under standards of good behaviour or leave to find another environment that best fits with their understanding of the good and the bad. Without these standards, conflict and resource waste cannot be avoided.

Most important, the ethics or standards of good behaviour will be the yardstick for deciding who is retained at the workplace and who should be released because they are counter to set objectives.

What is accountability?

Accountability is where "an individual or body, and the performance of tasks or functions by that individual or body, are subject to another's oversight, direction or request that they provide information or justification for their actions" (Accountability in Governance, The World Bank).[1]

The above definition suggests that reporting is a fundamental aspect of accountability and involves two distinct stages: *answerability* and *enforcement*. Answerability refers to the obligation to provide information about decisions and actions, and to justify them, to the authority tasked with providing oversight. In the corporate setting, for example, that would be the Chief Executive Officer being answerable to the Board of Directors; and the Board of Directors to stakeholders (shareholders, regulators, community, tax authorities, etc.). In the public domain, this obligation would be to the body tasked with providing oversight as well as to the public, the taxpayers.

The second stage, enforcement, suggests that the authority tasked with providing oversight can sanction the accountable entity or individual. Indeed, the oversight authority should take charge of both stages of accountability.

Providing information is the most effective way to demonstrate that managers and the body(ies) responsible for the governance of an organization delivered on respective stated commitments, requirements and priorities and made effective use of resources. Hence, it boils down to the need to report sufficiently and timely. By so doing, stakeholders can understand and make judgments on how the entity performs and whether it delivers value for money and has sound resource management.

There are general standards to reporting. The performance information and accompanying financial statements published by an entity should be prepared on a consistent and timely basis, generally by a specific date, every year. The reporting should be reliably anticipated. And to allow for comparison with other similar, peer entities, be prepared to use sector, national or international standards. International Financial Reporting Standards (IFRS) for corporates and the International Public Sector Accounting Standards (IPSAS) are examples of international reporting standards.

The concept and theory behind accountability

Dele Olowu (1993) emphasized that "public accountability is the requirement that those who hold public trust should account for the use of the trust to citizens or their representatives." Furthermore, Olowu observed that "public accountability signifies the superiority of the public will over private interests and tries to ensure that the former is supreme in every activity and conduct of a public official." Along the same lines, Mouftau Laleye (1993) said that "public accountability refers to sanctions and procedures by which public officials may be held to account for their actions."

From the above it can be ascertained how accountability refers to the notion that there are actions that public officials should be held responsible for while in office. For public officials to be held responsible for their actions, there must be certain norms and values that they are required to observe, alongside clear sanctions by which they can be punished for failing to adhere to, as well as rewards for complying with, acceptable norms and values.

The required norms and values for regulating and monitoring unethical behaviour comprise both written and unwritten (formal and informal) codes of conduct. The ethical codes of conduct for regulating accountability may be categorized into four groups. The first comprises personal self-imposed ethics, which emanate from personal beliefs and convictions on what is the right and wrong way of conducting oneself in public affairs. The second is self-imposed group ethics – the within-group, right or wrong ways practiced by group members in service to society. The third represents written ethical rules or conduct for public servants – ones not enacted by the legislature, but with administrative sanctions against offenders and a process for imposing such sanctions, e.g. standing orders or periodic instructions issued through circulars. The fourth group of ethical codes comprise enacted statutes or acts of the legislature or provision of a country's constitutions (Barlow, 1993).

Arising from its conceptualization, accountability is therefore considered a key determinant of the state of governance. To say the least, strict observation of accountability in the management of a public entity enhances good governance (Polidano & Hulme, 1997).

Relationship between ethics and accountability in governance

Ethics and leadership have often been thought of as mutually reinforcing concepts. Ethics, for the most part, can be considered as an internal set of moral codes and reasoning based upon societal and prescriptive norms (McDougle, 2006). In general, therefore, the ethics of leadership and leaders' degree of moral development are essential elements both in mainstream public and private sector leadership research (Bass & Steidlmeier, 1999; Howell, 1988).

Ethics as defined in the *Oxford Advanced Learner's Dictionary* (2000, p. 395) is the "moral principles that control or influence a person's behaviour." Ethics and public service values are unequivocally important elements in comprising the "body and soul" of public administration (Menzel, 2003).

In general terms, on the other hand, the business dictionary defines accountability as "The obligation of an individual or organization to account for its activities, accept responsibility for them, and to disclose the results in a transparent manner. It also includes the responsibility for money or other entrusted property."[2] Similarly, corporate accountability is defined as

> The act of being accountable to the stakeholders of an organization, which may include shareholders, employees, suppliers, customers, the local community, and even the particular country(s) that the firm operates in. In most jurisdictions, a body of corporate law has been developed in order to formalize these requirements.[3]

On the other hand, public accountability refers to the "obligation of authorities to explain publicly, fully and fairly, before and after the fact, how they are carrying out responsibilities that affect the public in important ways" (CCA, 2008, p. 2).

Governance refers to "sustaining coordination and coherence among a wide variety of actors with different purposes and objectives" (Jon Pierre, 2000). The actors range from political authorities and institutions, interest groups and civil society to non-governmental organizations and transnational entities. It encompasses the "nature of functioning of a state's institutional and structural arrangements, decision-making processes, policy formulation, implementation capacity, information flows, effectiveness of leadership, and the nature of the relationship between rulers and the ruled" (Landell-Miss & Serageldin, 1991; Johnson & Doig, 1999, p. 19). The broad definition of governance provides credibility to the contention that governance is much broader than government.

Accountability may likewise be referred to as strong or weak. The degree of weakness may be due to ill-defined ethical standards, be it those of public service and financial systems or an ineffective watchdog function (Langseth et al., 1997). This has the potential for an adverse effect on the system of governance overall (Kiwale, 2007).

Ethics are considered to provide the basis for accountability. Theoretically, accountability encompasses increasing transparency and legitimacy and improving policy implementation. That being the case, unambiguous ethical standards by leaders, public and corporate, are key to public confidence. This is a measure of good governance.

In general, therefore, leaders in the public sector are expected to maintain a level of ethical standards (beyond morality and integrity) to be accountable and serve societal interests. This is demonstrated through personal responsibility. In other words, the ethical role of the leader in a public entity can be summed up as follows: serve the public interest while being fair, honest, lawful, trustworthy and doing the least harm (McDougle, 2006).

It is important to emphasize at the outset that instilling ethics in human capital resources is of extreme importance. Making ethics a part of the everyday life of leaders would ensure that a culture of observing ethics does not only exist but also sustained. The appointment or election of credible leaders, ones with proven records of ethical conduct, goes hand in glove with rigorous enforcement of the ethical code.

Insisting on the general public's awareness of the codes of ethics that public leaders are required to observe, alongside the demand for accountability, must be the norm rather than the exception. Civic education is therefore key to attaining the goal. Both state and non-state actors have a role to play in informing the public of their role to ensure leaders' accountability, educate leaders of their legal obligation to adhere to the ethical principles and perform the ultimate oversight function.

The need to promote ethics across Tanzanian society is indisputable. Public and corporate leaders are indeed products of the society. Putting ethics at the front of societal values would help build the desired society. To that effect, a professional code of ethics and the adherence to them is important. Professional organizations and the private sector have a duty to ensure that their members abide by the set codes of ethics and where breaches occur, to impose appropriate sanctions.

Thus, a public-sector leader approaching the subject of ethics through an integrated approach to leadership is likely to value honesty and integrity and to act with impartiality in the exercise of authority while also demonstrating prudence in decision-making. Likewise, ethical expectations of public-sector leaders will quite possibly relate to a variety of factors associated with both transformational and transactional leadership (McDougle, 2006). To that effect, several attempts have been made to address the question of ethics and how they define the qualities of a public leader.

The famous Nolan Committee in the United Kingdom in 1995 outlined the 'Seven Principles of Public Life,' based on core values of the Weberian bureaucratic model advancing public duty over personal interest (see Table 2.1). Under the model, officials are guided by professional as well as personal codes of ethics that in all embrace ethics of neutrality and fairness, i.e. sense of duty trumping personal preferences (Weber, 1996; Du Gay, 2000). It has been argued elsewhere that the model unfortunately downplayed private motivations and external forces as well as social obligations, which are somewhat more impactful (Balogun, 2003; Miller & Le Breton-Miller, 2006).

The principles have been debated as well as adopted globally and form the basis for an analytical framework supporting the review of any systems or rules concerning ethics in public leadership (Tenga, 2010). The same applies to Tanzania, which adopted variations of the seven principles and elaborated these into its public service codes of ethics, as discussed herein.

Along the same lines, Lewis and Gilman (2005) identified five core ethical values of public service – accountability, impartiality, justice and fairness, beneficence and non-malfeasance (not doing harm). From this premise, it is asserted that the five values are a product of the role the public servant plays as the temporary custodian of public authority. The applicability of the values therefore differs, based on a country's context, economic system, political system and culture.

Table 2.1 The seven principles of public life

Principle	Description
SELFLESSNESS	Holders of public office should act solely in terms of the public interest. They should not do so in order to gain financial or other material benefits for themselves, their family or their friends.
INTEGRITY	Holders of public office should not place themselves under any financial or other obligation to outside individuals or organizations that might seek to influence them in the performance of their official duties.
OBJECTIVITY	In carrying out public business, including making public appointments, awarding contracts or recommending individuals for rewards and benefits, holders of public office should make choices on merit.
ACCOUNTABILITY	Holders of public office are accountable for their decisions and actions to the public and must submit themselves to whatever scrutiny is appropriate to their office.
OPENNESS	Holders of public office should be as open as possible about all the decisions and actions that they take. They should give reasons for their decisions and restrict information only when the wider public interest clearly demands.
HONESTY	Holders of public office have a duty to declare any private interests relating to their public duties and to take steps to resolve any conflicts arising in a way that protects the public interest.
LEADERSHIP	Holders of public office should promote and support these principles by leadership and example.

Source: Committee on Standards in Public Life, 1995

Public servants across the globe share values related to their professional status more than to their respective cultures (Shah, 2005).

Governance is an important attribute as far as the investment climate is concerned. In that respect, the measure of governance as propounded by Kaufmann, Kraay, and Mastruzzi (2003) comprises six components, namely voice and accountability, political stability, government effectiveness, regulatory quality, the rule of law, and control of corruption. According to the World Bank, in five out of six governance measures, Tanzania ranks above the average for peer group, i.e. low-income countries, whilst it underperforms when it comes to control of corruption (World Bank, 2004).

Public sector governance

> In order to achieve accountability, fairness and transparency of operations of Public Authorities and Other Bodies (PA & OBs), good corporate governance is of paramount importance.
>
> (Ludovick S. L. Utoh)[4]

Good governance in the public sector is the cornerstone for efficient and effective organizational performance and is underpinned by a number of accountability requirements. Governance encompasses the systems and structures by which an organization is directed, controlled and operated and the mechanisms by which it and its employees are held to account.

In the public sector domain, a slight variation of that description might apply. The Chartered Institute of Public Finance and Accountancy (CIPFA) defines governance as:

> the arrangements necessary to ensure that the intended outcomes for citizens, service users, and other public sector stakeholders, are delivered in a transparent and accountable manner that is efficient, effective, ethical, and sustainable.
>
> (CIPFA, 2014)

The single most important justification for good governance practices in the public sector is to ensure that SOEs/public entities act in the public interest. Acting in the public interest is not a matter choice for managers and their Boards of Directors; it is absolute necessity given that these use, to a varying degree, public resources, taxes and levies, subventions etc.

It follows, therefore, that acting in the public interest requires (a) a strong commitment to integrity, ethical values, and the rule of law and (b) transparency and effective stakeholder engagement. For the latter requirement, acting in the public interest is what brings about the need for accountable management. Public entities must be able to provide a functional means of public resource utilization such that stakeholders, including both the parliament and taxpayers, can make them accountable in terms of performance. In this regard, good governance and accountability need and support each other and, if done well, enhance the public's trust in our entities. Good governance encourages and can result in good accountability. In turn, accountability is a vital element of good governance.

To support the continued investment in public entities, taxpayers have to be convinced, among other things, that public entities act impartially and lawfully; public entities use public resources prudently; people have equity of access to their services; and people have access to useful information about public entities' activities and achievements. Many agree that the quality of public sector governance needs to and can be enhanced, since it is has fallen short. To that effect, there is need to raise standards at various levels. On one hand, clarity is required for differentiating governance and management, while on the other hand it is necessary to address all aspects pertaining to improvement of risk management.

In Tanzania, the expectation of accountability and transparency has been lost. This is because there is no well-established public management system with strong accountability foundations. The Controller and Auditor General (CAG) has repeatedly made this point over the years. In his 2012/2013 Annual General Report,[5] the CAG makes the following statement:

> In this era of increased need for accountability, transparency and good governance, informed decisions are very vital. To this effect therefore, my report will help to ensure that decision makers in the country are served with relevant, up-to-date information with technical recommendations on the financial reporting and public resources management of the Public Authorities and Other Bodies in the country.

The CAG goes further in his Executive Summary and states the following:-

> During the year 2012/2013 audit I have noted that there are 26 previous years' outstanding recommendations which were yet to be implemented out of 41 recommendations issued in the year 2011/2012 as summarized in chapter three (3) of this report. Some of the recommendations have remained unresolved for more than five (5) years indicating that those charged with governance have not fulfilled their responsibilities properly. Long outstanding recommendations lead to recurring of similar weaknesses, hindering the efforts of my Office of bringing about enhanced transparency and accountability over the use of public funds.

Such CAG summations in reports basically reflected salient issues as well as challenges related to public entities embracing emerging practices aimed at improving respective governance and accountability. They identified various elements of good governance that could be of use to public entities, including reporting standards that address both challenges and opportunities.

> It is . . . fundamental that public entities should be able to demonstrate what they are doing and why, when that is questioned. Public entities should expect to be tested, whether by members of the public, the media, or the courts. This is accountability in action, and public entities need to be ready to explain themselves. That has implications for how public entities operate on a daily basis: they need full and proper records of their work that show what decisions were made, who made them, and the basis on which they were made.
>
> (CAG, 2014)

Processes in a public entity have to be both right and have the appearance of being right. In absence of ethics, accountability and transparency, bad practices and corrupt tendencies are bound to thrive. Accountability as a mirror allows the public to get a view of whether resources are utilized appropriately and effectively – the right way.

The questions raised throughout prior discussion revolved around determining what the ethical way is and how it is relevant concerning Tanzania. It is even more important at a time when the public enterprises failed to deliver and are on a downward free-fall in performance and reputation. Lack of ethics has undone the hopes and dreams cherished in the mid-1960s when the public enterprises, the SOEs, were first established. The little that has been gained from these enterprises has been wiped out.

One cannot attribute ethics shortfalls to culture or public service principles alone. To an extent, the institutions themselves have played a major role as well. Indeed, cultural values may influence policy approaches to management and therefore necessitate change. Contextual institutional fit may deem necessary the redesign of or change in societal values along with respective expectations. It is no surprise, therefore, that different contextual policy relevant approaches to management may be called for (Munene, Schwartz, & Smith, 2000). Clarifying the thin line between public or private and professional or ethical requirements, as well as expectations, is important.

It must be highlighted that there are, at the same time, competing codes of ethics, in that what may be considered as private vice may in fact be infringing on public good. Much as it is important to acknowledge cultural differences and to respect differences in values, it does not imply that corruption, corrupt tendencies, conflict of interest, embezzlement etc. should be tolerated as an incurable feature. To address such issues, it is important to understand how requirements of private morality as well as social and economic realities in a society affect or influence the codes of conduct. The existence of unethical behaviour, unprofessional conduct and corruption may be symptomatic of malfunctioning institutions of the state, but at the same time they may be due to different reasons.

The big picture

When it comes to ethics, accountability and governance, at issue remains the questions, How do these influence public service delivery in public corporation entities? and Why is it important? Apparent failures of public corporation entities can result in huge economic and fiscal costs, necessitating putting in place an effective oversight function. This is of crucial importance because:

> Public corporation entities find themselves obligated (at times mandated) to fulfill political objectives or activities unrelated to respective core functions and objectives;
> When it comes to management, inefficiency and/or ill-managed public corporation entities can result in enormous economic costs. In some instances, the entities existence is a result of efforts aimed at addressing potential market failures;

A sustained negative impact on public finances can result from failing public corporation entities by way of guarantees, subsidies, low cost loans or direct capital injection.

Public corporations can become a conduit for circumventing fiscal controls and promote financial corruption (Allen & Vani, 2013). The entities have been known to be used via off-budget fiscal undertakings, provide for political patronage etc. thereby under-cutting the integrity of the set systems and processes.

Hellsten and Larbi (2006) argue that public morality weakens when the common understanding of the core meaning of moral is lost. Most of the time such a situation happens as private moral commitments supersede public morality, thus promoting negative trust. They refer to 'negative trust' as a situation where people believe that one cannot trust anybody to do their job in a more efficient and professional manner without self-interest (be it extra pay or expectation of *quid pro quo*).

It is this 'negative trust' which basically undermines public ethics and leads to the reversal of traditional ethical structures in public service delivery in countries like Tanzania. Consequently, there emerges a culture that promotes loyalty and trust among 'partners in crime' and 'ill-defined networks.' In effect, anybody striving to promote the traditional values by exposing corrupt tendencies and unprofessional conduct becomes a pariah. In other words, they are forced to embrace now common unprofessional and unethical practices, the absence of which may lead to social and professional costs, as the bad guys. The reverse social ethics lead to the fighters of unethical practices being the ones breaking the circle of trust when promoting public interest (Sengupta, 1982). Hence, the decline in support to public ethics as well as enforcement of impartiality and unprofessional behaviour comes as no surprise.

In recent decades, beginning with the abandonment of the Arusha Declaration and the subsequent embracing of economic liberalization, corporate/enterprise culture has changed so much so that personal gain trumps all other considerations.

Any simple desk research in Tanzania will reveal that the top ethical issues confronting our public companies today revolve around illegal political contributions to buy favours from politicians; health or safety violations; improper contracts; contract violations; anti-competitive practices; sexual harassment; corruption; defrauding the company; stealing by servant (stealing property coming into one's possession on account of one's duties) etc. They extend from simple etiquette, professional misbehaviour and lack of oversight (regulatory function) to sheer criminal behaviour. It thus stretches across public corporation bodies, from economic agencies to regulatory bodies as well as professional entities. All fall short somewhat when it comes to instituting ethics, accountability and governance.

Ethical behaviour and integrity are embedded in the organizational culture. It is the organizational culture which helps shape an employee's and an executive's behaviour. We choose to explain organizational culture as the shared practices, behavioural standards and assumptions that guide how people work and interact at the workplace. This remain debatable, but in our view it is among the simplest of descriptions.

Notes

1 Accountability in Governance – A note written by Risk Stapenhurst (Senior Public Sector Management Specialist, World Bank Institute) and Mitchell O'Brien (Consultant, World Bank Institute), http://siteresources.worldbank.org
2 http://www.businessdictionary.com/definition/accountability.html
3 http://www.businessdictionary.com/definition/corporate-accountability.html
4 Controller and Auditor General United Republic of Tanzania – August 2014.
5 Annual General Report of the Controller and Auditor General – *On the Audit of Public Authorities and Other Bodies for the Financial Year 2012/2013*.

Bibliography

Allen, R., & Vani, S. (2013). Financial management and oversight of state-owned enterprises. In R. H. Allen (Ed.), *The international handbook of public financial management* (pp. 685–706). New York, NY: Palgrave Macmillan.

ASME. (2011). *How to Create a Culture of Accountability*. The American Society of Mechanical Engineers (ASME). Retrieved July 4, 2016, from www.asme.org/career-education/articles/management-professional-practice/how-to-create-a-culture-of-accountability

Ayee, J. (1998). *Ethics in public service: Second pan-African conference of the ministers of civil service*. African Training and Research Centre in Administration for development (CAFRAD).

Balogun, J. (2003). Causative and enabling factors in public integrity: A focus on leadership, institutions, and character. *Public Integrity*, 5(2), 127–147.

Barlow, C. (1993). Ethical codes of African administration: Nature, content, limitation and required improvements. In S. Rasheed & D. Olowu (Eds.), *Ethics and accountability in African public services*. Addis-Ababa: UNICA and AAPAM.

Bass, B. M., & Steidlmeier, P. (1999, Summer). Ethics, character, and authentic transformational leadership behavior. *The Leadership Quarterly*, 10(2), 181–217.

CCA. (2008). *Citizens' Circle of accountability: The issue of public accountability: A summary for citizens*. Retrieved January 25, 2016, from www.accountabilitycircle.org/

Chapman, R. (Ed.). (1993). *Ethics in public service*. Edinburgh: Edinburgh University Press.

Chartered Institute of Public Finance and Accountancy – CIPFA (2014). Good governance in the public sector. IFAC/CIPFA project to develop an international framework. Retrieved from https://www.accountancyeurope.eu/wp-content/uploads/Carruthers1011201141210.pdf

Connors, R., Smith, T., & Hickman, C. (2010). *The Oz principle: Getting results through individual and organizational accountability*. New York, NY: Penguin Group.

Couzens, K. (1985). The principle of public service. In B. Williams et al. (Eds.), *Politics, ethics and public service* (pp. 43–51). London: Royal Institute of Public Administration.

Du Gay, P. (2000). *In praise of bureaucracy: Weber, organization and ethics*. London: Sage.

Hanekon, S. X. (1984). Ethics in the South African public sector. *Politician*, 3(2), 58.

Hellsten, S., & Larbi, G. (2006). Public good or private good? The paradox of public and private ethics in the context of developing countries. *Public Administration and Development*, 26, 135–145.

Howell, J. (1988). Two faces of charisma: Socialized and personalized leadership in organizations. In J. A. Conger & R. N. Kanungo (Eds.), *The Jossey-Bass management series. Charismatic leadership: The elusive factor in organizational effectiveness* (pp. 213–236). San Francisco, CA: Jossey-Bass.

Johnston, M., & Doig, A. (1999). Different views on good government and sustainable anti-corruption strategies. In S. Stapenhurst & S. Kpundeh (Eds.), *Curbing corruption: Toward a model for building national integrity*. Washington, DC: World Bank.

Kaufmann, D., Kraay, A., & Mastruzzi, M. (2003). *Government matters III: Governance indicators for 1996–2002*. Policy Research Working Paper Series 3106, World Bank.

Kiwale, C. (2007). Strengthening public accountability and governance in controlling corruption in Tanzania: The role of the Ethics Secretariat. In S. Tindifa (Ed.), *Public accountability and good governance in East Africa* (pp. 19–23). Kampala: Fountain Publishers.

Laleye, M. (1993). Mechanisms for enhancing ethics and public accountability in francophone Africa. In S. Rasheed & D. Olowu (Eds.), *Ethics and accountability in African public services*. Addis-Ababa: UNICA and AAPAM.

Landell-Miss, P., & Serageldin, I. (1991). *Governance and the external factor*. Proceedings of the World Bank Annual Conference on Development Economics. Retrieved February 15, 2017, from https://academic.oup.com/wber/article-abstract/5/suppl_1/303/1712183

Langseth, P., Stapenhurst, R., & Pope, J. (1997). *The role of a national integrity system in fighting corruption*. Economic Development Institute of the World Bank; EDI Working papers.

Lewis, C., & Gilman, S. (2005). *The ethics challenge in public service: A problem solving guide*. Hoboken, NJ: Jossey-Bass.

McDougle, L. M. (2006). *Understanding and maintaining ethical values in the public sector through an integrated approach to leadership* (Unpublished Doctoral Thesis). San Diego, DA: University of San Diego.

Menzel, D. (2003). Public administration as a profession: Where do body and soul reside? *Public Integrity, 5*(3), 239–249.

Merriam-Webster Inc. (2014). *Merriam-Webster's Collegiate Dictionary* (11th ed.).

Miller, D., & Le Breton-Miller, I. (2006). Family governance and firm performance: Agency, stewardship, and capabilities. *Family Business Review, 19*, 73–87.

Munene, J., Schwartz, S., & Smith, P. (2000). Development in Sub-Saharan Africa: Cultural influences and managers' decision behaviour. *Public Administration and Development, 20*(4), 339–351.

Painter, M. (2000). Contracting, the enterprise culture and public sector ethics. In R. A. Chapman (Ed.), *Ethics in public service for the new millennium* (pp. 165–183). Aldershot: Ashgate.

Pierre, J. (2000). *Debating governance*. Oxford: Oxford University Press.

Polidano, C., & Hulme, D. (1997). No magic wands: Accountability and governance in developing countries. *Regional Development Dialogue, 18*, 1–16.

Rasheed, S. & Olowu, D. (1993). *Ethics and accountability in African public services*. United Nations Economic Commission for Africa; African Association for Public Administration and Management (AAPAM); Nairobi: ICIPE Science Press.

Sengupta, P. B. (1982). Impact of corrupt environment on the formation of favorable attitudes towards corruption. *Social Defense, 18*(July), 5–9.

Shah, A. (2005). On getting the giant to kneel: Approaches to a change in the bureaucratic culture. In A. Shah (Ed.), *Fiscal management: Public sector governance and accountability series* (pp. 211–229). Washington, DC: World Bank.

TANU (1967). *The Arusha Declaration and the TANU's policy on socialism and self-Reliance*. Dar es Salaam: Government Printer.
Tenga, T. (2010). *The legal framework for the regulation of public ethics in Tanzania – a review*. Ethics Commission's MP Workshop, Morogoro.
United Nations Department of Economic and Social Affairs – UNDESA (2001). *Public service ethics in Africa Volumes 1 and 2*. New York, NY: UNDP – Regional Bureau for Africa, United Nations.
URT (1932). *Companies ordinance (Cap. 212)*. Dar es Salaam: Government Printer.
URT (1992). *Public Corporations Act, 1992*. Dar es Salaam: Government Printer.
URT (1995a). *Public Leadership Code of Ethics (PLCE) Act No. 13 of 1995*. Dar es Salaam: Government Printers.
URT (1995b). *Sheria ya Maadili ya Viongozi wa Umma, Na. 13, ya 1995*. Dar es Salaam: Mpiga chapa wa Serikali.
URT (1996). *Presidential commission of inquiry: Report on the state of corruption in the country*. Dar es Salaam: Government Printer.
URT (1999). *The national framework on good governance*. Dar es Salaam, Tanzania: United Republic of Tanzania, Steering Committee on Good Governance, President's Office, Planning Commission.
Weber, J. (1996). Influences upon managerial moral decision making: Nature of the harm and magnitude of consequences. *Human Relations, 49*(1).

3 The public sector code of ethics

Tanzania's constitutional structure has long provided a case for unambiguous ethical standards, statutory law as well as codes of ethics and conduct acknowledging the importance of governance. In effect, an Ethics Secretariat is established under Article 132 of the Constitution of the United Republic of Tanzania. The Secretariat is empowered and given authority to inquire into the behaviour and conduct of any public official for ensuring that the provisions of the laws concerning the ethics of public leaders are duly observed.

The correlation between ethics and accountability, and its effect on good governance, provides the impetus to gauge, on one hand, the magnitude of accountability and the public's expectations and, on the other, the strength or otherwise of the rules and regulations as well as societal norms. Dobel (1990) argues that accountability, personal responsibility and prudence are the keys to ethical decision-making for individuals in the public sector. In other words, the strength or weakness in accountability is related to how well defined ethical standards are. Ethics as the foundation of accountability requires a clear set of standards to judge governance, which is an important metric for building overall public confidence.

In keeping with the constitution, enacting codes of ethics for public officials, is basically recognizing that high moral and ethical standards are required in the conduct of and public service delivery. A code of ethics for guiding public officials is necessary to prevent conflicts of interest in public office, improve standards of public service, and promote and strengthen the faith and confidence of the people in their public institutions and machinery. For example, it is expected that a public official be independent and impartial; not use public office to obtain private benefits; avoid any action which creates the appearance that he/she uses public office to obtain a private benefit as well as that government policy and decisions are made through the established processes and the public has confidence in the integrity of its government and its public officials.

Apart from the constitution, numerous other reforms over and above the code of ethics have been put in place in Tanzania over the years. The core motive behind all reforms has been to strengthen public accountability and governance. They include reform programmes for public service, public finance management and the legal sector, as well as programmes for strengthening the Prevention and Combating of Corruption Bureau (PCCB); establishing the Presidential

Commission of Inquiry Against Corruption, the Commission for Human Rights and Good Governance (CHRAGG) and the Public Leadership Code of Ethics Act; and introducing the National Anti-Corruption Strategy Action Plan.

Tanzania's code of ethics

The leadership code enacted by TANU, the ruling party from independence to 1977, formed the basis of the initial discussion of ethics and leadership in contemporary Tanzania. The continuous reference to the leadership code in different arenas to date, be they political, social or academic, is no accident. According to Tenga (2010), gauged against the famed Nolan principles which have been embraced globally as the benchmark, some aspects of the leadership code would not withstand the litmus test when it comes to openness and accountability.

Historically, the issue dates to Tanzania's founding father, Mwalimu Nyerere, whose stance on ethics was well known. It was indeed Nyerere's quest for a 'national ethic' which subsequently led to including the 'Leadership Code of Ethics' in the famous Arusha Declaration (Msekwa, 2016).

Although the embracement of ethics in public life dates to pre-independence/ colonial administration days and onward during the era of the Arusha Declaration, it was in the mid-1990s that amendments were made to the constitution by the introduction of Article 132. The article enacted the Public Leadership Code of Ethics (PLCE) Act No. 13 of 1995 and enabled the establishment of the Ethics Secretariat, an extra-ministerial government department under the President's Office.

The core doctrine that informs the code of ethics extends from expectations of incontestable integrity to prohibition on solicitation and acceptance of gifts and benefits. Public leaders are, for example, expected to act and relate in a prudent manner insofar as decision-making and conflict of interest are concerned. The core doctrine also encompasses confidentiality, prohibition of misuse of government property and declaration of wealth and liabilities. In addition to the receipt of declarations of wealth by public leaders, the Secretariat is also mandated to receive complaints from the public, on breaches of the code of ethics, and to inquire into allegations of breaches of the code of ethics by public leaders, from members of the executive, legislature and judiciary branches of government to the police and the military (URT, 1995).

Specifically, the Ethics Secretariat mainly has the duty to:

a   receive declarations which are required to be made by public leaders under the constitution or any other law;
b   receive allegations and notifications of breach of the code by members of the public; and
c   inquire into any alleged or suspected breach of the code by public leaders who are subject to the Act.

The Act establishes a statutory basis for the development of standards of ethics for public leaders. It aims to strengthen accountability and governance of specified bureaucrats and politicians defined in a broad sense as public leaders (Kiwale, 2007). The public leaders mentioned earlier also include those serving in SOEs and agencies. Thus, the basic principles and provisions underlying the code in detail are as follows:

- Unquestionable integrity: Public leaders are obliged to act with honesty, impartiality and openness (transparency).
- Decision-making: Public leaders must act in accordance with the law and in the public interest.
- Avoiding situations of conflict of interest: Resolve conflicts of interest in favour of the public interest.
- Public scrutiny: Official duties and private affairs to be subjected to close public scrutiny (need for transparency).
- Private interest: Avoid conflict with leadership responsibility.
- Gifts and benefits: Refrain from soliciting or accepting economic benefit other than incidental gifts, customary hospitality or other benefits of nominal value.
- Preferential treatment: Refrain from stepping out of official roles to assist private entities or persons in their dealings with government.
- Insider information: Refrain from taking advantage of or benefiting from information obtained during official duties/responsibilities and not generally available to the public.
- Government property: Public leaders are not allowed to directly or indirectly use or allow use of government property for private benefit.
- Post-employment: Refrain from acting in a manner that can cause ridicule to the service or taking advantage of previous office (conflict of interest).
- Declaration of wealth: assets and liabilities: The principles and ethical standards prescribed in the PLCE Act No. 13 of 1995 aim to institutionalize accountability for public leaders, which will enhance transparency, openness and fairness in decision-making processes, which are pillars of good governance, and hence limit corruption and mis-governance practices. The Ethics Secretariat has the important role of ensuring effective and efficient public scrutiny, which is the bedrock of public accountability.

It remains indisputable that values and integrity are important for maintaining sustainable social systems and developing a national ethics agenda. There are, however, numerous challenges that need to be addressed: Where does one begin for ethics interventions? Do ethical standards align with the national development agenda? Are ethics interventions inclusive, participatory and collaborative enough to ensure and enhance accountability? Are ethical standards stipulated in different laws, rules and regulations and reflected in national socio-economic frameworks? How about a national policy on ethics? The responses to the questions were first brought to the fore in the Arusha Declaration and subsequently via other pertinent policy documents.

Sentiments have been aired across the board to understanding without a doubt that the present Leadership Code of Ethics Act is in serious need of review (Tenga, 2010). Factors that have arisen since its enactment justify this conclusion. Some of the factors include

- New enacted legislation including the Commission for Human Rights and Good Governance Act (2001) and the Prevention and Combating of Corruption Act (2007);
- The 2003 Public Sector Regulations providing for a code of conduct for all civil servants;
- The codes of ethics for Local Government Councilors in 2000;
- The National Strategy for Growth and Reduction of Poverty incorporating good governance as one of the three clusters of the strategy;
- The introduction and adoption by the government of the National Anti-Corruption Strategy Action Plan as a strategic policy along with a framework of action for preventing and combating corruption, thereby strengthening governance, transparency, accountability, integrity and efficiency and improving public service delivery; and
- Recent regulatory changes, in particular in the tendering and procurement area, have been introduced under the Public Procurement Regulatory Authority (PPRA) regulations, and as have mechanisms to address specific areas of concern.

The constitutionally directed content of Rules of Public Leaders Ethics appear to be the legal pillars for the formal codes of ethics. The constitution states that these rules shall:

- Identify office holders who shall be subject to the rules of ethics.
- Require such holders of public offices to make formal declarations concerning their assets income and liabilities.
- Prohibit conduct that portrays a leader as dishonest, practices favouritism or lacks integrity; or forbid conduct that tends to encourage corrupt practices in public affairs or jeopardizes public interest or welfare.
- Prescribe penalties which may be imposed for breaches of codes of ethics.
- Provide for procedure, powers and practice to ensure compliance with the code of ethics.
- Prescribe any other provisions necessary for promotion and maintenance of *honesty*, *transparency*, *impartiality* and *integrity* in the conduct of public affairs and for the protection of public funds and any other public property.

These requirements are in line with the earlier elucidated Seven Principles of Public Life: selflessness, integrity, objectivity, accountability, openness, honesty and leadership (Tenga, 2010).

Critical incident: Arusha Declaration, ethics and accountability

The turnaround in ethics and accountability for better or worse in Tanzania cannot be discussed in isolation of the revered Arusha Declaration. In effect, Tanzania's Development Vision 2025 acknowledges that, indeed, the Arusha Declaration was the premiere national vision (URT, 1999b). Without a doubt, the development vision and some of the policies for social and economic transformation are guided by the principles enshrined in the Arusha Declaration. It is the Arusha Declaration that brought to the fore and sought to realize a set of fundamental moral, ethical and civil values which stand the test of time (URT, 1999a).

The declaration brought about a code of ethics for leaders with the objective of separating business and politics, and providing a check on those in power from using their offices to accumulate wealth (Kinana, 2011). When asked as to why he agreed to the Arusha Declaration, Mwalimu Julius Nyerere said:

> A short time after independence a privileged group was emerging from the political leaders and bureaucrats who had been poor under colonial rule but were now beginning to use their positions in the Party and Government to enrich themselves. This kind of development would alienate the leadership from the people. So we came with a new national objective; we stressed that development is all about our people and not just a small and privileged minority. The Arusha Declaration was what made Tanzania distinctly Tanzanian. We stated what we stood for, we laid down a code of conduct for our leaders and we made an effort to achieve those goals.[1]

It can be said that the declaration failed to address the complex and dynamic nature of policies and incentive structures necessary to drive the development process; in other words, it underestimated the role of incentives and the magnitude of external pressures. State control of the major means of production, and the prospect of growth via a viable public sector investment as the engine of economic growth and development, dominated. Today, Tanzania enjoys national unity, social cohesion, peace and stability due to the declaration's elucidated core social values.

Some contend that the values of the Arusha Declaration, as well as the prevalent political and social-economic dynamics, are still relevant today across Tanzania society. Issa Shivji argues that "the Arusha Declaration was not made defunct overnight after the Zanzibar Declaration was passed, there were underground efforts to devalue the first declaration right from the early 1980s" (Shivji, 2013). The argument goes on further stating that social evils (typical of eroded ethics) like corruption were by-products of undermining and ignoring the important policy document that served as Tanzania's political, social and economic compass.

Tanzania's prospects of becoming a prosperous nation cannot be attained unless the country revives the values and principles of the Arusha Declaration and emphasizes adherence to leadership ethics and the promotion of human equality (Shivji, 2013). It is the hope of many that these values are appreciated and have been incorporated into the Development Vision 2025.

Ethics code – governance of parastatals and business ethics

Whatever the motivation for setting up a business entity, acceptable principles of business, either public or private, highlight the expectation of reasonable return as central. That being the case, shareholder dereliction, be it that of government or private business, is similar to dereliction of duty and is unethical or contrary to good business practice. The parastatal sector has cruised through the eras without having borne this in mind.

The application of outdated ideas goes back to the Ujamaa era. The environment at the time subdued such dereliction from being seen as such, which impeded innovativeness and creativity in governance. At the time, the mindsets of the leaders, as well as that of society, were influenced by the dogma that parastatals have no owner, for they belonged to the people. It was this deep-rooted belief that dominated the thinking about the 'sacredness' of the parastatals and their governance, then and on to today. Not much in terms of innovativeness has been taken into consideration by way of their context following economic liberalization. The shortfalls could as well be traced back to absence of or failure in strategic management.

It is noteworthy that the statutes of some parastatals did not, for instance, outline such mundane matters as board membership qualifications (Mwapachu, 1983). As a result, the Boards of Directors of the parastatals left many questions unanswered. For example, how free and autonomous are public enterprises in strategy formulation and management? It is not farfetched to conclude that the parastatals were nothing more than instruments in the implementation of the party and the government policies (Mwapachu, 2005).

El-Namaki (1979) was, during the time, of the assertion that "Several of the current symptoms of operational failure of some Tanzanian enterprises could be effortlessly associated with mediocre demonstration of managerial stamina by the respective boards." Bottom line, the buck stops with the boards and the boards were consistently weak (Mwapachu, 1983). Control of public entities at the time revolved around the ruling Party, TANU, and government's revered instruments; specifically the 1971 Party Guidelines (*Mwongozo*) and Presidential Circular No. 2 of 1969. The circular stipulated principles upon which public entities, and therefore their control, were established. Likewise, the party guidelines stipulated that:

> the conduct and activities of the parastatals must be looked into to ensure that they help further our policy of socialism and self-reliance. The activities of the parastatal should be a source of satisfaction and not discontent. The party must ensure that the parastatals do not spend money extravagantly on items which do not contribute to the development of the national economy as a whole.[2]

The control aspect insofar as these parastatals were concerned was put to the test. For example, in 1969 the party ruled against Karadha company's (a hire-purchase subsidiary of the National Bank of Commerce) decision to provide public loans for purchase of private vehicles. Likewise, the Tabora region's party executive committee decided to hand over some of the Tabora Regional Trading Company's business functions to private businessmen after being dissatisfied by services provided by the SOEs/parastatals (Mwapachu, 1983).

Strategic management encompasses continuous planning, monitoring, analysis and assessment of all that is necessary for an organization to meet its goals and objectives. Consistently analysing internal and external strengths and weaknesses, formulating, executing and evaluating action plans, and making changes where desired results fall short remained the Achilles heel of the parastatals. The shortcoming was vivid in their operational efficiency, cost-effective delivery and innovativeness.

The argument that parastatal managers lacked creativity and innovativeness has been advanced throughout the sectors across the economy. In many a case "managers played it safe and avoided risky and innovative decisions" because of the perceived lack of control. The counter to that has always been that such controls were imposed on parastatals for purposes of ensuring that they serve public interest, that is, ensuring that national goals and objectives are adhered to in implementation (Mwapachu, 1983).

In a business context, operational efficiency, the ratio between the input to run a business and the output gained from the business, is what is strived for. Strategies to accomplish the delivery of quality goods or services in the most cost-effective and timely manner are part of the efficiency formula. For a long time, this has not registered as far as public entities are concerned. Owners (the public), therefore, have been neither getting the most value for their money from deployed resources nor seeing efficiency from the elimination of waste in business operations.

With the apparent dilution of ethics in recent years, there have been new expectations on business ethics and governance ushered in part by the 'new leadership' under President Magufuli. It is important, therefore, to raise issues pertaining to ethics and governance at this juncture, so as to provide a useful background for an objective discussion of business ethics and corporate responsibility in the current economic environment, given the high public interest in light of corporate governance failures.

Ethics code, governance and accountability in a market economy

Bouncing off the definition of corporate governance, Mallin (2002) places responsibility as an element of ethics of care[3] beside mechanism of control through laws and rules. To the contrary, Gillan and Starks (1998) view corporate governance as the system of laws, rules and factors that control operations at a company. At the same time, corporate governance is depicted in the *Cadbury Report* (1992) as "the system by which companies are directed and controlled." The report is not merely concerned with the control mechanism but also the leadership required for directing the respective companies.

From a stakeholder perspective, corporate governance mechanisms can be categorized into typologies internal and external to the companies. These pave the way for two models of corporate governance, namely the "shareholder" model and the "stakeholder" model, to emerge (Mamun, Yasser, & Rahman, 2013). Yet another model of corporate governance is built on agency theory. Under this model, shareholders as principals delegate roles to managers as agents, and risk is shared between the two parties alongside concealed conflict of interest (Eisenhardt, 1989). Agency theory, however, is insufficient in explicating how managers must address non-direct shareholder interests such as political pressures and societal expectations from companies (Nwabueze & Mileski, 2008).

Within Tanzania's public corporation entities, a 'stakeholders' model was advocated in theory while in practice what was implemented was the 'shareholder' model. Much as the shareholder model seemed to fit right in, what was happening was that shareholders had abandoned what was theirs and the delegated agent became both.

Corporate governance, which surfaced as a critical part of modern management (Monks & Minow, 2004) and was viewed as a system utilized to shield investors' interests, was a no-man's entity in Tanzania. What happened defied Shleifer and Vishny's (1997) contention that suppliers of capital saw governance as a means to assure themselves a return. Neither was the situation congruent to La Porta et al.'s (2000) definition of corporate governance as a collection of investors' protective mechanisms against both the owners and their agents.

Instead of corporate governance being the mechanism to help entities reduce agency costs and better align the interests of owners and investors (Picou & Rubach, 2006), it deteriorated the very owners' and investors' positions, by way of bleeding resources right, left and centre. The adopted corporate governance mechanisms neither maximized shareholders' return on investment nor provided the requisite accurate information to shareholders to enable them to decide whether to continue to entrust the agents. The agents were not judged in terms of the entity's performance but rather on some form of cronyism, disguised as performance measurement.

As such, the way corporate governance was practiced in Tanzania was not regarded as "a set of relationships between a company's management, its board, and other stakeholders," as espoused in the authoritative body such as the *OECD* (OECD, 2004) which looks into a wider network of relationships including other stakeholders.

Myriad definitions address different stakeholders' roles in the context of corporate governance and its applicability in Tanzania. The definitions broadly view governance as a course of action or a means, as well as interactions among stakeholders that reflect numerous shades of ethics and accountability. What was witnessed with the erosion of ethics and accountability in public entities was partly a result of absence of governance guidelines, as the country shifted from Ujamaa as the guiding light to embracing a market economy. According to Kasalla (2002), erosion of ethics and absence of transparency resulted in a Tanzania that was akin to social promiscuity, as leaders across the sectors of the economy succumbed. The erosion, on one hand, inhibited the functioning of the market and, on the other, distorted the allocation and use of resources (Sitta, 2005). The pursuit of market-oriented policies, including divestiture of public enterprises, and the creation of

Enforcing the code of ethics

Tanzania's multitude of rules, laws and regulations as well as oversight mechanisms are aimed at preventing, investigating and sanctioning unethical practices. At face value, these should adequately provide the requisite tools to enforce the code. It is no secret, however, that when it came to the code of ethics, the government's internal control systems were inadequate, or were insufficiently enforced, to prevent abuses of power and authority – a common non-adherence to the requirements of the code of ethics. In the absence of adequate enforcement of the existing laws, rules and regulations, opportunities for abuse on a massive scale are likely to emerge and persist.

According to the Warioba Report (Warioba, 1996[4]), the current situation is a result of the failure to enforce rules and regulations, or the wilful circumvention of them, along with weaknesses of the institutional set-up to deal with enforcing the code of ethics. Placing emphasis on investigating and sanctioning unethical practice is critical. A special emphasis on enforcement and punishment can only be attained sustainably if the underlying causes are addressed (Klitgaard, 1998). Systemic non-adherence of the ethics code is indicative of public sector malfunction and consequent poor performance.

The main focus of public procurement legislation and regulations is to ensure transparency and accountability. These are most often the key motivations to individual and instructional probity, a key deterrent to collusion and corruption and a key prerequisite for procurement credibility. It is challenging, insofar as the code of ethics is concerned, when rules and regulations are not implemented or enforced.

Prior to the coming into being of the Public Procurement Regulatory Authority Act (and subsequent revisions), regulations and related legislation, the enforcement of procurement laws/rules remained passive and permissive. Since the Act's first passage, a number of challenges in the implementation of the law have persisted, even when Parliament repealed and re-enacted the Public Procurement Act in 2004 and 2011 (TPJ, 2016). The public sector was characterized by ever-increasing expenditure and procurement which consistently created opportunities for malpractice, corruption and wasteful public procurement. To be able to vitiate and minimize the chances of the malpractice and other ills, the enacted rules and regulations have incorporated oversight function that includes new procurement-related documentation. Indeed, enforcement of any law/rule requires proper awareness and orientation, which necessitates a revisit to bring them into conformity with other laws/regulations without straying from international best practices. Reviews may provide a second look at, among other things, increasing the vetting threshold of contracts by a procuring entity's legal officers, involving special groups in the public procurement, negotiating prices with the lowest evaluated bidders, providing a preference scheme to local contractors, local manufactured goods and local experts' involvement in joint venture agreements between local and foreign firms (TPJ, 2016), and most of all, providing value for money over time.

One of the biggest enforcement challenges has been the inadequate oversight function. Experience shows that accountability is not enforced. The parliamentary committee's oversight function, for instance, is dependent on annual audit reports of the Controller and Auditor General (CAG), the "public watchdog." It is evident and unfortunate that the implementation of CAG recommendations along with those of the parliamentary committee have been, if anything, sporadic. Again, the oversight function has no teeth! In absence of reliable and effective enforcement mechanisms, which will in turn rebuild public trust, the aspirations of the ethics code will remain a pleasing fleeting illusion to be pursued but never attained.

Erosion of corporate ethics and accountability

It is not an overstatement to say that the erosion of ethics and, as a result, accountability in public corporation entities in Tanzania followed the demise of the Arusha Declaration and the subsequent adoption of the Zanzibar Resolution. Some within Tanzania claim that as soon as the principles of good governance laid down by Mwalimu Nyerere were ignored, Tanzania's good governance (broadly speaking) started to be corrupted (Kassala, 2002). This could be seen from the growing economic callousness by those with economic power, or say in the distribution of the national cake, to the indifference in the suffering of ordinary citizens due to economic difficulties facing the nation. It was no surprise, albeit a bit too late, that President Mkapa sought to address the issue by starting with the public service.

> Tanzania stands at the threshold of a new era: The new era demands a transformed public service. This will be a service that is truly transparent and accountable to the public. The service will have zero tolerance for corrupt behaviour. The service will guide the Nation as it crosses irreversibly into a poverty-free zone in the 21st Century.[5]
>
> (President Mkapa, June 20, 2000)

The Public Sector Reform Programme (PSRP) launched in early 2000 aimed at transforming public service into result-oriented public service delivery. Among other things, it aimed to create a public service of the highest caliber and integrity, that is both responsive to and supportive of national efforts.

It is unfortunate, however, that for the most part the capacity to support the implementation of good governance was curtailed by weak monitoring and oversight functions (Morara, 2010). Government ministries responsible for monitoring particularly parastatals, and other mechanisms such as independent regulators, fell short in fulfilling their role. In any event, most were generally weak when it came to implementation and fell prey to external political influences. Policy measures in certain instances magnified the erosion of ethics as well. A good example is how the privatization policy as a reform measure was undertaken.

Code of ethics and privatization

In the early 1990s, Tanzania underwent major privatization of public entities, an important step to address shortcomings in governance including mismanagement and non-performance of the parastatals (Kabwe, 2011). Privatization embraced as part of the broad public sector reforms in Tanzania was touted as a good example of corporate governance solution, given the poor performance that public corporation entities registered over the years. The process continues today, and in the interim a number of reforms were instituted in the name of enhancing governance.

The legacy of privatization, however, is related to the state's failure to establish and require accompanied effective governance mechanisms (Morara, 2010), of which the code of ethics was to be part. Indeed, for successful privatization, good corporate governance is indispensable, as it balances shareholder expectations and rights with accountability, responsibility and trust, which are the three hallmarks of good corporate governance and which allow for the existence of an efficient post-privatization.

The reforms addressed such issues as the lack of effective, sound and adequate regulatory frameworks. This was followed with legislative measures to establish regulatory agencies to enhance regulatory processes, which consisted of putting in place rules and standards, as well as monitoring compliance and enforcement. This was a good initial point in promoting governance but fell short because of failure in effective application.

Privatization was also linked to another corporate governance challenge, namely the abuse of corporate authority. The abuse by boards and regulatory authorities included unjustified augmentation of executive benefits and privileges in varied forms of allowances.

Moreover, this was the time when governance was left in the hands of the greedy and corrupt, who corroded not only ethics but also public resources for own benefits. It was the time also that bureaucracy became inefficient and corruption crept in to entangle service delivery (Kinana, 2011). Corruption can and does indeed sabotage national development. It leads to a loss of government legitimacy and of public trust and support (Sitta, 2005).

Along with the aforementioned aspirations, other reform measures were adopted and implemented simultaneously, as Tanzania opted for a holistic strategic approach to improve governance. This is reflected in both the National Framework on Good Governance (NFGG) and the National Anti-Corruption Strategy and Action Plan (NACSAP) (Sitta, 2005). It was the NFGG that gave rise to the Accountability, Transparency and Integrity Programme (ATIP). ATIP aimed at supporting NFGG through strengthening the legal and judiciary system, enhancing public financial accountability and strengthening oversight and watchdog institutions.

NACSAP, which came about as a result of stakeholders' collaborative efforts to combat corruption, envisaged improving the quality of public service delivery through an effective and transparent system of procedure and regulations; enhanced organizational capacity to deliver a high quality standard of service; and increased public awareness of procedures, standards of services, codes of conduct and their rights in general.

As such, it has been realized that good governance has to become a critical element in the management and growth of the economy. To a large extent, economic crises and corporate failures have been closely associated with the lack of good corporate governance. Indeed, absence of sound corporate governance has fuelled corruption and cronyism and suppressed the making of sound and sustainable economic decisions. Corruption can and does sabotage national development and lead to a loss of government legitimacy and of public trust and support (Sitta, 2005).

Code of ethics and Tanzania's future

Current governance enhancement efforts at the national level, enshrined in the Development Vision 2025, are aimed for the future of Tanzania and tracks down to corporate level ethics and accountability. Governance in Tanzania will be enhanced if and only if it does away with outmoded ways (Kassala, 2002). There should be deliberate efforts to embrace the pillars of corporate governance including but not limited to transparency, accountability, integrity and respect for the rights of all stakeholders, not only in policy pronouncement (lip service) but also in action and all aspects of public life.

The Development Vision clearly highlights Tanzania's experience, which reflects the promulgations and aspirations of the Arusha Declaration, under which good governance was identified as one of the key prerequisites for attaining the development goals. Various policies aimed to build up governance capacities and leadership skills, as well as a developmental mindset within the requisite ethical framework, have a significant role to play toward national endeavours. The realization that good governance is essential for the attainment of the Development Vision deems necessary the adoption of strategies to build integrity by, among other things, promoting accountability and transparency.

Along the objectives, lately President John Magufuli has identified three specific ethics-related areas to which he has given top priority: (a) cutting wasteful and unnecessary public expenditure, (b) fighting impunity in public service delivery and (c) tackling corruption that has long plagued our nation (Msekwa, 2016).

In other words, these may be described as the three leading areas which have shown a clear, unambiguous demonstration of absence of leadership ethics in the governance system. The actions are clearly aimed at ensuring that the relevant actors in our governance system are made to comply with the stipulated leadership ethics requirements. Ethics is obligatory in a good leader. Ethics is the heart of leadership. Ethics is the guiding mirror in public service delivery across the economy.

Good governance means integrity, commitment and transparency in public service delivery. It implies the embracement of innovative, non-traditional approaches to addressing the numerous challenges. This calls for departure from old ways of doing things led by ethical and accountable leaders. Good leaders emanate from good citizens. Ethical leaders emerge from ethics and integrity embracing citizenry.

Notes

1 *New Internationalist Magazine*, 1998. Shivji, Issa (2012). Self-reliance and Self-sufficiency: nationalist reaction to globalist imposition. Paper for the International Conference on 'The Meaning of Sufficiency Economy: Theory and Practice in Society, Economy and Business', to take place on 16–17, February 2012, Bangkok, on the occasion of King Bhumibol's 84th birthday.
2 TANU Party Guidelines, 1971.
3 Ethics of care, also called care ethics, is a feminist philosophical perspective that uses a relational and context-bound approach toward morality and decision-making. The term *ethics of care* refers to ideas concerning both the nature of morality and normative ethical theory. The ethics of care perspective stands in stark contrast to ethical theories that rely on principles to highlight moral actions – such as Kantian deontology, utilitarianism and justice theory – and is not meant to be absolute and incontrovertible. www.britannica.com/topic/ethics-of-care
4 Government of the United Republic of Tanzania, *Report of the Presidential Commission of Inquiry Against Corruption*, November 1996.
5 President Mkapa at the launch of the Public Sector Reform Programme (PSRP), June 20, 2000.

Bibliography

Cadbury, A. (1992). *Cadbury report – Report of the committee on the financial aspects of corporate governance*. London: Gee & Co. Ltd.

Dobel, P. J. (1990). Integrity in the public sector. *Public Administration Review, 50*(3), 354–366.

Eisenhardt, K. (1989, January). Agency theory: An assessment and review. *The Academy of Management Review, 14*(1), 57–74.

El-Namaki, M. (1979). *Problems of management in a developing environment: The case of Tanzania (State Enterprises Between 1967 and 1975)*. Amsterdam; New York: North-Holland Pub. Co.; New York: Sole distributors for the U.S.A. and Canada, Elsevier North-Holland.

Gillan, S., & Starks, L. T. (1998). *A survey of shareholder activism: Motivation and empirical evidence*. Retrieved from SSRN https://ssrn.com/abstract=663523 or http://dx.doi.org/10.2139/ssrn.663523

Kabwe, Z. (2011). *Public enterprises in Tanzania: Challenges and prospects*. Comments presented to the CEOs Roundtable Dinner.

Kassala, C. D. N. (2002). *From corruption of good governance to good governance of corruption in Tanzania*. A Paper presented At the Debate on Corruption in Tanzania, Karimjee Grounds, Dar es Salaam (unpublished).

Kinana, A. (2011, March 4). *Keynote address to the "Legacy of Julius Nyerere: Economies, Politics and Solidarities in Tanzania and Beyond"*. Conference, Carleton University, Canada.

Klitgaard, R. (1998). International Cooperation Against Corruption. *Finance & Development, 35*(1), 3–6. Washington, DC.

Mallin, C. (2002). The relationship between corporate governance, transparency and financial disclosure. *Corporate Governance – An International Review, 10*(4), 253–255.

Mamun, A., Yasser, Q., & Rahman, A. (2013). A discussion of the suitability of only one vs more than one theory for depicting corporate governance. *Modern Economy, 4*, 37–48. http://dx.doi.org/10.4236/me.2013.41005

Monks, R. A. G., & Minow, N. 2004 (2002). *Corporate governance* (2nd ed. (reprint)). Oxford: Blackwell Publishing Ltd.

Morara, B. (2010). *Enhancement of corporate governance through privatization*. Nairobi: Privatization Commission of Kenya.
Msekwa (2016, June 2). Ethics is the heart of leadership: Why Minister Kitwanga's sacking was a big, good lesson. *The Daily News*, Tanzania.
Mwapachu, J. V. (1983). *Management of public enterprises in developing countries: The Tanzania experience*. New Delhi, Bombay, Kolkata: Oxford & IBH Publishing Co.
Mwapachu, J. V. (2005). *Confronting new realities: Reflections on Tanzania's radical transformation*. Dar es Salaam: E & D Ltd.
Nwabueze, U., & Mileski, J. (2008). The challenge of effective governance: The case of Swiss Air, corporate governance. *The International Journal of Business in Society*, 8(5), 583–594. Retrieved from https://doi.org/10.1108/14720700810913250
Nyerere, J. K. (1968). *Freedom and socialism*. Arusha: Oxford University Press.
Picou, A., & Rubach, M. (2006, April). Does good governance matter to institutional investors? Evidence from the enactment of corporate governance guidelines. *Journal of Business Ethics*, 65(1), 55–67.
Polidano, C., & Hulme, D. (1997). No magic wands: Accountability and governance in developing countries. *Regional Development Dialogue*, 18, 1–16.
Shivji, Issa (2012). Self-reliance and Self-sufficiency: nationalist reaction to globalist imposition. Paper for the International Conference on 'The Meaning of Sufficiency Economy: Theory and Practice in Society, Economy and Business', to take place on 16-17, February 2012, Bangkok, on the occasion of King Bhumibol's 84th birthday.
Shivji, I. (2013). *Revive Arusha Declaration, else prosperity will remain elusive*. Retrieved June 6, 2015, from: http://azimiolaarusha.blogspot.com/2013/10/prof-issa-shivji-revive-arusha.html
Shleifer, A., & Vishny, R. W. (1997). A survey of corporate governance. *Journal of Finance*, 52(2), 737–783.
Sitta, S. (2005). *Integrity environment and investment promotion: The case of Tanzania*. Presented at the OECD Addis Ababa Conference.
TANU (1967). *The Arusha Declaration and the TANU's policy on socialism and self-reliance* (1st ed.). Dar es Salaam: TANU, Publicity Section.
TPJ (2016). Publication of Public Procurement Regulations 2016. *Tanzania Procurement Journal*. Retrieved from https://ppra.go.tz/index.php/news-archive/531-publication-of-public-procurement-regulations-2016-very-close
Tenga, T. (2010). *The legal framework for the regulation of public ethics in Tanzania – a review*. Ethics Commission's MP Workshop, Morogoro.
URT (1932). *Companies ordinance (Cap. 212)*. Dar es Salaam: Government Printer.
URT (1992). *Public Corporations Act, 1992*. Dar es Salaam: Government Printer.
URT (1995). *Public Leadership Code of Ethics (PLCE) Act No. 13 of 1995*. Dar es Salaam: Government Printer.
URT (1996). Presidential commission of inquiry: Report on the state of corruption in the country. Dar es Salaam: Government Printer.
URT (1999a). *Development Vision, 2025*. Dar es Salaam: President's office, Planning and Privatisation Commission, Government Printer.
URT (1999b). *The national framework on good governance*. Dar es Salaam, Tanzania: United Republic of Tanzania, Steering Committee on Good Governance, President's Office, Planning Commission.
Warioba (1996). *United Republic of Tanzania: Presidential commission of inquiry: Report on the state of corruption in the country*. Dar es Salaam: Government Printer.

4 Corporate evolution and challenges

In the world of business, evolution is part of the real world, and businesses evolve mostly from low to high value added, taking companies to new heights. At the country level, the corporate sector is the engine of growth, as value creation and value addition ensue. Value addition activities in the manufacturing sector, for example, have been a characteristic feature of the evolving corporate sector. In the case of Tanzania, the quest to build a manufacturing foundation early on after independence as a basis for industrial development continued to be a major component of its development strategy. The industrial sector was expected to take the lead in economic transformation to a more dynamic economy. This called for structural change and sustained income growth and for the emergence of what was envisaged to be a formidable corporate sector in Tanzania.

Evolution of the public corporations (parastatal)

From the end of colonial rule to the present day, the public corporation in Tanzania evolved in numerous phases. Phasing calls for analytical approaches in understanding institutions and pertinent policies in the ever-changing context that can explain what went into their development, rise, fall and, in some cases, ultimate demise.

Corporate evolution occurred through the phases in which development strategies traversed, from the post-independence mixed economy (1961–66), through state-led import substitution (1967–85) and the reform period (1986–95), to the current period under which industrialization occupies an elevated role in economic transformation endeavours.

Upon independence in 1961, Tanzania inherited a small and undiversified industrial sector. Like many other newly independent African states, it was characterized by a small private sector, which was more involved in traditional trading activities. A higher proportion of the private sector comprised traders, brokers and merchants rather than industrial investors or entrepreneurs. As a result, given the smallness (scale-wise) of the private sector at the time, state involvement was justified. The small private sector was dominated by non-indigenous entrepreneurs. Like in many African countries, ethnically the dominant trading class constituted non-indigenous African players: Asians in East and Central Africa and the Lebanese in West Africa. To advance what was therefore a proactive approach to economic well-being, the establishment of state-owned enterprises became a logical and valid policy proposition. The leadership saw state-owned enterprises as the viable solution to address shortfalls in scale and involvement of the majority population as well as skill development and technology transfer. This was a rational and beneficial approach from a social and economic perspective, to address the "entrepreneurial gaps" faced by the indigenous private sector. In effect, government involvement in economic activities was seen as the natural order of affairs (Gibbon, 1995).

Upon independence, Tanzania, under the late first President Mwalimu Julius Nyerere, embarked on efforts to create its own 'distinct national identity' and settled on a development model based on African socialism that was premised on equity and self-reliance. The ultimate objective was to guarantee that welfare growth benefits much of the population. The particular visualization of welfare growth embodied the people's increased access to social services, such as schools, healthcare and water supplies, across the nation, in both rural and urban areas.

Alongside what appeared to be strong sentiments of "economic nationalism" among independent African countries, the evident genuine weakness was the subordinate status of African private enterprises and that African economies were largely in the hands of foreigners. The coming into being of state-owned enterprises was to enable the state to carry out economic activities that private entrepreneurs could undertake and minimize the dominance of foreign enterprise. These were the war cries, motivations and rationales of many African countries for creating state-owned enterprises and the subsequent emergence of the relatively large and at one point dominant state-owned enterprise sector in countries like Tanzania.

At independence in 1961, then Tanganyika's economic development was largely the result of private sector initiative, with the colonial government providing requisite administrative services and infrastructure. It is no surprise that its participation was limited to the purchase of minority stake and the establishment of crop marketing boards for main export crops including cotton, coffee and sisal. Of all the entities with government shareholding, it was the diamond mine, the salt mine and the meat-packing plant in which it had majority stake (World Bank, 1988).[1] The shares were held then as has become customary since, by the Treasury Registrar. Even in the case of the three undertakings, to a large extent the government remained inactive in terms of the entities' management, regulatory as well as monitoring aspects.

By 1966, about 43 enterprises were government 'owned' (World Bank, 1988). A large proportion of the companies' assets were in the electricity and mining sectors, only 10% in manufacturing and the rest spread over sectors such as construction, tourism, agriculture, commerce and finance. The trend continued until the 1967 Arusha Declaration milestone. A number of enterprises were added to the government's portfolio, in line with the aspirations of the newly adopted Arusha Declaration. The entities included the National Housing Corporation, the National Insurance Corporation and the National Development Corporation (NDC). NDC's holding company-like status was meant to specifically facilitate the management and promotion of state-owned entities in the same manner as was the case of several additional marketing boards and financial and banking institutions.

Domestic resources were inadequate to meet all the goals, hence the need to look outside for investors. Overall, the government's policy to attract foreign investors came under the assumption that the main thrust in industrial and other investments was to come from private investment. The public sector was merely to fill in shortfalls left by private investments – as a gap filler or a necessity where an opportunity is not attractive enough to investors. In order to encourage private investors, the government introduced a number of incentives, including guaranteed repatriation of profits. In effect, the First Five Year Development Plan – FYDP (1964–69), with its ambitious public investment programme, could not escape private sector dominance. Its implementation thus worked on the assumption that 75% of the investments in the industrial sector would originate from private players (FYDP). In later years, however, the government reliance on private investment fell through as the inflow of private capital was far less than expected and continued to flow into traditional areas rather than broadening and diversifying the industrial base, as anticipated.

The Arusha Declaration laid down a new social-economic orientation. It encompassed state control of important industries as part of the effort to put the commanding heights of the economy in the hands of the masses. Alongside this new orientation was collective production in Ujamaa villages (*Ujamaa* may be literally translated to "familyhood"), meeting the population's basic needs and the emphasis on development endeavours based on own abilities and resources (self-reliance).

The period was one that placed extra emphasis on self-reliance and even more emphasis on the attainment of social objectives, e.g. employment generation and rural-urban equality. The economic blueprint, on the other hand, emphasized public ownership of the means of production, central planning and control, the principal instruments to attain set objectives. The philosophy was spelt out in Tanzania's economic blueprint, the Arusha Declaration. It advocated for public ownership of means of production with the goal of gaining control of the economy, to mobilize resources to serve a number of socio-economic objectives, including:

- to promote self-reliance;
- to force the pace of economic development by mobilizing and generating surpluses for investment that might otherwise be used for consumption or leave the country;
- to change the pattern of development, placing more emphasis on rural and agricultural development and production to meet basic needs;
- to distribute the fruits of development more equitably by increasing productivity, employment and the standards of living of the masses, concentrating on the production of basic needs and eliminating profiteering and exploitation; and
- to accomplish these ends efficiently, that is, at minimum cost to the economy (World Bank, 1988).

It is no surprise, therefore, that along with the Arusha Declaration was a rapid explosion of 'public sector' institutions (the parastatals) and assets. The number of these institutions rose 70% (from 43 in 1966 to 73 by the end of 1967). There were 380 in 1979 and over 450 by the 1990s (PSRP, 2008).

Tanzania's development vision as envisioned in the Arusha Declaration consisted of three major components, namely the creation of Ujamaa villages, the creation of an extended parastatal sector, and government control of and intervention in the market process.

The 1972 *Villagisation Programme* was the official modus operandi for the creation of Ujamaa villages. It involved mobilizing the population dispersed over wide areas in rural Tanzania into prior identified locations. The intention was to ease the delivery of social services to the rural population and to increase efficiency in agricultural production. In the case of the latter, individual household farming was replaced with communal and state farming. Although the villagization move was voluntary early on, it later (the beginning of 1974) became mandatory. To the apparent dismay of the leadership, the implementation pace of the villagization programme was unsatisfactory (Scott, 1998).

It was unfortunate that the villagization programme did not bring about the envisaged increased efficiency in production but instead led to a progressive decline in agricultural productivity. In effect, communal efforts did not produce as well as when the farmers were engaged in production as individual households.

The second key component of the development strategy was to put in place a large parastatal sector as a means for stimulating overall economic development. At the onset of the Arusha Declaration, the government began a campaign to nationalize all notable foreign-owned operations from the production, distribution and finance sectors and created new state-owned companies. With a special focus on import substitution, the leadership intended through the 1975 Basic Industry Strategy, among other things, to develop domestic heavy industry to replace the importation of inputs used in the production of domestic consumer goods.

The public sector (parastatal) role in Tanzania

The public sector in Tanzania has a large impact in the development of the country's economy. Public expenditure comprises a major part of the gross domestic product (GDP), and public sector entities are the major employers and significant market participants. Through a political process, the public sector determines the outcomes it wants to achieve as well as the types and levels of intervention. The intervention may be through legislation or regulations, delivery of goods and services, income redistribution via tax regimes or social security payments and the assets ownership in state-owned enterprises.

The emergence of the dominant public sector is traced back to 1967, following the adoption of the Arusha Declaration and its aspirations. The government of the day pledged to build a socialist economic management system stressing the importance of active state intervention in the nation's economic life, via ownership of the means of production. It further prophesized that although private

48 Corporate evolution and challenges

investment is to be encouraged, by and large, economic activities are to be promoted and owned by the state. It emphasized public ownership of industrial and commercial property. Among assets listed as "major means of production" are:

> the land; forests, mineral resources; water; oil and electricity; communications: transport; banks; insurance; import and export trade; wholesale business; the steel, machine-tool, arms, motor car, cement and fertilizer factories; the textile industry; and any other big industry upon which a large section of the population depend for their living.[2]

As a first step in implementing the Arusha Declaration, the government announced in February of 1967 the nationalization of nine commercial banks, eight import-export firms and seven milling firms with associated food manufacturing interests. Act No. 1 of 1967 was the Act "to establish the National Bank of Commerce and to vest in the Bank the Assets and Liabilities of Banks hitherto carrying on Banking Business in the United Republic." It did not affect, however, the status of the People's Bank of Zanzibar and the then National Cooperative and Development Bank of Tanzania. By the same token, the State Trading Corporation (STC) was created to undertake all export-import business of the nationalized import-export businesses.

Sector-wise, the parastatals were more important and dominant in some sectors than others, reflecting to a certain extent the priority of the time. In effect, 30%, slightly less than 30% and 14% of the assets in the parastatals were found in energy and mineral sector, industry and trade sector and agriculture sector, respectively. At the same time, for instance, the parastatals boasted of generating 47% of manufacturing sector's value addition and job creation as well as 37% and 68% of the same in the transport sector (World Bank, 1988). Forty percent of the assets acquired via nationalization were in the commercial sector, 36% were in manufacturing and the rest was split between agriculture and finance. With the growth of the public sector, institutions came along the introduction of regulations and controls. The propagation of such controls and related policies adversely affected the private business climate. By the early 1980s, the parastatals had grown to more than 400 companies (Fischer, 2006).

The development of the parastatals was also accompanied by a strong anti-private sector drive. As Henley (1993, p. 463) notes, "what was left of the private sector was placed at a disadvantage relative to the public sector." The then new Leadership Code of 1971 disallowed people in leadership positions and public employees from having a second source of income either in private business or from renting property. This further reinforced the growth of an environment hostile to private sector development. As many authors point out, the situation contrasted with that of the country's neighbours, Kenya for example, where civil servants were encouraged to have private sideline income sources (Fischer, 2006). Nonetheless, it is important to note that from the start, mismanagement, embezzlement and widespread inefficiency were the characteristic feature of almost all public enterprises (Fischer, 2006; Lofchie & Callaghy, 1995). Many reasons have been brought forth to explain and illustrate this, to no satisfaction. On a closer look, however, certainly and most obviously a lack of management experience, unclear strategy and non-existent controls and oversight have featured repeatedly.

The emergent parastatal sector was diverse in nature. It ranged from large operations of between 1000 and 6000 employees to natural monopolies (e.g. Tanzania Harbours Authority – now Ports Authority and TANESCO), and non-commercial educational institutions to firms in every conceivable line of business. One-third of the institutions were under the Ministry of Trade and Industry, and many of them were administered by the National Development Corporation, then the country's largest holding company. In nearly every line, Ministry had parastatals under their authority. The period was marked with a mixture of social and commercial objectives guided by political directives, which negatively impacted the attainment of efficient and profitable operations. This was manifested via poor investment decisions, poor and inadequate reporting systems, deficient boards etc., as described briefly hereunder.

Poor reporting systems remained a critical deficiency with the parastatals. It was the inadequate financial reporting and monitoring systems that contributed to insufficient monitoring and inadequate follow-up function.

Deficient Boards of Directors was reflected via revealed faulty supervision, as the first line of a proprietor's defence. Boards generally failed to perform their core functions as policy-makers, performance evaluators and management supervisors. "Boards do not ensure managements achieve set targets of performance. Even where targets are set, weak boards often accept inadequate explanations from the managements for shortfalls in performance" (Tanzania Audit Corporation, 1986, p. 15).

Poor investment decisions at the outset were compounded by a noticeable lack of managerial agility, i.e. managers lacked the flexibility and autonomy to address changing market conditions, rendering the production units to miss out in terms of optimization. Coupled with inadequate capitalization, poor investment decisions could not be reversed with ease.

It was common to see many ill-qualified and untrained parastatal managers who largely owed their positions more to political networking than to sheer technical skills and capabilities. It came as no surprise, for example, that in absence of an effective monitoring function, executives misused or used firm's resources for personal gain. The generally weak management that emerged from the sector was the result of the dysfunctional system and was a major cause for its continuance.

Price control

One other key component was the extended government controls and interventions in markets. Based mostly on the ideology from the adopted socio-economic blueprint, Mwalimu Nyerere's government raised strong concerns and reservations about the ability of the free market in allocating economic resources. It linked arbitrary price movements to greed and as a characteristic feature of the capitalist system. The creation of the National Price Commission in 1973, following the enactment of the Price Control Act, was in line with those sentiments (Semboja & Rugumisa, 1988).

It suffices at this juncture to state that the systematic departure from the market price mechanism in favour of controls aggravated the situation. Interventions such as the overvalued exchange rate may have contributed to the major economic distortions and severe imbalances in the 1980s. Coupled with other factors such as the 1979 war with Uganda, all these exacerbated shortages of necessities and economic imbalances, as the state continued to intervene in the markets.

Corporate governance in Tanzania

It remains undisputed that public institutions (parastatals included) fell short of the aspirations espoused in the Arusha Declaration, in terms of contribution to the set social-economic objectives. On the other hand, whatever positive gains accomplished were not optimally attained, i.e. they were attained at a much higher cost. Numerous reasons have been brought forth to explain the parastatal sector's disappointing performance which, for purposes of our discussion here, basically boiled down to failures in governance and hence the consequent policy implications.

In addition to a variety of external factors on the governance front, the disintegration of the East African Community (EAC), and its consequent effects, was high on the list and the impact far reaching. In many areas, it implied starting from scratch in circumstances where progress had been made via common East African Community-wide institutions.

Most of all, however, corporate governance is better explained by the overall policy environment within which economic activities take place. The fact that centralized administrative regulations to control the economy prevailed and governance emerged within that very framework led to the pursuit of unfitting policies. But even where appropriate policies were in place, the extensive deployment of regulatory mechanisms to attain policy objectives led to the emergence of numerous other challenges.

In hindsight, it can be asserted that the government failed not only to monitor performance, but also to act on the deluge of information on its hands. As losses amassed and holes filled via budgetary transfers and subsidies, the public entities became immune to shortcomings, thereby further eroding the governance function.

The governance system

The governance system that emerged from the framework consisted of several overlapping layers (Tenga, 2010) of control (representative of a bureaucratic nature).

1   Institutional Managers at operating companies' level were theoretically generally accountable for day-to-day operational and administrative decisions. However, in reality, they had to obtain external approvals from higher-ups before executing decisions.

2   Boards of Directors (or Management Committees) were responsible for reviewing corporate plans, financials and operating results. This governance function was weakened by irregularity in meeting and failure to address performance-related issues, focussing instead on minor administrative issues.
3   Sector holding corporations were to manage the affairs of respective subsidiaries, to take actions to avert and minimize losses and to expand business. Performance at this level was very much dependent upon the needed expertise and guidance. In somewhat counterproductive ways, the hierarchical structure provided for empire building notwithstanding national priorities or mandates.
4   The Board of Directors at each holding corporation functions in a manner similar to that of an operating company but answerable to the parent ministry.
5   Parent ministries were to approve corporate plans, financials and capital expenditures as well as supervise performance and take corrective action. Absence of expertise at this level rendered the implementation of such corrective measures moot in practice.
6   The ministry responsible for Finance and Economic Affairs approved investment projects and annual plans, provided budgetary support and assessed financial performance as the general overseer. In effect, the office of the Treasury Registrar, the overseer of public investment had minimal role in all of this.
7   Ultimately the buck stops with the executive, i.e. the responsibility for the whole system lies with the president (assisted by the cabinet) and the National Assembly; the two towering pillars of the government machinery. Much as this upper echelon is supposed to focus on general guidelines and overall strategic issues, often they seem to intervene (and interfere) in lower-level decision-making.

The hierarchical structure was dotted all over with a multitude of implementation agencies. The Standing Committee on Parastatal Organisations (SCOPO), for instance, was mandated to set up parastatals' organizational structure, determine uniform parastatal remuneration levels as well as supervise budgetary allocations. SCOPO's mandate resulted in limiting parastatals' freedom and ability to compete with the private sector in attracting a quality workforce. Independent of SCOPO, the Permanent Labour Tribunal (PLT) was tasked with the administration of an across-the-board bonus system, hinged on adherence to the stipulations of the National Policy on Productivity, Incomes and Prices (Tenga, 2010).

Down the road, especially beginning with the Mkapa era, several reforms took place. Notable was the Executive Agency Act No. 30 of 1997, which facilitated the creation of executive agencies under various government line ministries. This was part of a broader reform programme with the objective of addressing challenges associated with inefficiency and untenable costs via affordable, effective and efficient institutional set-up. Executive agencies were to enhance public service delivery by adopting effective private sector techniques (Ntukumazina, 1998). The emerged model provided the impetus for public service delivery via operational autonomy, to enable result-based accountability (Sulle, 2010) and enhanced managerial autonomy. Result-based accountability was to be linked to a set of clear incentives for results and sanctions for poor performance (Moynihan, 2005) and not meeting set objectives.

To date, the executive agencies have gradually developed respective institutional identities (Sulle, 2012). Revenue generation and retention became more of a motivator which, other things being equal, may entice the agencies to develop better management processes, thus building a case for efficiency-driven argument behind their establishment.

It is important to note that the hierarchical structure rested on the assumptions of well-organized machinery – machinery with adequate resources, managerial capacity, regulatory systems, reward mechanisms and related policies. The reality, however, could not be further from the assumptions.

Governance, resource availability and managerial capacity

At some point, Tanzania had more parastatals than did many other countries with greater administrative and managerial talents (Temu & Due, 2000). The underfunding and understaffing of the public institutions, because of the tendency to spread thin the limited resources, kept inefficient institutions alive but only at a great economic and social expense. This was seen as a choice, devoid of any reasonable justification.

From agency theory, principals, i.e. owners, delegate responsibilities to agents, i.e. managers or employees, who manage firm assets on their behalf. For one, there exists information asymmetry, i.e. managers or other agents have greater access to strategic information than do principals, who are not willing to bear the cost of directly monitoring the agents due to steep agency costs. Generally, principals are risk neutral and willing to bear greater risks than are agents, because their asset wealth is more likely to be diversified between corporate assets and other equities/investments. Agents are more risk averse than principals, because most of their wealth is concentrated in the firm and received in the form of pay and opportunities for promotion. This was not the case in Tanzanian corporate governance, because it did not apply. Rather, it was evident through moral hazard, i.e. the agent was tempted to take (and some cases succeeded in taking) advantage of information asymmetry with principal and act opportunistically (defined as making decisions not aligned with principal's interests) and use the firm resources to maximize the agent's wealth (often at the expense of the principal).

When it comes to governance, deficient in or in absence of a performance-based reward and punishment mechanism, it is true that the public sectors' separation of ownership and management functions held managers accountable for performance but failed in giving them the autonomy necessary to perform and deliver. The regulatory system failed to address this and as a result, neither performance nor management was well undertaken.

Generally, the motivation behind an employees' engagement is the evenhanded give and take an employee is motivated to have in an equitable exchange with the employer (Adams, 1963). To address inequity or the appearance of it, an employee may reduce inputs (reduce effort), try to influence managers' or co-workers' inputs or withdraw emotionally or physically (engage in absenteeism, tardiness, sabotage etc.).

Governance shortfall is therefore seen via employment and compensation policies through which the resultant parastatal sectors' low productivity, ineffectiveness and inadequacy can be traced. Three attributes emerge as important in the Tanzanian context overall, namely lack of high-quality human resources for senior staff, managerial and board membership positions, overemployment at lower levels and general absence of motivation. These three elements are largely explained by the employment and compensation policies and have in turn left scars in hiring, firing and remuneration settings.

National Framework on Good Governance

The 1999 National Framework on Good Governance in Tanzania summarized the governance policy. It emphasizes that good governance is critical to the success of Tanzania's development strategy and brings forth numerous approaches to enhance governance. They include shifting management responsibilities and production from the state to the private sector; the devolution of power and resources from the central government to local authorities; re-organizing ministries and other government agencies to make them more efficient and effective; and proactively attacking financial malpractice such as corruption and fraud in the public sector (URT, 1999a).

The framework acknowledges that governance in a Tanzanian perspective is the set of rules, institutions and practices that sets limits and provides incentives for individuals, organizations and businesses (URT, 1999a). According to the framework, three major good governance dimensions exist, viz. political, economic and administrative/managerial. It is within these dimensions that different stakeholders exhibit the virtues to nurture good governance. The framework defines governance as a network and interaction of public and private bodies that have a role to play in the formulation and implementation of public policy and the delivery of public services.

As part of consolidating the broad framework, in September 2011, Tanzania committed itself to and joined the Open Government Partnership (OGP) initiative. OGP's objective is "to make government business more open to its citizens in the interest of improving public service delivery, responsiveness, combating corruption and building greater trust" (Kombani, 2013).

OGP is built on transparency, citizen participation, accountability and integrity as well as technology and innovation, all considered key pillars of good governance. That being the case, embracing OGP invoked the government's commitment to practice good governance as elucidated under the principles.

While transparency has remained one of the utmost priorities of Tanzania since independence as espoused by Mwalimu Nyerere, citizen engagement which is to ensure community involvement in decision-making has left a lot to be desired despite years of leaning socialist.

54 Corporate evolution and challenges

In his inaugural address to Parliament in 2005, Tanzania's fourth President, Jakaya Kikwete, highlighted the significance of integrity to public officials:

> I ask the Public Ethics Commission not to shy away from asking each one of us to account for our assets and wealth. The Commission should be proactive. I will help it to build the capacity to do so, if indeed that is the problem.[3]

To that effect, several integrity and accountability enhancement measures have been instituted over the years to assist in the fight against corruption as well as in improved service delivery. It was expected, therefore, that the aspirations would eventually seep down to all institutions involved in public service delivery, including the corporate public entities. The measures went over and above notable legislation such as Public Leadership Code of Ethics Act, Prevention and Combating Corruption Act, Commission for Human Rights and Good Governance Act, Public Procurement Act and the Public Audit Act.

The above notwithstanding, it is debatable whether the lackluster performance was the result of a poor degree of enforcement or the product of unnecessary regulation going over and above the desired oversight function into having negative impacts.

Inadequate laws and regulations enforcement or too many regulations?

Several policies impacted public service delivery and thus the requisite production of goods and delivery of public services. Whereas production by public entities was marred by a range of policy-related issues, from competition from low-priced imports to price setting (and consequent effect on quality), service delivery failed due to absence of policy directions.

In Tanzania, it has always been the characteristic feature of the market that substandard imports are sold alongside the domestically produced quality goods. This area had massive negative impacts on the public production units. Much as laws and regulations exist, lack of enforcement and loopholes made it possible for the low-priced imports to undercut the market, with dire consequences for the domestic producers. Adherence to quality standards by domestic manufacturers meant failing to compete in what became a tilted playing field in favour of imported goods. Indeed, if the market were a level playing field, more could have been attained by way of investment into diverse production units and, subsequently, skills development, transfer of technology and overall enhancement of domestic production of goods and services to the public (Wangwe et al., 2014).

It is not a surprise for producers in the private sector, therefore, to indicate the negative impact of what they consider to be over-regulation because of a multitude of duplicate regulatory functions. Not only does enforcement of these rules and regulations overlap, but also compliance translates into additional costs. Reforms aimed at synchronizing regulatory processes in effect did not resolve either the burdensome cost or related bottlenecks that impact public service delivery.

Twisted accountability

The notion of accountability as applied to that elucidated earlier comprises three distinct aspects: *transparency, answerability* and *controllability* (Bovens, 2005).[4] Leaders are fully accountable when they exercise their powers in a way that is transparent, in the sense that it enables others to see whether all is done in accordance with the relevant rules and mandates; they are answerable in the sense of being obliged to provide reasons for their decisions and actions; and *institutional checks or control mechanisms* are in place to prevent mismanagement and abuse of power and ensure that corrective measures are taken in cases where the rules are violated.

From a stakeholder perspective, accountability implies that a firm providing an account of itself would be more about creating a positive impression and signifying that it is in line with community interests (Munro & Mouritsen, 1996).

Likewise, according to Stewart (1984), for accountability to exist, there has to be a power relationship. The relationship is between the donor entity and the recipient entity – the "bond of accountability." This infers that the information is gauged against a set of standards or expectations, as well as sanctions and rewards, accordingly. Accountability, therefore, presumes a subject's responsibility and an answerability for actions undertaken (Chapman & Dunshire, 1971).

In Tanzania, the extensive government involvement in the provision of social service was constrained by the low level of economic growth in the late 1970s and 1980s. The state's grip on resource allocation and control over the actions of economic agents loosened (Ndulu & Mutalemwa, 2002). The 1980s, often referred to as the lost decade for sub-Saharan Africa, was evidence to that with declining annual growth (Moss, 2007). In some quarters it was ascertained that the causal factor behind the failure of Africa's economies was basically a crisis of governance (World Bank, 2000).

Despite the general belief that governance matters and that there are strong causal relationships between good governance and development outcomes (Kaufmann et al., 2003), what emerged from Tanzania's experience was a twisted aspect of governance and accountability. The twisted accountability left a lot to be desired – from performance and programme accountability to corporate social responsibility and discouragement of the local businesses via taxation. Indeed, more needed to be done.

Performance and programme accountability

Performance accountability scrutinizes the performance of an officer, or an organization, to ascertain whether the set goals and objectives have been attained. Stewart (1984) points out that the stated goals may not always be fully known by the stakeholders, and this lack of information affects their ability to hold the relevant parties to account.

The processes employed are vital for the attainment of set objectives and should be part of the board's strategic planning and monitoring responsibilities. This goes along with setting, monitoring and evaluating company goals and objectives and taking corrective actions when and as required. These are aspects of performance accountability exercised at the company level.

In the case of corporate Tanzania, it is not an overreach to conclude that there was no performance accountability. Going by the CAG's annual general audit and performance reports on public entities over the years, one of the major discussion categories has been the performance and implementation of recommendations. In one of the recent draft reports, it was noted that there is "increased need for accountability, transparency and good governance" for informed decision-making by those entrusted with "stewardship to be accountable in the collection, utilization and management of public resources" (CAG, 2016).

Programme accountability, similar in nature to performance accountability, examines the attainment of set goals and objectives in specific programmes (Stewart, 1984). It applies to all organizations irrespective of whether they are public or private sector, not for profit or otherwise. In the context of the stakeholder approach, relevant stakeholders may also hold the leadership (management and the board) accountable for the policies and activities of the entities for which they are answerable. Typical features in public entities, namely lack of proper project planning, design and management including inadequate or lack of project risk assessment have been featured (Mochal, 2003) as potential factors, as were lack of proper governance and project management practice alongside inadequate management capability (Morgan & Gbedemah, 2010).

Corporate social responsibility

Across Tanzania, corporate social responsibility (CSR) has for a long time been viewed from the perspective of philanthropy, i.e. understood in terms of philanthropy (doing well and doing good with part of the profit) and thus in most cases referred to as charitable community support projects. It is only in recent years that the practice of CSR has evolved. Significant growth in 'CSR buy-in' has been reflected by the number of enterprises that have an explicit CSR policy. In effect, CSR and sustainability have become cross-cutting issues that are ingrained within both corporate operations and strategy (Lauwo, 2013).

CSR in the present-day business world generally refers to but also goes beyond sustainable business performance, i.e. the principle to generate profit itself in a responsible and sustainable way (Mader, 2012). All phases of Tanzania's administrations have consistently worked on new legislation and regulations as a way to enhance public accountability and good governance and to foster good CSR practices (Lauwo, 2013). To date, what can be summarized is in line with Shivji's (1976) argument that to promote CSR reporting in the name of protecting public interest in Tanzania is curtailed by incapacity.

For instance, the Companies Act 1932 – Cap 212 (as amended), which basically lays the foundation for addressing governance issues, was first enacted in 1929 and remained in force until 2002 when it was amended (Lauwo, 2013). Although in some aspects the amended Act required directors to advance corporate disclosure and to act in good faith to uphold the best interests of the company, primary has been the financial interests of shareholders rather than stakeholder interests, which have remained secondary.

Significant changes were made in the Companies Act (2002) as well, to accommodate global developments into domestic law as far as accounting disclosures, corporate governance and directors' duties are concerned. Section 183(1), for instance, provides that "matters directors of the company must have regards to in the performance of their functions, which include, having regard to the interests of the members, company's employees' and stakeholders." Despite this requirement, as highlighted above, shareholder interests are held superior to general stakeholder interests. Furthermore, much as the Act requires annual disclosure of, for instance, directors' remuneration, it remains silent and non-obligatory on disclosure of pertinent issues such as occupational health and safety, product integrity, environmental sustainability and interaction with local communities, job discrimination, whistle blowers, etc. emanating from actions by corporate bodies (Curtis & Lissu, 2008; Lauwo, 2011, 2013).

Several laws and regulations have also been put in place to impose obligations on companies in respect of a variety of other issues, via regulatory frameworks. They include environmental protection, occupational health and safety, labour standards, disability, non-discrimination etc. Not much can be said in a positive way in terms of the ability of these provisions to promote good governance, corporate responsibility, public accountability, and transparency (Lauwo, 2013).

Taxation pain

Corporate Tanzania has been one (if not the only) stakeholder group to have been visibly impacted by tax reforms in Tanzania. For a long period of time, the claim has been that there is a tendency of tax authorities to target corporate taxpayers rather than broaden the tax base. In turn, the tax authorities argue that there is nothing new in what it does: it is merely enforcing compliance, which corporate Tanzania has enjoyed laxity in implementation for an extended period. It is unfortunate, however, that the targeted approach does more harm and discourages compliance rather than promotes it, at least in the short run. As a result, there has always been a 'cat-and-mouse' relationship between the two parties. In fact, there is a widespread perception in the business community that the revenue authorities have concentrated on known corporate taxpayers. The effectiveness of the Tanzania Revenue Authority regarding this group is illustrated by studies conducted on the Tanzanian manufacturing sector. Until 1995, taxation was not an issue raised by manufacturers as thorny with negative impacts to output and performance, let alone governance. Since then, however, it has become one of the main issues of concern, in addition to the fact that the formal sector business has been impacted by the multitude of overlapping local and central government taxes and levies (Luoga, 2001).

Indeed, the perception by the overall corporate Tanzania is of a tax system that is unfair and has thus become a major hindrance to the development of voluntary compliance and a level of trust with the tax authorities. This is further evidenced in part by the rate at which tax grievances are taken to the courts of law (Luoga, 2001). Trade and industry umbrella organizations, such as the Tanzania Chamber of Commerce, Industry and Agriculture (TCCIA) and the Confederation of Tanzania Industry (CTI) etc., have repeatedly presented their grievances to the authorities to prove the arguments they raise. Twice, the demands from the business community have resulted in changes to the existing tax laws (Rakner, 2001), indicating validity of the arguments.

Corporate waste and its pain

Inefficiency in the corporate bodies, including public entities, is a sure ticket to any entity's demise. This and the inability to adapt to changing economic circumstances over the past two decades have in turn generated a wave of organizational innovation, witnessed globally in recent years.

In Tanzania public corporations, the entrenched bureaucracy coupled with inefficiency culminated in the demise of quality and organizational accountability and led to the witnessed massive waste. It is when waste becomes severe that it has multiplier effects and triggers other shortfalls across the economy. This is even more evidenced in performance.

Corporate performance is gauged every day but more revealed via annual reports. These reports are important in identifying deficits and shortfalls with the view to addressing them and thus enhancing service delivery. The performance evaluation framework, insofar as public entities are concerned, has however been inadequate. The limited nature of the framework failed to provide for sufficient levels of accountability.

Indeed, with regard to public entities, regulations require that annual performance reports are produced and evaluated by the relevant oversight organs; these include the relevant Committees of the Parliament and the Controller and Auditor General's National Audit Office (NAO). The Parliamentary Parastatal Organisation Accounts Committee (POAC), for instance, was responsible for the oversight of public entities and other bodies as per Section 38 of the Public Audit Act 2008, which sets in motion the working relationship between the NAO and the respective parliamentary oversight committees.

Despite efforts by the NAO and the POAC, among others, we have witnessed over the years continued corporate waste and absence of and failure to institute corrective measures. It has been customary that the adoption of one appropriate corrective measure this year will be followed by additional waste.

The corporate waste referred here is a direct result of a lack of integrity. Public integrity has been upheld neither across public service delivery processes nor within the public resource management framework. Systemic failure to track waste and abuse of resources or potential conflicts of interest has led to the high price that Tanzanians have been paying and will continue to pay until formidable and sustainable corrective action is in place.

In recent years, for instance, the CAG's reports have shed light on how entrenched the absence of accountability, mismanagement, abuse of resources, conflict of interest, among other ills are. Subsequent parliamentary committees' efforts to provide the requisite "checks and balances" has not produced results that go hand in hand with the objective of minimization of corporate waste. Many efforts have been put in place, including privatization of parastatals, to eliminate waste, but there is not much to show yet.

Parastatal sector reforms

During the early days following Tanzania's independence, the need to establish parastatals was from the premise that the private sector then lacked not only the capacity to generate the needed economic growth but also the ability to efficiently allocate resources. This changed with the adoption of Tanzania's socio-political and economic blueprint, the Arusha Declaration. By the mid-1980's, a steady decline in parastatal sector performance had registered and normalized such that to survive, most firms in the parastatal sector relied on borrowing and government subsidies (PSRC, 1994). The inevitable reform measures and policy changes that ensued thereafter entailed, among others, the proliferation of privatization and the demise of SOEs.

In 1992, the government made an official pronouncement of parastatal sector reform as a national policy. Under the policy, one of the fundamental objectives was for the government to revert to and enhance focus on traditional roles of government, i.e. the maintenance of law and order and the provision of economic and social infrastructure, ensuring a level playing field for efficient economic competition and a balancing of economic and social activities (Waigama, 2008). It completely divested from direct involvement in economic ventures.

Operationalizing the policy, the Parastatal Sector Reform Programme (PSRP) was adopted in the context of being part of the broader reforms introduced from the mid-1980s after the sectors' disappointing performance. The policy reforms entailed trade liberalization, removal of foreign exchange controls, the elimination of price controls, interest rates and the financial sector reform in general (including opening for the return of private banks). The role of the private sector was enhanced as a decision-maker, alongside tax reform and civil service reforms (PSRC, 1993). The parastatal sector reforms were meant to reduce its overall dominance and at the same time promote the role and the importance of the private sector across the economy.

As far as Tanzania's development endeavours are concerned, it was clear that parastatal sector reform was not only inevitable but also needed and indeed unavoidable. Tanzanians in general, workers and peasants as well as producers and consumers alike, were being short-changed and ill-served by the majority of the parastatals. Likewise, as the owner, the state's return on investment was inadequate whilst misuse of investments was rampant across the sectors.

The reform programme (PSRP) was in large part driven by four main pragmatic arguments, namely the extent of the attainment of the original objectives of state ownership; the immense cost and sustenance of the objectives; investment opportunities being missed by public sector firms pre-occupied with survival; and rampant assets misuse (PSRC, 1994).

It is important to realize that among the original objectives of state ownership was to ensure that the corporate sector of the economy was removed from the hands of foreigners and minorities that were dominant at independence. By the time the parastatal sector reforms came around, all parastatal sector management was Tanzanian, with a qualified and experienced professional cadre, able to take the corporate sector forward into the future. With this realization, and following privatization measures, for over the past two decades there has been a dramatic diversification of ownership (PSRC, 1994). With the policy, it was hoped to register growth in the private sector, stimulating new entrepreneurs across different sectors of the economy.

The cost of maintaining the parastatal sector has been immense and to the point of being unsustainable, given the estimated capital invested over the years. Instead of earning dividends, the government as the owner had to continuously bear the fiscal losses incurred, year in and year out. The annual losses at one point averaged upwards of 7% of GNP, almost half the level of new investment in the country (PSRP, 2008). Even with the profitable parastatals, it was difficult to generate cash, whilst many benefitted from tax exemptions and debt forgiveness, thereby transferring the losses across other sectors of the economy. Many parastatals ran well at the outset, but in absence of funds for re-investment, their luck ran out. On the other hand, new parastatal start-ups were neither innovative nor profitable. A survey undertaken in 1992, for example, revealed that of every 10 parastatals, six would never be able to meet their currently maturing obligations and were not credit worthy (PSRC, 1993); the reforms signalled that it was time to go.

Indeed, the parastatal's under-performance created ripples across the economy. Among the most notable was the banking sector. Ironically, the loss-making parastatals were given priority at the will of the government. This, as expected, weakened the banking system's portfolio (with non-performing loans) over the years and eroded the capital base. Thus, the sustained losses impacted not only the other commercial entities but also the poorest with the least access to finance. In other words, because of the parastatals poor performance, consumers were left to fend off poor-quality high-priced goods, banks were left with unpaid loans and the government year in and year out was left continuing to cover the sectors' accumulated losses (and was deprived of revenue). These results did not imply that these enterprises had no potentials; many could be turned around under new ownership as well as new leadership (PSRC, 1993).

The assertion that resources were misused has been brought forth as one of the compelling reasons behind the parastatal reforms. Sale of assets to meet current obligations was a common feature, against all regulations and principles, as was workforce pruning, work stoppage, pilfering of assets and other desperate measures.

While aware of the many problems parastatals faced and their ultimate demise (inevitable as it was), no one can dismiss their achievements and contribution to the economy. The economic and business history of Tanzania cannot be written without a chapter on the parastatal sector's role. Much was gained through the influence of the parastatal and respective corporate experience, waste and all.

Tanzania public corporation setting today

Governance issues in public entities have a structural dimension revealed through the government's multiple roles as an owner, regulator, adjudicator and executive, with apparent conflicting objectives. The ambiguity brought about by the roles at times led to the government extending the public entity's function beyond public policy. Decisions not based on an economic basis, including, for example, the provision of subsidies, grants and bail-out packages at a cost to the public enterprise, have offered the government reasons for continuing to extend controls.

By the late 1980s, peer countries across the globe embarked on a sell-off of public enterprises, embracing the opening of economies and market-determined production policy objectives (Giugale, 2014). Similarly, having earlier resisted the Washington Consensus policies,[5] Tanzania went through privatization as the government sealed its decision to transfer part of its functions and responsibilities to the private sector. This implied that both the government and the private sector had to find optimal ways to adjust to new ways of doing business in a market economy.

The transition to a market economy in Tanzania aimed at the emergence of a more pluralistic society. That notwithstanding, it realized the importance and need for an inclusive approach toward the private sector. The government, however, failed to provide an amicable environment for the flourishment of the sector. For one, preparations fell short in that public officials altered their roles to become facilitators of private sector development. This deemed necessary a change in the mindset of public service provision to accommodate and facilitate private sector development. The new policy provided the platform for the private sector to be able to identify obstacles from unreliable power supply to uncooperative government bureaucrats and systems along the process, to circumvent what became unnecessary institutional voids.

With diminished government involvement in the economy (outside its traditional role) alongside the introduction of market economy policies, the private sector was expected to take the lead in anticipation that the private sector would grow. This, however, did not materialize because sector-led growth largely has been hampered by an atmosphere of mistrust. Whereas the public sector is stigmatized with the idea that working with the private sector is indicative of its apparent failure, the private sector, on the other hand, is undeveloped and is characterized with limited ability to deliver (GIZ, 2013). Efforts to improve private sector participation and collaboration as set out in numerous policy pronouncements, including Development Vision 2025, continue and have since been well expressed in its key development plans.

Economic liberalization and other policy measures required strong visible governance and good economic management. The changes were not for the want of new policy alone but for one that does not repeat past mistakes. In recent times, there has been an increase in regulatory bodies, most of whom tout their own corporate governance guidelines leading to conflicting and/overlapping or confusing objectives, where zero or minimal coordination efforts exist. In corporate

Tanzania, where only a few public listed companies exist, with most companies not listed, and the agency problem is non-existent, i.e. principals and the agents are often the same people, thus render corporate governance a different life of its own.

The evolution on corporate public entities and the challenges encountered in Tanzania are a culmination of the policy environment that was defined by the various milestones. From the governance perspective, the main relational issue of corporate governance in Tanzania rests with the need to protect the interests of the stakeholders at large.

Certain aspects of the reform ideas that were compatible with local values were infused while the ones that seemed incompatible were ignored. Some of the approaches under the reforms were accommodated based on the 'eyes-on, hands-off' stance to provide some flexibility to the governance process, which resulted in improvement despite economic and institutional constraints. Indeed, under the reforms was the enormous pressure to infuse new management and governance approaches to enhance performance of the public sector, in service delivery, although some old ways were never abandoned (Sulle, 2010).

The complexity arising from the corporate governance model in the public corporation entities and the business environment is compounded by shortfalls in enforcement of regulations and/or recommendations and issues raised by the oversight bodies.

Given that corporate governance is, in essence, a soft issue, the challenges of making governance norms mandatory and ensuring its embracement across the sector is today important in the sectors' development, as corporate entities internalize the norms to be observed in letter and in spirit.

Notes

1 World Bank (1988). *Parastatals in Tanzania: Toward a Reform Programme*. Washington, D.C.: World Bank.
2 The Arusha Declaration and the TANU'S Policy of Socialism and Self-Reliance (1967).
3 Dr. Jakaya Mrisho Kikwete in his inaugural speech to Parliament on December 30, 2005.
4 Mark Bovens (2005). Public accountability – a framework for the analysis and assessment of accountability arrangements in the public domain (unpublished work, 2005). Utrecht School of Governance, Utrecht University. Draft made for CONNEX, Research Group 2: Democracy and Accountability in the EU.
5 Washington Consensus is defined as:

> [. . .] a set of economic policy recommendations for developing countries and Latin America, in particular, that became popular during the 1980s. The term Washington Consensus usually refers to the level of agreement between the International Monetary Fund (IMF), World Bank and the US Department of the Treasury on those policy recommendations. With the onset of a debt crisis in the developing world during the early 1980s, the major Western powers, and the United States in particular, decided that both the World Bank and the IMF should play a significant role in the management of that debt and in global development policy more broadly.

When the British economist John Williamson, who later worked for the World Bank, first used the term Washington Consensus in 1989, he claimed that he was actually referring to a list of reforms that he felt key players in Washington could all agree were needed in Latin America. However, much to his dismay, the term later became widely used in a pejorative way to describe the increasing harmonization of the policies recommended by those institutions. It often refers to a dogmatic belief that developing countries should adopt market-led development strategies that will result in economic growth that will "trickle down" to the benefit of all.

(www.britannica.com/topic/Washington-consensus)

Bibliography

Adams, J. S. (1963). Wages inequities, productivity and work quality. *Industrial Relations*, 3, 9–10.
Bovens, M. (2005). Public accountability Chapter 8 pp. 102–208. In Ewan Ferlie, L. E. Lynn & C. Pollitt (Eds.), *The Oxford handbook of public management*. Oxford University Press Inc., New York.
CAG. (2016). *The annual general report of the controller and auditor general on the audit of public authorities and other bodies for the financial year 2014/2015*. Dar es Salaam: Office of the Controller and Auditor General, National Audit Office.
Chapman, R., & Dunsire, A. (1971). *Style in administration: Readings in British public administration*. London: Allen and Unwin.
Curtis, M., & Lissu, T. (2008). *A golden opportunity? How Tanzania is failing to benefit from gold mining*. Dar es Salaam: Christian Council of Tanzania.
Fischer, P. (2006). *Rent-seeking, institutions and reforms in Africa*. Boston, MA: Springer.
GCAP (2014). *Infographic: Tanzania's mobile money revolution*. Retrieved August 1, 2016, from www.cgap.org/data/infographic-tanzanias-mobile-money-revolution
Gibbon, P. (Ed.) (1995). *Liberalised development in Tanzania: Studies on accumulation processes and local institutions*. Uppsala: Nordiska Afrikainstitutet.
GIZ (2013). *Cooperation with the private sector in Tanzania: German federal ministry of economic cooperation and development: Country report 2013*. Retrieved from https://www.giz.de/fachexpertise/downloads/giz2013-en-tanzania-country-report.pdf.
Henley, J. (1993). Privatization in Africa: Prospects for Tanzania. In T. Clarice & C. Pitelis (Eds.), *The political economy of privatization*. London: Routledge.
Kaufmann, D., Kraay, A., & Mastruzzi, M. (2003). *Government matters III: Governance indicators for 1996–2002*. Policy Research Working Paper Series 3106, World Bank.
Kombani, C. (2013). *Open government partnership in Tanzania: A paper presented in Rabat*. Morocco. Retrieved from www.opengov.go.tz/files/publications/attachments/6KOMBANI_Tanzania_en_sw.pdf
Lauwo, S. (2011). *Analysis of Corporate Social Responsibility (CSR) and accountability practices in a developing country context: A study of mining industry in Tanzania* (PhD Thesis), University of Essex.
Lauwo, S. (2013, July 10–July 12). Silences in corporate social responsibility reporting and the potential of alternative forms of reporting: A case study of the mining industry in Tanzania. In *The 8th international conference in critical management studies*. Manchester: University of Manchester. Retrieved September 18, 2016, from. www.escholar.manchester.ac.uk/api/datastream?publicationPid=uk-ac-man-scw:198817&datastreamId=FULL-TEXT.PDF

Lofchie, M., & Callaghy, T. (1995). *Diversity in the Tanzanian business community: Its implications for growth*. USAID Mission, Dar es Salaam, Tanzania. http://www.sscnet.ucla.edu/polisci/faculty/lofchie/tanzaniabusinessstudy.pdf.

Luoga, F. (2001). *Taxpayers' rights and obligations: A survey of the legal situation in Tanzania*. Draft report, submitted to the Taxation, Aid and Democracy Research Programme.

Mochal, T. (2003). Poor Planning is project management mistake number one. *TechRepublic*. Retrieved November 12, 2016, from www.techrepublic.com/article/poor-planning-is-project-management-mistake-number-one/

Morgan, A., & Gbedemah, S. (2010, February 2). *How poor project governance causes delays*. Paper presented to the Society of Construction law, London.

Moss, T. (2007). *African Development: Making sense of the issues and actors*. Boulder, CO: Lynne Rienner Publishers.

Moynihan, D. (2005). Why and how do state governments adopt and implement managing for results reforms? *Journal of Public Administration Research and Theory*, *l*(15), 219–243.

Msekwa, P. (2016). Ethics is the heart of leadership: Appreciating President Magufuli's refreshing stance on leadership ethics. *The Daily News*, Tanzania; May 12, 2016.

Munro, R., & Mouritsen, J. (Eds.). (1996). *Accountability: Power, ethos and the technologies of managing*. London: International Thomson Business Press.

Ndulu, N. J., & Mutalemwa, C. K. (2002). *Tanzania at the turn of the century: Background papers and statistics*. Washington, DC: World Bank and Dar es Salaam: Government of United Republic of Tanzania.

Ntukumazina, D. (1998). Civil service reform in Tanzania: A strategic approach. In S. Rugumamu (Ed.), *Civil service reform in Tanzania: Proceedings of the national symposium*, Dar es Salaam.

PSRC (1993). Parastatal Sector Reform Commission: *Master Plan*, Government Printer, Dar Es Salaam.

PSRC (1994). Parastatal Sector Reform Commission, *1993 Review and 1994/95 Action Plan*, Government Printer, Dar Es Salaam.

PSRP (2008). Implementation Completion and results report (IDA-33000 IDA-3300A), on A credit to the United Republic of Tanzania for. Public Sector reform Project. Report No: ICR0000677. Public Sector Reform and Capacity Building (AFTPR), Eastern Africa Country Cluster 1, Africa region, the World bank.

Rakner, L. (2001). The politics of revenue mobilisation: Explaining continuity in Namibian Tax policies. *Forum for Development Studies*, *28*(1).

Scott, J. (1998). *Seeing like the state: How certain schemes to improve the human condition have failed*. New Haven: Yale University Press.

Semboja, J., & Rugumisa, S. M. H. (1988). Price control in the management of economic crisis: The national price commission in Tanzania. *African Studies Association*, *31*(1), 47–65.

Stewart, J. (1984). The role of information in public accountability. In A. Hopwood & C. Tomkins (Eds.), *Issues in public sector accounting* (pp. 13–34). Oxford: Philip Allan.

Sulle, A. (2010). The application of new public management doctrine in developing world: An exploratory study of autonomy and control of executive agencies in Tanzania. *Public Administration and Development*, *30*(5), 345–354.

Sulle, A. (2012). Result-based management in the public sector: A decade of experience for the Tanzanian executive agencies. *Journal of Service Science and Management*, *4*(4), 499–506.

Tanzania Audit Corporation (1986). *Tanzania Audit Corporation Eighteenth Annual Report and Accounts for the year Ended 30 June; TAC*. Tanzania: Dar es Salaam.

TCRA (2014). *Tanzania Communication Regulatory Authority (TCRA) annual report accounts for the year ended 30th June 2014*. Accessed on August 2, 2017. Retrieved from: https://www.tcra.go.tz/index.php/publication-and-statistics/reports.

Temu, A., & Due, J. M. (2000). The business environment in Tanzania after socialism: Challenges of reforming banks, parastatals, taxation and the civil service. *The Journal of Modern African Studies, 38*(4), 683–712.

URT (1932). *Companies ordinance (Cap. 212)*. Dar es Salaam: Government Printer.

URT (1992). *Public Corporations Act, 1992*. Dar es Salaam: Government Printer.

URT (1995a). *Public Leadership Code of Ethics (PLCE) Act No. 13 of 1995*. Dar es Salaam: Government Printer.

URT (1995b). *Sheria ya Maadili ya Viongozi wa Umma, Na. 13, ya 1995*. Dar es Salaam: Mpiga chapa wa Serikali.

URT (1996). *Presidential commission of inquiry: Report on the state of corruption in the country*. Dar es Salaam: Government Printer.

URT (1999a). *Development Vision, 2025*. Dar es Salaam: President's office, Planning and Privatisation Commission, Government Printer.

URT (1999b). *The national framework on good governance*. Dar es Salaam, Tanzania: United Republic of Tanzania, Steering Committee on Good Governance. President's Office, Planning Commission.

URT (2000). *Privatisation in Tanzania, annual review 2000/2001 and action plan 2001/2002*. Dar es Salaam: PSRC.

Wangwe, S., Mmari, D., Aikaeli, J., Rutatina, N., Mboghoina, T., & Kinyondo, A. (2014). *The performance of the manufacturing sector in Tanzania: Challenges and the way forward*. WIDER Working Paper 2014/085, United Nations University World Institute for Development Economics Research, Helsinki.

World Bank (1988). *Parastatals in Tanzania: Toward a reform programme*. Report No. 7100-TA. Country VI Department, Africa Region, July 27, 1988.

World Bank (2000). *Can Africa claim the 21st century?* Washington, DC: World Bank.

5 Governance failure and corporate waste cases analysis

Based on contextual reflections, one can look back at milestones along the long journey taken by Tanzania's corporate SOEs to comprehend the different but related attributes that have charted the fate of these enterprises. In this chapter, five individual cases of SOEs are described and analysed in depth from the perspective of corporate governance failures and the resulting waste. The cases touch on a variety of stakeholders, ranging from gatekeepers to regulators. The chapter also reviews governance mechanisms and performance.

In each case, we to begin with a background (a chronological perspective of sorts) and weave through the leadership phases in Tanzania in terms of how the different governance-related aspects were given prominence, before addressing the magnitude of waste associated with the respective entity. The conclusions reached are basically reverting to try to see how successful the particular case has been.

The case of Air Tanzania Company Limited (ATCL), as seen over time, is one of the most grossly tolerated wastage of public resources that typifies the tragedy of the commons in economics. This is seen through failure of the company to adhere to generally accepted basic principles of corporate governance, tolerating financial abuse and sins of omission as well as of commission.

The Tanzania Communication Regulatory Authority (TCRA), on the other hand, presents a case of waste by a regulator, as a result of the failure of not only enforcing the regulations on the books (a governance function), but also being tolerant of non-optimal use of resources. The CAG reports claimed that the regulator had failed to monitor the telecom industry and failed to gather the requisite and much-needed revenue for the state, for it to be able to channel the same toward development endeavours.

We then have the Tanzania Electric Supply Company Limited (TANESCO) case that represents an infinite waste to the nation, once again resulting from failure to abide by basic governance principles. Consecutive policymakers, line ministries, TANESCO directors and consecutive managements tolerated an adverse situation, which was public knowledge. This was not the case of who bells the cat but rather a case of which of the cat's nine lives goes first. TANESCO's nine lives seem to have been around for too long. The case of Tanzania Leather Associated Industries (TLAI), on the other hand, is a case of negligence at the highest level, resulting in waste across an entire sector and untold cost to the nation due to failure in corporate governance.

Well-intentioned plans went to waste because of basic failings in sectoral governance and leadership. This extended from policy and operational failings due to lack of clarity to pure disregard of the sector's economic potential.

The case of the Tanzania Ports Authority (TPA) represents another governance failure by the keeper of the nation's trade and economic gateway. It reflects a lack of foresight and appreciation of a divinely inspired opportunity in terms of geographical advantages. It seems as if no one saw to it that the performance objectives were realistic and adhered to, or that realistic and strategic focussed goals were set and risks were well managed. As a result, the nation has so far failed to realize the immense economic potential that exists in abundance across the sector.

In all these cases, there were common issues. They ranged from governance-related themes such as failures in resource management and risk management, management framework shortfalls and ill-informed (non-evidence-based) decision-making to regulatory oversight failures and policy shortcomings. All the data and information used in these cases came from publicly available sources. We look at each of these, one by one.

Air Tanzania Company Limited– case of public waste

For a long period of time, due to deteriorating financial performance, ATCL has been in major financial distress. A performance review of this public entity reveals persistent losses over the past decade with the consecutive ATCL managements unable to come up with any proven turnaround strategy (CAG, 2016). ATCL presents a sorry case of unacceptable tolerance to wastage of public resources. The national carrier has repeatedly been in intensive care over such a long period and has become "a heavy burden to the government and taxpayers."[1].

Starting with the partial privatization of the then Air Tanzania Corporation (ATC) to South African Airways, no viable solution to the challenges facing the company has come to fruition. Instead, it has continued to be a spout of massive resource waste through exorbitant management, maintenance and operating costs that arose, among other reasons, from unfeasible aircraft lease arrangements.

The ATCL privatization process

As part of the economic liberalization and consequent privatization policy, in 2002 the Government of Tanzania placed 49% of its shares in the then ATC and entrusted its management to South African Airways (SAA). Subsequently, a new entity in the name of ATCL was incorporated under Cap 212 as a private limited liability company.

At the time, ATC's fleet comprised two aircraft, a company-owned B737-200 and a B737-300 operated under a dry lease. The privatization exercise also entailed downsizing the workforce by about 50%, from 493 to 251 employees.

Furthermore, several good faith measures were instituted by the government. To ensure that the new operational structure began with a clean financial slate, the government assumed all of ATC's liabilities by placing them under ATC Holding Company, a wholly owned government entity created to take over assets of ATC that were not directly linked to ATC's core business and all of the outstanding liabilities.

The objective then was to institute the structural changes that would usher in new ways of doing business, bring about ATCL's efficiency and enhance productivity towards eventual profitability. It is unfortunate, however, that the anticipated turnaround could not be realized, and instead, according to the nation's Controller and Auditor General (CAG, 2016), the privatization resulted in financially overburdening the company. The CAG report highlighted the following adverse outcomes from the process:

- Increased management costs because of management fees charged by and paid to SAA;
- Increase in maintenance costs due to fees due and paid to South African Technical (SAT), a subsidiary of SAA;
- Increased operational costs, e.g. catering etc.;
- High technical human resource capacity turnover, especially of engineers; and
- High leasing costs paid to SAA on leased aircraft.

After four agonizing loss-making years, the government in 2006 decided to repurchase the 49% shares from SAA and reverted to sole ownership of the national flag carrier. By that point in time, ATCL had incurred losses estimated at almost TZS 25 billion and become insolvent with a negative equity of TZS 6.9 billion (CAG, 2016). The Civil Aviation Authority Director General at the time is quoted as saying, "Air Tanzania was in a worse state than before it was taken over by SAA."[2] Such was the extent of damage to the company from lack of diligence and duty of care.

The CAG report further noted that it was evident that ATCL's privatization did not consider the immediate objectives and repercussions, nor likewise, how these related to longer-term objectives, which include the development of the market demand within the airline industry. Moreover, there was no evidence of a government-initiated preliminary assessment of the benefits accruing to ATCL from the joint venture with SAA. Furthermore, the CAG's post-privatization review revealed as well that the government did not carry out any comprehensive analysis to identify potential costs and constraints toward the attainment of the long-term objectives.

Privatization is not the only issue that bedevilled ATCL at the time. Absence of an enterprise risk management framework, lack of effective turnaround strategy and technical challenges were significant among other factors that deepened the challenges ATCL had been facing.

Absence of an enterprise risk management framework

The absence of a risk management framework had much to do with explaining the state of affairs at ATCL. Such a framework not only aligns the principles of sound corporate governance but also the management of risk as an important strategy for the attainment of organizational goals and objectives. Enterprise risk management (ERM) is defined by the Committee of Sponsoring Organizations (COSO) as

> a process, effected by an entity's board of directors, management and other personnel, applied in strategy-setting and across the enterprise, designed to identify potential events that may affect the entity, and manage risk to be within its risk appetite, to provide reasonable assurance regarding the achievement of entity objectives.[3]

The CAG 2016 report also noted that ATCL had not established a risk management function in its various structures. There are no processes for assessment of risks facing the company, such as a structure to oversee the whole process within the risk management cycle. The absence of a risk management framework impaired the company's ability to identify, analyse or control exposure levels to systemic and operational risks. It was indeed the failure to anticipate the potential operational risk that led to ATCL ceding to the unprofitable aircraft lease.

Technical challenge – aircraft lease loss

In October 2007, ATCL signed a dry lease agreement with M/s Wallis Trading Co. Ltd for leasing an Airbus A320 without adhering to the formal standard operating procedures[4] required under such transactions. As part of the procedures and as a standard risk management practice, both the company's technical unit as well as the Tanzania Civil Aviation Authority (TCAA) were required to assess the quality of the aircraft in accordance with international civil aviation standards, prior to entering into the lease agreement and undertaking the registration.

In this case, it is understood that both the ATCL's technical unit and TCAA conducted their investigations well after the lease contract had been signed. The findings of the investigation revealed that the aircraft did not meet the required standards. It was crucial that the weaknesses were rectified prior to handing over the aircraft to ATCL.[5] At the same time, the legal advice from the Tanzania Attorney General's office about the lease dating back to 2007 was not heeded. Table 5.1 summarizes the chronology of events pertaining to ATCL's aircraft lease transaction and challenges that arose subsequently.

Technical challenge – key aviation certifications

The aviation business requires attaining certain minimum thresholds or standards. The primary area of concern should be to ensure that the airline abides by the rules that make it qualify as an airline. Of serious concern, among many

70 Corporate waste cases analysis

Table 5.1 Chronology of events – ATCL aircraft lease

Date	Detail	Note
Oct 2007	Beginning of lease contract	Monthly rent at USD 370,000
Feb 2008	Completion of TCAA mandated maintenance by the lessor M/s Wallis Trading Co. LTD	
Apr 2, 2008	Release of USD 60 million letter of guarantee from the government	Lessor previously not willing to release aircraft without the guarantee
May 2008	Release of aircraft	ATCL cumulative rent amounted to more than USD 2.5 million
Dec 2008	Aircraft sent to Mauritius Air for technical checkup	Costs of over USD 590k incurred
	Aircraft transferred to Air France for crucial comprehensive C12+ checks	Cumulative rent at more than USD 3 million
		Owner contribution only USD 300,000
Oct 2010	Maintenance was completed	Aircraft could not be returned due to ATCL failure to settle the bill
Oct 17, 2011	Agreement on lease termination reached	Cumulative rental fee amounted to over USD 15 million
		Along with interest and other charges amount owed totalled USD 42,459,316

Source: Author's summations from various CAG reports

others, was ATCL lacking the prerequisite aviation certifications, including the standard but very important IATA Operational Safety Audit (IOSA) certification (CAG, 2016).

Going by the standard operating procedures, it was required that by the end of December 2008 the airline be IOSA compliant. ATCL, however, could not pay for the consulting services estimated at USD 1 million to be able to meet the requirement. As a result of being non-compliant, ATCL was in December 2008 suspended from the International Air Transport Association (IATA) and consequently remained only as a clearing house member.[6]

To compound the problems, while failing the IATA standards, ATCL did not fully meet the equally important Air Operator Certificate (AOC) requirements. The acquisition of a full AOC in 2010 required payment of about USD 1.4 million, which was mainly for the purchase of a minimum requirement for aircraft spare parts, putting in place an Approved Maintenance Organisation, purchase of maintenance software, as well as facilitating pilots' and engineers' training. The failure to acquire the certifications clearly risked the company's flight operations and safety, as well as posing extra difficulty in the envisaged fleet modernization for an overdue route network expansion program and other strategic endeavours.

Ineffective turnaround strategy

ATCL performance failures have been attributed to both internal and external factors. External factors included the ever-increasing competitive environment, an increase in prices of inputs and changes in market demand. The internal factors included failures in management, in financial decision-making, and in coping with or ignoring new industry trends. That notwithstanding, in the case of ATCL there was no turnaround strategy aimed at building the airline into a true national carrier, one that operated profitably and was accountable to the public through its service offerings. As one of the consequences, the airline had been fast losing its air operations market share to the point where by 2011 it had the lowest of the top five operators with 0.4%. This was well behind the private operators such as Precision Air (58.8%), Coastal Travel (21.8%) and Zan Air (4.2%) (TCAA, 2011).

A turnaround strategy entails a process of transforming a non-performing, loss-making company into a profit-making entity. Indeed, such corporate turnaround is a structured, well-planned methodological approach for a company's revival, and its attainment adheres to a step-by-step approach. The approach takes time, investment and the involvement of a competent workforce (CAG, 2016). The turnaround strategy is one that would enable ATCL to re-organize itself, structure and human resource-wise, to become competitive – that is, to improve quality, efficiency, effectiveness and performance in service delivery on a continuous basis and be able sustain these gains for the long haul.

The CAG's, 2016 review indicated that the distressed ATCL had critical human capital challenges as its Achilles heel (see Table 5.2). Largely, ATCL had aged personnel in most of the key and critical functions including quality and safety, aircraft engineers and pilots; under-qualified staff and an inferior physical resource base; and no succession plan to speak of, factors that brought its long-term sustainability into question. Table 5.2 summarizes the human capital at the material time.

The above staffing levels, totalling 270 employees, were a clear sign of lack of enterprise or effective governance, considering that at the time the company operated only two aircraft.

Table 5.2 ATCL human capital

Category	Number	%	Remark
Permanent staff	127	55	Staffing core functions
Contractual staff	54	23	Staffing core and support functions
Temporary staff	50	22	Staffing auxiliary support functions
Close to retirement	39	31	Permanent staff over 55 years[7]

Source: CAG Report (2016) and authors' calculations

Other challenges revolved around the company's highly indebted position to the extent that it failed to meet its operational costs and honour maturing obligations. Typifying SOE non-performers, ATCL has been characteristically dependent upon unpredictable subventions from the parent Ministry. The situation was worsened by the company's huge maintenance costs, its inability to comply with the mandatory regulations, e.g. IATA, IOSA and other mandatory regulatory training for its technical personnel, as well as its difficulty in refurbishing and facilitating resources for enhancing services.

It is notable, although not shocking, that ATCL's own staff have not had a very positive view of their company. Reporting on a "Customer Satisfaction Survey" for the company, the CAG noted that staff rating at ATCL was very poor in all six areas of the survey covering leadership, general management practices, human resource management, financial services, work environment and general comments (CAG PA & OBs, 2010/11).[8]

Governance, waste and ATCL's deteriorating financial performance

Government ineffectiveness, seen in the lack of accountability, downright neglect, irresponsibility, non-adherence to ethical principles and at times sheer apathy, culminated in inefficiency and waste, and therefore was largely responsible for ATCL's plight. Poor resource deployment is partially because public spending is a complex, multifaceted process, which is not transparent to the general public. The foregoing was proven beyond doubt by the magnitude public resource waste incurred by ATCL's extended saga as a result of inefficiency, absence of accountability and sheer ineptitude.

It is well known that one of the many challenges facing ATCL for the past several years, and perhaps the major one, is financial distress. The company's unaudited financial statements indicate that ATCL has had losses for almost a decade (nine years to be precise). Looking back (hindsight is always 20/20), it was all about failure in governance, i.e. the lack of accountability, the absence of a risk framework and poor resource management.

Risk framework

Every public entity faces a variety of positive and negative uncertainties which can affect its success in attaining set objectives, as well as in terms of value for money. Each entity has to remain active in seeking to recognize both threats and opportunities and to decide how best to respond to them, including how to set internal controls.

It was thus crucial for ATCL to identify the existing as well as potential risks and come up with mitigating measures. A risk management plan would have helped it attain set objectives and, among other things, ensure value for the money.

Notice, for example, that a significant portion of ATCL revenue is realized from the sale of tickets. Since 2007, the company's revenue has been fluctuating year after year. Whereas between 2008 and 2013 revenues decreased drastically, averaging a mere TZS 5.9 billion, the two-year period between 2014 and 2015 revenues improved to register record sales of TZS 16.24 billion and TZS 15.01 billion, respectively. On the other hand, ATCL expenses have been fluctuating significantly year after year, recording the highest at TZS 85.11 billion in 2008.

The absence of a risk management framework certainly exacerbated ATCL's situation. Such a framework should have prepared the company for what was an eventuality, including the potential loss trend, and put in place mitigating measures. One cannot emphasize enough how important it is to capture all of the organization's potential risks, so they can be evaluated in context. In the case of ATCL, some of the risks were certainly missed and hence the enormous consequences.

Starting with, for instance, the identification of high-impact, low-probability risk, onward to opportunity risks, end-to-end risks, and cumulative risk, would enable the facilitation of a systematic approach to risk mitigation. By so doing, ATCL could have certain standard responses to risk including preventive, corrective, directive and detective controls, viz.:

- Preventive action by way of hands-on measures to limit undesirable outcomes without the imposition of unnecessary costs.
- Corrective controls to address damaging aspects of obvious risks, including contingency planning.
- Directive controls in the sense of measures designed to specify the way in which a process is carried out to rule out some obvious potential damage.
- Detective controls via the identification of damages so that remedies could be instituted immediately.

Indeed, in this situation, a stitch in time would have saved nine. The idiom carries a simple but powerful message: there was no need to procrastinate (if governance failure qualifies as such). In part, it was the delayed action to come up with a viable, long-term resolution on the part of the government that made matters worse for the company.

Resource management

For better and effective resource management, it is important that each public sector entity establishes governance arrangements appropriate to the entity's business, scale and culture. Such a structure should combine efficient decision-making with accountability and transparency. This would help in the attainment of the entity's objective in both the short term as well as the long term.

A review of ATCL's past strategic plans, including the most recent 2015/2020, as well as the plan and budget 2015/2016 alongside the company's financial forecast, reveals once again evident shortfalls in management of the meagre resources. According to the CAG, the strategic plan's sole purpose (it appears) is to support a plan to obtain USD 20 million in term loan funding from the TIB Development Bank. The 2015/2020 strategic plan document places emphasis on bringing the company to sustainable operations through the acquisition of a

74 *Corporate waste cases analysis*

new aircraft fleet. The funding requirement would facilitate the purchase of a Bombardier DHC8Q400 for USD 24,500,000 and one Boeing B737NG for USD 80,000,000. According to the CAG's report, the plans fall short in terms of governance aspects, as it identifies significant inconsistency in the strategy and lack of clarity with respect to the attainment of its objectives (CAG, 2016).

Again, the strategic plan 2015/2020 did not acknowledge or address governance challenges that brought the company to its knees in the first place.

Observations, insights and lessons

It is crucial to understand that the airline industry as a whole has never been viewed in a favourable light by many investors. One anonymous industry analyst went so far as to say, "this industry has been viewed as something close to a gambling casino; [investors] see it as a labor intensive business being run by ego-driven managers. The market believes it's a lousily managed business" (Sheth, Allvine, Uslay, & Dixit, 2004, p. 261). When we identify ATCL as an unacceptably tolerated case of public waste, we are cognizant of what the industry has been through. We in turn ask the reader to recognize the logic behind the situation faced by ATCL. From a governance perspective, the situation called for (a) timely governance-related decision-making and (b) commitment to a definite course of action.

Logically, ATCL's recovery process had to start somewhere and certainly sooner before the company almost collapsed. Perhaps most minimally, the earliest possible point could have been a turn-around strategy (say in 2006) and recognition of the various adverse impacts that accumulated to the failure, to address the challenges and the consequences arising in a timely manner.

Absence of a commitment because the problem is not "well-defined" or because it has yet to prove costly enough or commercially beneficial might lead to an inherent and unmanageable problem. On the other hand, if a commitment exists, because the government has acted to approve the way forward or has legally bound itself to fulfilling those commitments, then there is a possibility to see light at the end of the tunnel.

Internally, as it had been revealed, there was no evidence that ATCL had a business case prepared to ascertain the overall implications of the adopted measures toward its recovery. Of concern is that since 2007, ATCL has been experiencing financial constraints, suggesting that it has been unable to strategically plan for business revival, revamp and expansion.

One thing remains clear. Weak, ill-performing public institutions, such as ATCL in this case, can seldom be expected to reform themselves in the absence of external pressure. Unlike their private counterparts, public entities are often inadequate at mobilizing public pressure for specific institutional reform.

In essence, effective decision-making informs the need to actively manage the identified risks and opportunities. Likewise, appraising an alternative course of action using varied approaches including ascertaining the feasibility of attaining value for money is inevitable. Where appropriate, evidence-based

Corporate waste cases analysis 75

decision-making is what is desired to reach decisions among both policy and/or project choices, steering initiatives and taking stock at each critical point.

Poor governance hinders effective resource use. While quantitative estimates of overall waste and inefficiency could at times be seen as speculative, there is total agreement that the saving of public funds could in substantial ways boost economic and social impact in resource-dire areas such as education, health and infrastructure. It is no surprise, therefore, that a segment of society views efforts to revive ATCL as a class issue. This is the one that argues with sarcasm that "our Bombardier runs on the ground," commenting on recent efforts to acquire new aircraft to revive ATCL instead of mobilizing resources for better public transportation by road or railways.

Duality in air travel development and tourism promotion cannot be underestimated. In looking at the two sectors from a development perspective in a country such as Tanzania, it is obvious that it is an irreversibly interdependent relationship. Indeed, given the current tourism model, one cannot simply survive without the other. The success and growth of one industry inspire growth and progress of the other.

ATCL is not alone. Well-intentioned turn-around strategies have been undermined in the past by inefficiency, wrong-headed priorities and outright graft. The rationale for a turn-around strategy would enable ATCL to perform its functions efficiently. For this, it needs to pursue multiple objectives: improved provision of quality services; provision of efficient services; embracement of business best practices; increased quality via adoption of modern technology and techniques; and increased revenues.

Different organizations, public and private, take different approaches to address the same opportunities or risks. Embedded in each public sector entity's systems should be arrangements for recognition and managing opportunities and risks. ATCL's board should have evaluated its respective desired risk appetite, bearing in mind legal obligations, policy decisions, business objectives, as well as public expectations. Risk assessment to gauge prevalent and potential risk is what has been amiss with ATCL. Consequently, any resolution brought to the table should bear that in mind.

Waste by regulator: the Tanzania Communications Regulatory Authority

The Tanzania Communications Regulatory Authority (TCRA) is a quasi-independent government body regulating the communications and broadcasting sectors. The Authority, a statutory body, was established as part of the government policy reforms in the communications sector with the aim of improving the availability of the information and communication services to the public as well as allowing for the entry of new players and services into the market.

TCRA was established under the Tanzania Communications Regulatory Act No. 12 of 2003 to regulate the electronic communications, postal services, and management of the national frequency spectrum in the United Republic of

Tanzania. The Authority became operational on November 1, 2003, and took over the functions of the now-defunct Tanzania Communications Commission (TTC) and Tanzania Broadcasting Commission (TBC).

Telecommunications is one of the fastest growing sectors in Tanzania. The growth emanates from not only the increase in mobile phone customers airtime but also the expansion of broadcasting as well as Internet-related services. That notwithstanding, the sector's low contribution to the economy raises questions. In 2015, for example, the sector grew by 12.2%, but it only contributed 3.6% to Tanzania's GDP (Collings, 2016).

TCRA has outlined a set of core values. They include professionalism, respect, empowerment, innovation, integrity, accountability, teamwork, objectivity, efficiency and non-discrimination, all enshrined as guiding principles of its daily functions as well as toward the attainment of long-term objectives. It has also highlighted the importance of quality in operations and service delivery. Among TCRA's quality objectives are:

i   To maintain an effective Quality Management System complying with International Standard ISO 9001:2008;
ii To achieve and maintain a level of quality which enhances the TCRA reputation with stakeholders;
iii To ensure compliance with relevant statutory and regulatory requirements; and
iv To endeavour, at all times, to maximize stakeholder satisfaction with their services.

It is important to highlight at the outset that TCRA is ISO 9001:2008 certified, implying that there were no major non-conformities and it thus met the threshold espoused in the seven quality management principles, namely customer focus, leadership, engagement of people, process approach, improvement, evidence-based decision-making and relationship management.

Looking at TCRA from the ISO 9001 perspectives as a regulator in terms of applicability, it may have fallen short in governance, especially in respect to four of the seven principles, viz.:

a   Principle 4 – process approach, i.e. a desired result is achieved more efficiently when activities and related resources are managed as a process.
b   Principle 5 – improvement, i.e. improvement of the organization's overall performance should be a permanent objective of the organization.
c   Principle 6 – evidence-based decision-making, i.e. effective decisions are based on the analysis of data and information.
d   Principle 7 – relationship management, i.e. an organization and its external providers (suppliers, contractors, service providers) are interdependent and a mutually beneficial relationship enhances the ability of both to create value.

The ISO 9001 standard is generic, and its parts must be interpreted with care to make sense within a particular organization. Indeed, it has been customary across sectors to work toward standardizing interpretation of guidelines in respective marketplaces. Some argue that the standard is seen as prone to failure when a company is interested in certification before quality (Seddon, 2000). As such, instead of enhancing quality improvement, the certifications are more often than not based on contractual necessities (Barnes, 2000; Henricks, 2001). This is an area of interest when looking at TCRA, the regulator, from a governance perspective.

According to the latest annual report of the Controller and Auditor General, at TCRA, numerous governance-related shortfalls were evident, translating to a waste of public resources by the regulator. Among others were a number of aspects related to the implementation of the Telecommunication Traffic Monitoring System (TTMS). The report revealed that no feasibility study was carried out, no business case developed and no proper assessment of risks undertaken for TTMS implementation. Also noted was the lack of proper communication among project key stakeholders, an unwarranted weakness that resulted into the exclusion in the TTMS's contract bills of quantities (BoQ), some of the key modules responsible for revenue assurance. To cap it all (mundane as it may seem), there were also inherent failures in the preparation and operationalization of the annual action plan.

It will therefore be helpful to look at these various aspects as a way to gauge governance shortfalls and ascertain the magnitude of waste by regulator, how it came about and lessons to learn therefrom.

Implementation of TTMS project

TCRA entered into an agreement with Societe Generale de Surveillance (SGS) to undertake a Telecommunication Traffic Monitoring System installation project under a build, operate and transfer (BOT) arrangement. For TCRA and the government, the monitoring system represented an important step forward in the regulation of telecommunications, which is a crucial and strategic sector in Tanzania's socio-economic development endeavours. The system provides the authorities with the technological solutions to independently measure and analyse key aspects of the telecom sector. But by so doing, it not only ensures regulatory compliance but also efficiently facilitates the exhaustive levies collection.

The TTMS is considered not only ground-breaking, but also one of the paramount accomplishments of the country's communication sector (TCRA, 2014). It comprises several other components, including the volumetric and the billing of the international traffic entering Tanzania, as well as the detection and elimination of international communications by-pass fraud. Since becoming operational, TTMS has yielded concrete outcomes. Through its acquisition and operationalization of the TTMS, the TCRA has positioned itself as one of the most progressive regulatory authorities in Tanzania, so much so that former President Kikwete urged the country's other public institutions to emulate it and be able to demonstrate similar efficiency and strategic thinking (Global Voice Group, 2014).

The TTMS allows the government to leverage a crucial resource, the telecom sector, to create new revenue streams. Given the rapid growth of mobile telephony in Tanzania, the TTMS across the board not only facilitated the government's new revenue collection efforts but also enabled mobile operators to increase their revenues as well. The government estimated that the project would generate an additional TZS 20 billion per year in revenue, solely through the monitoring of international incoming calls (TechMoran, 2014). Moving from nothing to that high amount annually was a commendable and a very promising feat indeed. It is obvious, therefore, that the opportunity cost – the cost of passing up the next best choice – is enormous. The importance of such telecoms traffic monitoring systems to a poor country like Tanzania cannot be underestimated. The multiple benefits extend beyond revenue protection and optimization, to providing tools for regulatory enforcement and high-level business analytics that will facilitate informed decision-making for policy and business decision-makers. The benefits are a global trend that Tanzania stands to benefit from.

The world has continued to witness sustained growth rates across the telecom sector, and this could possibly persist into the future. For example, Ericsson's predictions indicated that by 2018 smartphone subscriptions would exceed four billion, as mobile broadband works toward the seven billion subscriptions threshold (Ericsson Mobility Report, 2013). Other global projections likewise indicate a ten-fold 4G subscription growth within five years (88 to 864 million, between 2012 and 2017) (Pyramid Research, 2013). Consequently, with the projected escalation in users, traffic and applications, it is expected that revenues across the telecom sector would equally increase. In effect, revenues from traditional telecom operators are likely to decline. Some studies indicate that by 2020, they are likely to lose up to 6.9% to VoIP service (Obiodu & Green, 2012).

The cloud computing (another closely related potential area) market, worth USD 18 billion in 2011, was estimated to double by 2013 and quadruple soon after, mostly due to cloud-stored big data initiatives, which are presently responsible for 75% of global data centre traffic (ITU, 2014). In effect, it is estimated that by December 2017, yearly IP traffic globally is projected to go beyond the zettabyte mark (1.4 zettabytes). This is attributed to the incursion of pay TV and video streaming as well as other media-rich content services (CISCO, 2010). The youth comprise the major consumer group of these and future services in the Tanzanian market. They are part of the monthly four billion hours of YouTube video binge watching, Facebook's 30 billion pieces of shared content and 400 million daily tweets (McKinsey Global Institute, 2013).

The coming reality of the Internet of Things (IoT) and machine-to-machine (M2M) communications will significantly back the expected growth. By 2017 it is expected that there will be tremendous growth in devices, e.g. TV growth will register 42%, tablets 116%, smartphone 119% and business Internet M2M modules 86%. Indeed, it was projected that wireless device traffic would for the first time exceed wired device traffic in 2014 (CISCO, 2010).

In a world with increasing technology-aided fraudulent practices, it is important for governments to institute protective measures to optimize revenue streams. Having TTMS enables control over data and further modernization as well as empowerment through appropriate governance machinery. The new revenue streams can be channelled to appropriate areas for poverty reduction and other sustainable development endeavours, including education and health systems, infrastructure development etc. Tanzania, like many other countries, will be an active participant in this changing marketplace.

The glowing picture painted by that detailed above might lead one to the impression that all was rosy in terms of governance and optimal resource utilization. In effect, that was not the case from day one; not with the absence of a feasibility study, ineffective utilization of various TTMS modules, lack of communication between key stakeholders and failure to undertake a risk assessment. We discuss these attributes as contributing to waste in the following section

Missing feasibility study

Given the potential of the telecommunication industry and its role across the economy, conducting a feasibility study ahead of implementation was imperative.[9] The aim of a feasibility study (though not a perfect science) is to ascertain the economic viability, financial and technical feasibility as well as social desirability of a project. In an objective and rational manner, it exposes the strengths and weaknesses of a proposed venture, discloses opportunities and threats present in the environment, identifies the resources required, and ultimately evaluates the prospects for success of a project.

According to the CAG report (CAG, 2016), no evidence was presented to either justify the contractual project costs amounting to USD 100,000 for undertaking the feasibility study or to substantiate that a comprehensive business case was prepared to support the decision to implement the project.

A feasibility study would have incorporated salient contextual aspects related to the Tanzanian market in particular and the international market in general. For example, the International Telecommunication Union (ITU), for one, recognizes that each member state has the sovereign right to allow or prohibit certain forms of alternative calling procedures in order to address their impact on its national telecommunication networks; the interests of consumers and users of telecommunication services; and the need of some member states to identify the origin of calls. Further, it recognizes that some forms of alternative calling may impact the quality of service (QoS), quality of experience (QoE) and the performance of telecommunication networks and the benefits of competition in delivering lower costs and choice to consumers. Moreover, it acknowledges that there are a myriad of stakeholders impacted by alternative calling procedures, and that the understanding of what is an alternative calling procedure has evolved over time (ITU, 2014).

Given the above mentioned and more, in the absence of an all-inclusive feasibility study and business case, there was at the beginning the risk that a project may be implemented without taking into consideration the varied needs of not only the TCRA but also other stakeholders. Again, this is contrary to standards espoused under ISO 9000 principles for which TCRA had been certified. Successful project implementation calls for finding flaws before project launch and for making modifications accordingly. If the flaw cannot be addressed or shaped to better fit and appears to be truly fatal, it may be optimal to abandon and avoid wasting meagre public resources. Better yet, a feasibility study facilitates asking, "What if?" and probing, testing and experimenting, an opportunity worth pursuing. That was not the case with TCRA. It is no wonder that major issues arose in the implementation of an Airtime Revenue Monitoring Solution.

The Airtime (Automated) Revenue Monitoring Solution

The Automated Revenue Monitoring System (ARMS) was developed to meet the growing needs of regulatory and tax authorities for effective telecom revenue control and verification systems. This product allows for the instant capture of all the telecommunications charging data events, billing events and usage events. It also ensures verification of the total turnover of the telecom operators, the licensing fees and taxes related to the turnover and the deduction of airtime bonuses, among others, in an accurate and efficient manner. Accurate information on market dynamics leads to better governance of the telecommunications sector, market growth, increased revenue for both government and the service providers, and better competitive pricing for consumers.

In 2014, through consultation meetings between the TCRA, TRA, Ministry of Communication, Science and Technology (MoCST) and Ministry of Finance (MoF), a committee was formed to develop recommendations to agree collectively on the modalities for implementing ARMS successfully. According to the CAG report (CAG, 2016), the committee's recommendations emphasized the full engagement of TRA in the TTMS agreement as a key stakeholder. In essence, TRA should take over the procurement of the system, including entering into contract with the consultant.[10] The actual recommendations issued by the committee stated as follows:

- Since the TRA is the main beneficiary of ARMS, TRA may consider being incorporated as a part of the TTMS agreement;
- TRA to enter into agreement with ARMS provider for provision of ARMS services;
- TRA may look for a best technology which can lead to direct access of information from telecom operators. Some of the options are:
- TRA can link with all operators and use TCRA racks available at operators' sites. This will involve setting up links between different operators and the TRA central site;
- TRA can use the existing infrastructure (links and racks) at TCRA, which will involve accessing all the information from TCRA HQ;
- TCRA to provide to TRA all information on the current TTMS capabilities so that TRA can be aware of the functionalities of TTMS. This will help TRA in developing further requirements as needed for ARMS;
- TCRA to invite TTMS consultant for further clarification on the TTMS contract implementation of ARMS within the TTMS agreement framework; and
- In case TRA becomes part of the TTMS contract, TCRA and TRA will need to agree on the appropriate ARMS procurement procedures.

Ironically, all these recommendations could have been identified by the feasibility study and incorporated appropriately in the overall project. Despite the powerful and worthy recommendations and obvious oversight in the implementation of TTMS, the committee did not consider aspects of governance and management of the ARMS project.

Given that this project spans across multiple agencies with distinct reporting structures, leadership and management, the marriage of varied objectives related to the multiple agencies should have been given prominence. The committee's recommendations notwithstanding, adherence to public procurement regulations across government agencies should have prevailed first and foremost. Public Procurement Regulatory Authority (PPRA) regulations have specific procedures related to PPP procurement (such as the TTMS) which stipulate under Article 369, for instance:

1 Subject to the provisions of the Public Private Partnership regulations, the contracting authority shall carry out a feasibility study before undertaking the procurement of a solicited PPP project.
2 The contracting authority shall not proceed with the procurement phase of solicited PPP or private sector participation project if the feasibility study indicates that the proposed project will not deliver value for money or improve the quality of the public service.

Even further, such measures would have come in handy, especially in relation to procurement continuous monitoring, contract and performance audits. Article 379 (negotiation, agreement and award), specifically, stipulates that:

i Where a contracting authority selects a private partner, the contracting authority shall comply with the procedures under the Public Private Partnership regulations in negotiating with the private party, drafting, approving, vetting and signing of the agreement.
ii The mechanisms for monitoring implementation of the project, reporting, dispute resolution, processes for remedying deficiencies, provisions for handling default by either party, and finally handing back requirements if the project is prematurely terminated shall be as specified in the Public Private Partnership regulations.

It is apparent that adherence to transparent governance came short and, as a result, even the contingency position fell through. Streamlined governance in a well-regulated economic sector is a primary requisite to attract investors and investment. This is of crucial importance for the economy of a country like Tanzania with its many development needs and priorities.

Ineffective utilization of TTMS modules

TCRA's implementation of TTMS to monitor international and interconnect telecommunications traffic from licensed operators entailed installation of five separate modules: the Local and International Traffic Monitoring System, Fraud Management System, Quality of Service Monitoring Platform, Mobile Money Monitoring Platform and Device Detection System, also known as Central Equipment Identity Register (CEIR). According to the CAG report (CAG, 2016), whereas some of the modules are effectively utilized, others leave a lot to be desired.

Local and international traffic monitoring

The Local and International Traffic Monitoring System is indeed a valuable module to TCRA more than to any other entity. That notwithstanding, however, its usage could have been expanded to the TRA, for instance, for use in verification purposes with respect to telecom operators and local and international calls revenue. Unfortunately, that was not the case, thus the monitoring of local and international traffic was left unattended.

Fraud management and quality of service

The use of TTMS's Fraud Management System is closely linked to the Local and International Traffic Monitoring System, rendering its utilization within acceptable levels. Whereas the Quality of Service Monitoring Platform fits pretty well in TCRA's core activities, there is still room for improvement via reassessment of the rules around the quality of services offered by telecom operators and the existing technical capability that the subsystem is providing.

Today, communication networks provide the interconnectivity between different regions across the world. These networks are growing and with time more and more traffic will be routed between different sources and destinations per second. Communication through Internet Protocol networks has provided new opportunity for entities small and large to get into varied types of telecom business. Some are able to offer relatively cheap rates on international traffic and by-pass the legal routes. This grey traffic – a term used for illegal termination of international communication traffic in any country – causes huge revenue losses not only to legal telecom companies but also to the government in terms of fees and taxes (Khan et al., 2015) because of failure to monitor the traffic. For purposes of our discussion here, grey traffic is extended to include false reporting by telecom companies to unethically cheat on the regulator and deny the government due revenue.

Mobile money monitoring

The Mobile Money Monitoring Platform, which provides visibility to mobile payment transactions over time, can be used more extensively. Tanzania's mobile money industry growth rate is astonishing, and the environment is one of the most conducive for financial inclusion. The industry is one of the most well developed in the world, setting its mark with growing competition and interoperable systems among service providers. The number of people with access to formal financial services has quadrupled, with 38 million mobile money accounts and 8.9 million active mobile money users at an average transaction value of USD 19 (CGAP, 2014).

The TTMS component or subsystem provides the technical capability that could dramatically improve the regulation of mobile money banking and monitoring, as well as its innovation. The Bank of Tanzania (BoT) could be among both the subsystem's potential contributors and its beneficiaries. With the addition of a few business analytics variables on top of this module, important and pertinent questions related to money supply –including mobile money velocity relative to monetary base, the impact of default or failure in the mobile money platform hosted by telecom operators, the impact on the exchange rate as a result of cross-border mobile transactions, money laundering and illicit transactions through mobile money and cross-border currencies – could be optimally investigated. Today the BoT has enabled mobile money service to (pay interest) share profits. Indeed, only one principle guided the Bank of Tanzania when it was time to address what to do with interest (held in trust by banks) earned by customers of mobile network operators (MNOs): the benefits of the interest should accrue directly to the customer. The innovative approach came from none other than the MNOs themselves based on the BoT set criteria of how best to benefit the customer. Initially, the decision was frowned upon by Tanzanian banks, as the measure meant a direct competition by MNOs offering tangible customer benefits. They feared possibly massive funds outflow from the banking sector and into mobile money wallets. A year and a half later, there is no indication of the outflow and, in fact, the opposite happened in terms of flows into the banks. Banks ended up teaming with MNOs through another innovation that links mobile money wallets with bank accounts. It is unfortunate, however, that the TRA was yet to use the module to effectively establish tax revenue due from transaction costs being charged by mobile operators.

Device detection and identification system

The Device Detection and Identification System provide the capability to evaluate the authenticity of mobile devices used in mobile operators' network. This subsystem fits well in the core activities of TCRA. Its successful implementation, however, requires broader participation of stakeholders from the telecom sector, such as mobile customers and telecom operators.

Indeed, the utilization of TTMS could have further been enhanced by bringing along the other potential beneficiaries and important players in the economy, such as the Bank of Tanzania and the TRA, as well as by developing business capability through modification of TCRA's rules and processes.

Lack of proper communication among project key stakeholders

In accordance with the CAG report, the implementation of the TTMS was overshadowed by a lack of proper communication among the key public sector stakeholders. They include the Bank of Tanzania, Tanzania Revenue Authority (TRA) and Tanzania Telecommunication Company (TTCL). (CAG, 2016). This weakness resulted in public waste due to failure to include in the TTMS contract's bills of quantities some key modules responsible for revenue assurance, i.e. ARMS. Consequently, TCRA and TRA had to plan to have a separate agreement with the TTMS consultant to include this module within TTMS by adding some system functionalities that would enable TRA capabilities to performing revenue assurance across the telecommunication industry. The move would entail additional costs, which would have been minimized or eliminated if this was taken care of earlier alongside the installation of the five currently operating modules.

Despite assurances and contractual agreement with the consultant, at the time of the CAG's reporting, the consultant had not installed the necessary component to be able to capture domestic revenue accruing to telecom companies. The objective of the installation per contract was "CAG (2016, p94)." Consequently, the objective was not attained and the project failed to eliminate and prevent revenue loss to both the operators and the United Republic, thus occasioning at a minimum a loss of more than USD 2,722,605.50 (provision per contract).

Failure to conduct project risk assessment

From the foregoing discussion, it was evident that the TCRA and other key stakeholders had not clearly specified their requirements in terms of deliverables from the start of the project; they instead concentrated on inputs and the mechanics of delivery. Such inherent weakness could have exposed stakeholders and the government to the potential risk of ending up with a project that does not meet their real needs. As such, the failure to conduct risk assessment at the beginning and along the process was a failure in governance.

In its report, the CAG indicated that it could not ascertain whether the TCRA carried out appropriate or any risk assessment and whether it provided for the allocation of the TTMS project risks between the two parties (CAG, 2016). Appropriate allocation of risk among project players, whether public or private as was the case here, is a key requirement if the public/private finance and concessions approach is to deliver optimal value for the money. Successful management of the assessed risk over the lifetime of the project is *sine qua non* for any successful project implementation.

A successful project should benefit from workable, commercially viable and cost-effective risk sharing. Differing interests and objectives among parties necessitate coming up with effective risk allocation, an integral part of a project's success. An oft-quoted approach to efficient risk allocation places each risk on the party best able to manage that risk. Much as this is a useful rule of thumb, it remains a gross over-simplification. This is because it is only meaningful if risk is borne by the party that has an interest in managing it proactively or will obtain resources needed to address risk issues as and when they arise to minimize their impact on the project, has access to the right technology and resources to manage the risk when it crystallizes, can manage the risk at least cost and most of all delivers value for money (Delmon, 2011, p. 96).

The CAG could not ascertain whether the TCRA had optimally transferred the relevant project risks to the private party in the PPP endeavour (CAG, 2016). This was especially crucial after a determination had been made as to the transfer cost and who was better placed to bear and manage which risk etc. Indeed, the management of risk in PPP is complex and intensive, but mechanisms to address the risks have been developed. What is important as a risk mitigation measure is to organize the project and assess it efficiently. Performance of due diligence will help identify risk gravity, risk interface and risk management priorities.

Some of the questions raised in the CAG report relate to the determination of the appropriate remuneration for the consultants, given that there was no evidence of a cost-benefit analysis having been conducted. Similar questions were raised concerning the contingency amount set aside for the TTMS project, contrary to regulations or norms.

Preparation and operationalization of annual action plan

An action or operational plan details the activities to be carried out by an entity or project, including time frames, planned inputs and funding sources, in order to generate outputs in relation to the outcome. It also serves as good reference for monitoring progress later in the year. The planned activities are derived from the strategic plan, which integrates the strategic objectives of an entity (CAG, 2016).

A review of TCRA's action plan and performance reports for the year 2014/15 by the CAG revealed that, contrary to requirements of the standards it is supposed to adhere to, some agreed action plan activities were not implemented or achieved as planned. More important, some activities earmarked for implementation lacked relevant performance indicators, baselines and targets (CAG, 2016). Also noted was that TCRA had neither prepared an action plan framework to address identified challenges nor decided on how to measure the performance achievements.

Non-achievement of the activities planned to be executed in the respective year may hinder the Authority to achieve its main strategic objectives. Likewise, absence of performance indicators, baselines and targets for planned activities suggests that the Authority might not be in a position to measure actual performance of its activities against its targets, and hence fails to achieve the intended objectives.

Observations, insights and lessons

When President Magufuli disbanded the TCRA Board of Directors and let go its Director General soon after taking office, it came as no surprise to those with prior knowledge of the potential that existed at TCRA and the apparent waste by the regulator. To a regular citizen, nonetheless, it was not as clear, given the pace the president was moving at and the aura TCRA had been able to build for itself as the exemplary regulator.

The CAG reports claimed that the regulator had failed to monitor the telecom industry and failed to gather the requisite much-needed revenue for the state, for it to be able to channel the same toward development endeavours. The president estimated that the regulator was responsible for occasioning a loss of US $180 million in tax revenue since 2013, when the traffic monitoring system was installed but failed to be utilized effectively. That is no small amount in terms of wasted resources.[11]

Some of the flaws elaborated above were systemic governance failures, whilst others can be categorized as negligence, apathy and incompetence. Some faults, however, call for measures and approaches that are beyond the governance structure and stakeholders' expectations. These are highlighted here under:

Verifying project viability through feasibility studies provides for extensive analysis of objective, funding source as well as project scope including political buy-in. It likewise entails the identification of legal risks and regulatory and political challenges over and above technical, financial and economic assessment prior to the development of the procurement process.

Absence of accurate information leads to ill-informed decisions and consequent adverse impact. Availability of timely and accurate information on telecom sector market dynamics leads to better governance, market growth, increased revenue and competitive pricing. Lack of transparency, which is key to good governance, exacerbated the situation and made it worse for the telecommunications sector.

Thanks to the amendments made under the Finance Act of 2016, there has been an increase in compliance level on money transfers as well as on telecoms revenue. The strategy on expanded revenue generation focuses as well on products in the telecommunication sector via the telecom revenue assurance system.

Tanzania is not the only country in the region or sub-Saharan Africa to adopt a revenue assurance technology. It has been deployed and successfully operated in Rwanda, Liberia, Guinea-Conakry, Congo-Brazzaville, Gabon, Central African Republic, Togo, Senegal and Ghana. The system has afforded governments new revenue streams to tap into and channel toward respective development priorities. To ensure a sustained revenue stream, monitoring is important. Challenges will emerge and be addressed along the way, and innovative ways will be fostered. The expected role of a regulator like TCRA is to facilitate compliance, and nothing short of that is acceptable. TTMS has proven its worth as a tool for good governance by a regulator like TCRA. As a compliance monitoring tool, it provides the TCRA with the upper hand, availing timely and accurate data to facilitate the enforcement of regulations and collection of revenue.

For TCRA, the regulator, nothing is more important than the need to improve its operational efficiency, which is part and parcel of good governance. It is ironic that the TCRA does not have an action plan with which to gauge performance as well as strategic objectives. Good governance includes having in place baselines, benchmarks, indicators and targets that hold all parties accountable and effecting the means to weigh performance of activities at a specific point or place or across the board.

Operational efficiency also hinges on collaborative efforts and communication among the key stakeholders. Failure on the part of TCRA to involve other key stakeholders at the initial stages of a project led to the adoption of costly measures and shortfall in terms of intended deliverables. Without incorporating stakeholders at the outset, it is not possible to ascertain if what is put up would address and meet real and not perceived needs. The relationship between TCRA and other regulatory agencies such as the BoT and the TRA as presented in this case reflects failure in governance by way of communication amongst stakeholders, leading to the waste of resources.

Going forward, a clear understanding of the mechanisms and rules governing Public Private Partnership arrangements is necessary for facilitating a project's realization of value for money. That being the case, it is crucial that preparations do not miss such important attributes as a comprehensive feasibility study and a detailed business case in advance of the decision to implement any major project. This will ensure that projects are successfully implemented, and the intended national objectives and project benefits are realized. As Mazzucato emphasizes, the role of the state should move from taking on risk with courage and vision to actually benefiting from taking risk and not "taking it away from someone else, who then captures the returns" (2015, p. 64).

Immeasurable resource waste: Tanzania Electric Supply Company (TANESCO)

TANESCO is mandated to generate, transmit, distribute and sell electricity to the Tanzania mainland and sell bulk power to the Zanzibar Electricity Corporation (ZECO), which in turn sells it to the public in the Islands. In fact, TANESCO owns most of the electricity generation, transmission and distribution facilities in the Tanzania mainland (TANESCO website[12]).

In relative terms, with the connection of approximately only 20% of households (mostly in urban areas), electricity access in Tanzania is considered low (Harper, 2015) by any standards. In Tanzania, like many other Global South countries, lack of electricity (as a source of energy) represents one of the basic characteristics of underdevelopment, which in turn affects the productive capacity of an economy (Nyang'oro, 2016). The government targets to raise availability to above the current 36%[13] and has identified various approaches, including placing emphasis on renewable energy in rural areas via Public Private Partnerships, towards that goal.

Policies to facilitate measures such as power purchase agreements (PPAs) have been put in place to accommodate independent power producers.

Since the 1990s, the Government of Tanzania has been working to reform the electricity sector. The reforms revolved around the state-owned electricity generation, transmission and distribution services. In 1993, the reforms embraced measures to liberalize electricity generation by opening it up to independent power producers (IPP) to sell electricity to TANESCO (Kapika & Eberhart, 2013).

This marked the beginning of what we consider one of the largest forms of resource waste by a public entity in Tanzania, which left the Tanzanian state and its people mired in debt, litigation and government resignations against a backdrop of alleged corruption. At the same time, costs to the consumer and government have significantly increased (Harper, 2015).

The genesis

The beginning goes as far back as 1994 when Tanzania went through a severe power shortage leading to frequent power outages and consequent power shedding, which from that point forward became the norm. As such, TANESCO's brand tag-line, "We light up your life," has since become a misnomer. With time it was apparent that shortages and the lack of electricity was having a major negative impact on economic activities and the government could not ignore the problem (Nyang'oro, 2016).

Most of the electricity generation capacity in Tanzania is hydro based, which, as nature would determine, is prone to droughts. Between 1992 and 2010, for instance, the country experienced droughts eight different times (1992, 1994, 1997, 2000, 2003, 2004, 2005 and 2009). The drought was the reason for the consequent massive power shortages Keller (2010a). Unambiguously, in more recent years, the power sector has been facing serious difficulties emanating from a growing power generation deficit caused by below average hydrological conditions and insufficient development of new generation capacity given ever-increasing demand. At the peak of the crisis, it was common for some areas to experience up to 12 hours of power outage per day.

That notwithstanding, Tanzania has not been able to attract investments in additional power generation capabilities. In more recent years, there has been an addition of only 300 MW, which falls short of projected demand (Kapika & Eberhart, 2013). TANESCO's immediate resolution to reduce power shedding was to enter into high-cost short-term contracts via private emergency power projects (EPPs). The move to shift to EPPs reduced load shedding and could be considered timely and necessary at the time, although it left a lot to be desired in terms of economic viability, since it significantly increased the average unit cost. The resulting effect was a consequent increase in financial gap and cumulative arrears to TANESCO's suppliers, the EPPs, as well as to IPPs.

In reality, however, the current story began in 1995, when TANESCO entered into what was to be a 20-year agreement under the auspices of Public Private Partnership (PPP) with Independent Power Tanzania Limited (IPTL), a joint venture between a Malaysian company and a local investor. The agreement entailed the purchase of 100 MW of power from the IPTL diesel-fuelled Tegeta plant in Dar es Salaam. From the start, the deal was mired in contestations around cost, environmental impact, and the fact that the assessed basis for the need of additional generating capacity was not the extension of access to the masses (Harper, 2015).

Resource waste begins

Numerous direct or indirect players were involved and/or complicit in facilitating wastage of public resources, as a result of failure in governance. The net extends from TANESCO itself (and by extension the government) to IPPs, EPPs and other public entities.

TANESCO remains the major culprit among the identified when it comes to the waste of resources in the sub-sector and its multiplier effect across the economy. Interestingly, the envisaged reform which every stakeholder believed started with TANESCO's restructuring has never come to fruition. In the World Bank's and other partners' circles, there has been a feeling of frustration with not only the pace of change and turn-around, but also the reality that the decisions undertaken seem to sink the utility even further. Ironically, it also included a period (1988–2000) during which power tariffs were increased by over 100% in nominal terms, to an average $0.09/kWh, at the time among the highest in Africa (World Bank, 2011).

Several pseudo-change elements were embraced, including an independent management contract. Contracting out TANESCO's management to a private sector contractor, NetGroup Solutions, did not improve matters either, much as there was some noted success in debt recovery rates, for instance, during their tenure. Although the process of engaging them was shrouded in allegations of impropriety and lack of transparency, the engagement itself was another unjustified unnecessary outflow of resources (Hall, 2007).

It remains a fact, nonetheless, that it was during NetGroup's term that there was noted improvement in the utility's financial and operational performance. During the time, TANESCO revenues rose from meagre monthly revenues of between US $10 and US $12 million in 2001 to about US $16 million per month in mid-2004 (Ghanadan & Eberhard, 2007). During the private management contract, however, technical performance was not as stellar, as it was dotted with system losses, poor quality and reliability of supply as well as lack of improvement in the rate of new connections (Kapika & Eberhart, 2013), objectives that were laid down to be attained in the engagement.

In 2006, the government opted out of renewing NetGroup's contract, citing that "it was dissatisfied with the quality of management provided by NetGroup Solutions" and adding that "the government was obliged to listen to the views of the public following complaints about the quality of service being offered by TANESCO" (TANESCO website). The bottom line was that if the outsourcing of management at TANESCO was a scientific experiment, the results were below expectations and nothing to be proud of.

Independent power producers – Songas and IPTL

IPPs first entered the Tanzanian landscape in 1993 when the government extended invitations for bids pertaining to the exploration of the Songo Songo natural gas reserves. The project was planned to entail, among other things, infrastructural development for gas extraction, gas processing, gas transportation via a pipeline and the construction of a gas-to-power plant in Dar es Salaam.

The Songo Songo invitation received little interest from investors for various reasons, including risk concerns at the time. Given that this was the first such investment undertaken in Tanzania, it could have enhanced the apparent concerns on the part of potential investors. It is said that only two of the 16 invitees submitted bids (Gratwick et al., 2006). After a series of delays in negotiations (which commenced in 1994), the venture eventually came to fruition with the finalization of the PPA. Commercial operations began in 2004 with the conversion of the jet-fuel plant to natural gas processing. All the while, it is important to note, the project incurred interest charges pertaining to start-up activities, i.e. allowance for funds utilized during construction.[14]

Likewise, the memorandum of understanding entered soon thereafter in 1994 between the Tanzania government and IPTL was a fast track measure aimed at arresting a dire situation in electricity supply in the country.[15]

In 1998, before the IPTL's Tegeta plant began generating electricity, TANESCO filed a grievance against IPTL at the International Center for Settlement of Investment Disputes (ICSID), claiming termination of the power purchase agreement due to violations of some aspects of its implementation. In the plea, it asserted that its entitlement to contract termination or alternatively reduction in tariff rates was based on two material facts. First, the contract was entered contrary to laid down procedures and second, the high charges could not be justified (Harper, 2015).

In 2001, the ICSID reached a verdict, turning down TANESCO's request for termination of the 20-year long-term contract, but granted power tariff reduction to mirror actual plant-related costs (Kapika & Eberhart, 2013). This provided for commercial production of electricity at the plant to begin on January 15, 2002. According to the agreement, therefore, the duration of the contract runs through 2022.

By the time of the ICSID ruling, TANESCO had incurred USD 40 million in capacity charges (Farlam, 2005) when the plant operated at less than 10% capacity. Ironically, whilst the average consumer was charged between US $0.7 and US $0.9 per unit, TANESCO paid IPTL more than US $0.12 per unit and a statutory monthly payment of US $3 million under the PPA (Farlam, 2005). IPTL in turn sued TANESCO in a New York court demanding US $70 million in unpaid capacity charges (Kapika & Eberhart, 2013).

Within a couple years of operation, the two IPPs were producing around 30% of generation capacity (Kapika & Eberhart, 2013), but costing TANESCO about 90% of its revenue (CAG, 2009). It is important to note the year-to-year variation in total electricity generated by IPPs and the fact that costs vary in relation to TANESCO's hydro-electric power generation performances, which are dependent on the whims of nature (i.e. rainfall). In drought years (e.g. 2005/2006), for example, IPPs represented over 50% of consumption, whereas in a normal year like 2007 they represented only 20%. Costs remained high nonetheless due to the nature of 'capacity charge payments.' The CAG noted in the annual report that TANESCO is extensively overloaded with liabilities pertaining to unjustifiable charges entered into with the PPAs, in violation of the Public Procurement Act and its regulations (CAG, 2009).

Emergency power providers

In 2006, TANESCO resorted to renting emergency power plants from multinational companies to alleviate power shortages. Following a severe drought in the country, the new government approved resorting to emergency power projects (EPPs) as emergency power supply sources during the severe drought period that faced the nation.

The tender issued by TANESCO provided for a relatively short period (12 months) during which emergency power supply would be needed, but this could be extended depending on the ensuing power supply situation. Contrary to this assertion, the contracts reached with the EPP multinationals were extended from 12 to 24 months, thus contradicting the whole idea behind the need for "emergency power supply" (Mwakyembe Report, 2008).

In all, TANESCO ended up engaging several different EPP multinationals that qualified, including Aggreko, Alstom and Richmond Development. Aggreko provided 40 MW of gas-fired power between October 2006 and October 2008, and Alstom between March 2007 and March 2008 provided 20 MW. Richmond Development was contracted to provide 100 MW fuelled by Songo Songo gas for a period of two years that ended being mired in a major political scandal.

Richmond Development was to first provide 20 MW by September 2006 and add the remaining 80 MW in February 2007. The initial 20 MW were provided a month late and only after the government provided an advance to the company (Gratwick et al., 2007). As it turned out, Richmond had neither the technical capability nor the capacity to fulfil the contractual obligations. Consequently, the contract was taken over by Dowans Holdings. Dowans was able to provide the contracted 100 MW, but by then the drought was over and the EPPs were no longer needed. As per contract, however, TANESCO was still obligated to pay capacity charge dues.

In due course, the government went ahead and cancelled the contract in alignment with the findings and recommendations of a parliamentary committee (and subsequent parliamentary resolution) which proclaimed,

> Richmond had neither the experience, nor the expertise, to deliver on the short-term agreement, and was in addition, financially and legally incapacitated [and that] the tender process and contract with Richmond for the emergency power production of MW 100, later being taken over by Dowans Holdings S.A on 23rd December 2006, was procedurally flawed and against

national laws and hence resulting in favouritism, embezzlement and the possibility of corruption.

(Mwakyembe Report, 2008)

Although the government cancelled the contract to abide with Parliament's resolution, citing default notices for lack of performance, TANESCO still had contractual obligations to honour. Subsequently, Dowans Holdings, which Richmond Development had passed the contract on to, took TANESCO to the International Chamber of Commerce (ICC), alleging breach of contract. On November 15, 2010, ICC co-arbitrators ruled in favour of Dowans Holdings and ordered TANESCO to pay US $123.6 million to the company in settlement of its claim.

It came as no surprise, therefore, when TANESCO reported a loss of more than US $100 million the following year. The loss was partly a result of the EPP project and was ultimately borne by the Tanzanian consumer. TANESCO applied to the regulator EWURA for a 155% tariff increase but was granted only a 40% increase. It thus had to resort to borrowing US $200 million from financial institutions to offset, among other expenses, capacity charges demanded by independent power producers, although the plants were operating below full capacity (van Niekerk & Hall, 2013).

Other

Other factors behind TANESCO's costly waste relate to institutions, decision-making and approaches of ill-informed governance and the consequent negative impacts. They include regulatory governance challenges and the emergence of EWURA, the implementation of PPP in Tanzania and from inside TANESCO and the function of the Board of Directors and top management.

Regulatory governance

As far back as 1999, the government sought to put in place a framework to regulate different sectors of the economy to enhance competition and efficiency. Subsequently, the Energy and Water Regulatory Authority Act (EWURA Act) of 2001 came into being. Due to unforeseeable circumstances, however, it was not until 2006 that EWURA, the institution, became operational. As such, there was a five-year limbo of undefined modus operandi, direction and oversight as far as the sectors incorporated in the legislation were concerned. The importance of an independent regulatory body cannot be over-emphasized when it comes to project success with respect to enhancing transparency, efficiency and a sense of purpose.

Thus, when the majority of the TANESCO-related waste took place, the much-needed independent regulatory body EWURA was not in place yet. The cost of this shortcoming was evident in all critical issues related to the electricity sector, including generation planning and investment, procurement, PPAs, pricing and tariffs. The absence of a regulator in the IPP and EPP processes left a distinct mark with a high possibility of impacting the future of the sub-sector and the economy as a whole. Overall, much as today EWURA is premier in regulatory credibility, much of the independence, accountability and transparency shrouding the operations of IPPs and EPPs can be linked to its absence back then.

Public Private Partnership

Tanzania's PPP policy identifies PPP as a viable means to address constraints related to the financing, management and maintenance of public goods and services delivery via the involvement of the private sector. PPPs can enable the government to fulfil its responsibilities in efficient delivery of socio-economic goods and services by ensuring efficiency, effectiveness, accountability, quality and outreach of services (URT, 2010).

Songas and IPTL were the first initiatives in the energy sector in Tanzania, conceptualized as PPP propositions to help alleviate the situation. Songas preceded IPTL, but due to delays and the pressing need, IPTL much sooner became a viable proposition to help. Some of the reasons behind the delay are attributed to the absence of PPP guidelines, legislation and regulations in Tanzania, thus rendering decision-making rather difficult and complex.

When it comes to implementation, Songas is considered to have been more successful than IPTL, which has caught the wrath of stakeholders from the very beginning. IPTL does not represent the best in PPPs in Tanzania. If anything, it set a bad precedent for the adoption of PPP not just because of the alleged corrupt practices and high cost of electricity, but also because it was adopted without a proper feasibility study and without the consultation of necessary stakeholders. If TANESCO had followed proper procedures, the government would have found that the problem to be addressed went beyond insufficient generating capacity. Apparently, TANESCO had in place strategies toward getting enough electricity, but it ended up purchasing electricity at a price it could not afford.

The government subsequently adopted a step-by-step process to PPPs, structured and guided by regulations within a legal framework. This sets out the roadmap, from inception entailing a feasibility study (and consequent approvals), procurement (including value for money) and contract management. The litmus tests for the regulator covering all phases are affordability, value for money and appropriate risk transfer.

Carrying out a thorough feasibility study was a *sine qua non* for IPTL and all PPP projects. A feasibility study compares public sector with private sector provision and takes into account affordability, value for money and risk transfer. It uses accurate information in its calculations and projections and considers all the financing options before committing to one model. Moreover, it would involve all the necessary stakeholders, identify all pertinent project risks and devise risk mitigation strategies.

Generators' imports

The energy crisis and high cost of energy caused economic agents to resort to using expensive power sources to minimize the negative impacts of power rationing. Electric generators have become the norm as commercial and industrial businesses and individual residences had to have their own generators to make up for the limited access to and supply of electric energy.

The high penetration rate of generators is a demonstration of businesses' and consumers' willingness to pay for electricity, despite the high cost. On average, generator power is four times the price of grid power. To many economic agents, the unreliable and intermittent supply of grid power justifies incurring the cost and thus making the additional price for generator power a necessary and acceptable cost of doing business. This new normal is a cost to the economy adding to the cost of inefficiency and wastage of resources.

TANESCO management

Political and regulatory environments have the capacity to significantly impact corporate governance systems. One characteristic feature at TANESCO is the high management turnover. Management turnover may be the most dysfunctional problem for an organization and may translate to loss due to lack of continuity or succession planning. At TANESCO, the average tenure for the Managing Director is three years. Although not directly linked here, executive turnover and its link to performance have been the focus of a growing body of research (Kato & Long, 2006), and TANESCO's governance woes fit right in.

While it is true that it is difficult to ascertain the effectiveness of corporate governance systems, it is easy to jump to the conclusion of management underperformance whenever top management is replaced, especially when a firm records poor performance. We are not in any way suggesting that management should not be held accountable for a firm's operations and poor performance. If, however, exogenous factors dominate, such as in the case of TANESCO, questions arise as to how one gauges performance and determines the level of accountability of the top management in a corporation's failure. To that effect, questions may arise as to the role of the Board of Directors and its effectiveness.

In TANESCO's case, it is imperative that executives are held accountable for the firms' performance, and this seems to have been the case. Replacements of chief executives have been attributed to failure to meet set goals and objectives. It is unfortunate that, in some cases, the removal has resulted in creating more harm than good to the institution. In effect, not all replacements necessarily resulted in enhanced performance. It follows, therefore, that the fundamental problem at TANESCO goes beyond how individual executives perform, to incorporate such pertinent issues as policy and regulatory environment and overall corporate good governance. The governance framework has been ineffective and leaves a lot to be desired, having failed to deliver performance improvements.

Observations, insights and lessons

The importance of energy to any economy cannot be overstated and even more so to a developing country like Tanzania. Indeed, the industrial structure is essentially the same in each national electric service industry (i.e. generation, transmission, distribution, system operation end-user supply and related services), much as there could be differences related to ownership and regulatory environment. It extends from a classic natural monopoly – transmission – to possibly the most innately competitive – retail last mile distribution – and heterogeneous in terms of organizational and ownership structures. What transpired with TANESCO at the centre and culminating to massive waste of resources as well as economic cost to the nation is without a doubt a case of governance failure.

The most memorable had been the contracts between TANESCO and Richmond Development Company LLC as well as IPTL, which came with political ramifications. Although it has been portrayed that the contracts TANESCO entered into with the IPPs and EPPs gave the other parties undue benefits, while impairing TANESCO and eventually customers and taxpayers, public governance systems and weaknesses cannot escape their share of blame. From lack of sector-wide long-term planning to poor contract negotiating and management skills to implementation, much was lacking in the implementation of these projects to address growing energy demands. Indeed, consequently, the burden of power generation has been too heavy on the public and curtailed efforts aimed for better lives for the populace. It is imperative that the government has in place and adheres to concrete medium- and long-term plans on how to avert power production and supply shortfalls and the massive related costs.

The CAG reports year in and year out noted that TANESCO is overburdened by the liabilities imposed by various power purchase agreements, mostly entered into without compliance with the requirements of the Public Procurement Act and regulations. These have resulted into the company paying more than what it charges its customers, thus operating at a deficit and accumulating losses consistently.

TANESCO has been mired in costly legal wrangles that were uncalled for, had the issues been take care of at the outset. The Richmond and IPTL arbitrations were especially costly to the Tanzanian taxpayer in terms of direct and indirect costs. Although hindsight is always 20/20, we can comfortably say that all the shortcomings could have been avoided from the beginning by adhering to good governance principles.

Conducting a proper project feasibility study would have adequately posed the right kind of questions to ascertain viability, social desirability and the need for the independent power producer. The study would not only address cost aspects and value for money, but also technology and demand power as well as affordability issues at the very start.

It should be borne in mind that at the advent of IPPs, the operating environment was devoid of transparency and an independent regulatory body, and much as they were promoted as PPP propositions, their implementation was experimental in nature since there existed neither PPP legislation nor guidelines or regulations. The need for the projects notwithstanding, the rushed nature of the implementation was worse for the projects and the economy than the alternative would have been. Given that the decisions were shrouded by lack of transparency, absence of proper bidding and corrupt practices made it even more difficult, as evidenced by the costly effort in trying to exit from the entanglement of such bad deals.

Closely related to the absence of a feasibility study was the absence of risk mitigation measures and strategies. Risk mitigation strategies are essentially financial strategies whose details are found in a thorough feasibility study. A feasibility study should have clearly elucidated the PPP proposition's strategic and operational attributes and outlined the proposed allocation of financial, technical and operational risks between the public and the private parties.

It is crucial to understand how complex, demanding and time-consuming PPP propositions are. It is also crucial, however, to emphasize that under the right conditions and in the right sectors, they can offer significant benefits to government, the private sector and consumers. PPPs have the potential to provide for efficient public service delivery whilst minimizing and avoiding the costly and politically contentious privatization as we have come to know it.

It is no surprise that neglecting facts and not being cognizant of the shortcomings inherent in the private sector, especially in a PPP proposition where the public party negotiates from a point of weakness/desperation, resulted in massive resource waste as witnessed in TANESCO's case. It is important to note likewise that electricity cannot be efficiently stored, once produced; it must be consumed as it is produced. In other words, no producer can charge a premium for the provision of a reliable supply (Megginson, 2005).

Whereas it is imperative, for instance, that executives be held accountable for firms' performances and that the failure to meet set goals justify being replaced, in some cases their removal renders more harm than good. In the case of TANESCO, replacements of executives have not led to improvements in performance as envisaged. The case suggests that there may be fundamental problems at TANESCO, which cannot be resolved by mere replacement of executives; it entails more than that. That being the case, corporate governance can be considered to have been ineffective, as successive executives all failed to deliver improvements in performance. Generation, with its limited scale economies at the plant level, can be potentially competitive, as can system operation and end-user supply. Governance improvements at TANESCO can go hand in glove with restructuring efforts that ensure the various sub-units are technically and administratively feasible to minimize resource waste.

Waste across an entire sector: the Tanzania Leather Associated Industry (TLAI)

Tanzania's abundant livestock resources rank it third in Africa. Yet, despite the enormous potential across the leather industry, the sector has registered markedly dismal performance. Indeed, the vision for the sector and its potential continue to remain largely unrealized. What has come to characterize the leather industry in Tanzania exemplify broader failures in governance and the waste of resources of the highest magnitude, of any sector of the economy.

The recent history of Tanzania's leather industry cannot be written without a narrative of the well-intentioned objectives. This begins in the 1970s following the adoption of Ujamaa as Tanzania's economic and social blueprint, under Mwalimu Julius Nyerere, to economic liberalization and the subsequent failures in governance of the 1980s–1990s. As part of the socialist aspirations, a high development priority was given to the leather sector during the period 1975–1995. This was evidenced by the establishment of several tanneries and leather-related industries under the TLAI. The industries were important parts of the overall leather value chain, producing processed semi-finished and finished leather products. Although these industrial units did not always run efficiently and at a profit, they operated under protective economic policies and produced a significant amount of leather products for the domestic and export markets (URT, 2016).

Informed by the import-substitution industrialization policy, the government managed to secure development finance from the World Bank to set up government-run leather sector parastatals. The loans amounting to more than US $40 million were utilized, for example, to set up the industrial leather cluster in Morogoro. In addition to the tannery was a shoe factory, a leather goods facility, a leather-board factory (which never took off) and a related canvas mill. In hindsight, some see the industrial cluster as one of the most notorious cases of resource waste, evidencing gross inefficiencies and absence of accountability in not only public investment, but also governance. Indeed, the leather industry in Tanzania presents an empirical puzzle that is relevant to development and governance (Erixon, 2005).

Until the mid-1990s, the government-owned domestic tanneries and leather industries used to process hides and skins for the local as well as export markets. In order to make the sector more efficient, dynamic and profitable, however, all tanneries and leather industries were privatized in the early 1990s. The objective for their privatization has, however, not been realized. Since their privatization, most have become non-functional, and most of the hides and skins are now exported raw or in wet-salted form, thereby losing the opportunity to earn additional income from value addition in processing, as envisaged.

Leather industry as a case of resource waste

From a governance perspective, the aim is to encourage better service delivery and improved accountability by establishing a benchmark for good governance in the public sector (IFAC, 2013), acting in the public interest for public good. Achieving good governance in the public sector also requires defining outcomes in terms of sustainable economic, social and other benefits; determining the interventions necessary to optimize the achievement of intended outcomes; developing the capacity of the entity, including the capability of its leadership and the individuals within it; managing risks and performance through robust internal controls and strong public financial management; and implementing good practices in transparency and reporting to deliver effective accountability (IFAC, 2013).

Evaluating Tanzania's leather sector using the above-mentioned requirements reveals evidence of waste, negligence and a total failure in governance. For unexplained reasons, the envisaged outcomes did not materialize. Not only were the well-intended interventions either ill-timed or ill-fated, but also the capacity development was unreal, the risk never managed and accountability never practiced. The Tanzania Leather Sector Strategy (2016–2020) acknowledges the many shortcomings since the 1990s, which rendered the sector uncompetitive. It attributes this to, among other things, the ill-fated liberalization process, lack of public sector investments and failure to attract foreign direct investments (FDI) in the most vibrant stages of the leather value chain. Despite thriving global demand for leather products, Tanzania's leather sector performance has been lackluster. Its weak performance in comparison to African peer countries, for example, is unexplainable in light of the large and growing livestock population, resources and value addition potential.

During the mid-1980s, the government hurriedly divested its leather parastatals with a view to promoting future industry development through the private sector. Assistance mobilized from development partners was meant to complement private sector efforts, to be able to grow the leather industry and the overall leather supply chain.

The poor state of the Tanzania hides and skins, as well as the leather industry itself, spans from livestock production and slaughter facilities and practices, to tanning and processing, to laws, regulations and policies related to livestock production practices, to industrial investment, exports and imports. Today, Tanzania's leather industry remains largely as undeveloped as it was 40 years ago. During the same period, the relative performance in the leather value chain by the countries of South East Asia and India reveals tremendous development and growth (Muchie, 2000), taking advantage of growing trends in the current globalization era.

The World Bank's Morogoro Industrial Complex Project completion report cited project-related deficiencies as reasons for failure in addition to macroeconomic conditions (distorted price, cost and foreign exchange relationship). The deficiencies included over-ambitious project conception, implementation inexperience, insufficient expertise and lack of professional competence, to mention but a few (World Bank, 1990). The report acknowledges that everything went wrong, from project conceptualization, scope and procurement to project management and implementation. It remains a classic case of failure in governance that continued to adversely impact the entire leather value chain.

Mostly, despite pouring tremendous amounts of resources into the sector to supplement 'private sector' development, efforts to enlarge the leather industry at different levels across the sector all but failed. Three decades down the road, neither the government nor the individual development partners and multilateral donor agencies that provided support have anything to show in terms of aspired outcomes in the Tanzanian leather industry and overall leather value chain development. In effect, it can be surmised that it was not until the adoption of the Hides, Skins and Leather Act of 2008 that serious efforts to revive the leather sector began in earnest.

Sub-optimality in sector governance

Sub-optimality and shortfalls in governance, i.e. interventions, outcomes and risk management, across the leather sector can be seen through key factors that cut across the industry sub-sectors, viz. raw hides and skins production, collection, and commercial tanning and leather finishing to manufacture of leather goods, in the beginning, the middle and the end of the value chain, as indicated hereunder.

The beginning – hides and skins collection

It is common industry knowledge that the quality of leather begins with animal husbandry, slaughtering techniques and collection methods. The Tanzanian leather industry, however, has been lacking in these areas. They are at the outset characterized with damaged hides and skins due to disease, brand marks, and ground drying, and consequently low off-take rates and collection. These were among the foremost challenges facing the leather industry at the most basic level of the leather value chain (UNIDO, 1997). Interventions at this level were aimed to primarily improve the quality of hides and skins and increase their collection. Its success hinged on training in methods of slaughtering and leather handling; construction of modern slaughter slabs and curing sheds; quality grading and monitoring of the skins and hide quality and quantity. It is important to highlight that a higher proportion of presently available animal slaughterhouses are not organized, for successful value addition across the sector.

The government's decentralization measures, including the decision to dilute extension services, made it especially challenging to maintain the output of hides and skins at the requisite levels and monitor to assure quality. According to investigations undertaken by the UNIDO Africa Leather programme, at least 60% of defects in Tanzanian hides and skins are attributed to defects caused during slaughter. Poor handling and preservation procedures account for the majority of defects. Subsequently, the significant loss in quality of the hides and skins due to post-slaughter activities has contributed to the poor image of the exports (UNIDO, 2007) and the consequent decline in exports.

The middle – operations management, capacity and the environment

In the middle of the value chain, where most of the activities take place, the waste of resources was rampant. Obvious pieces of evidence presented themselves in terms of operations management, capacity building and environmental protection, among others, as highlighted hereunder.

Operations management

Across the board, from management to operations, skills shortfall is apparent across the sector. Some things were amiss despite heavy investment in skills development via training early on. The government had invested in a variety of leather technology and operation skill sets across the sector.

100 *Corporate waste cases analysis*

The case of Moshi Tanneries' operational hiccups due to a string of ill-timed decisions, for example, reveals a lot of the obvious skill shortcomings. The company identified a need for and imported a new boiler. The boiler was stuck at the Dar Port for lack of funds to clear it from the port. In an apparent 'oversight,' the company had not made a budget allocation for such expense. The management was occupied with other issues while the boiler was stuck at the port and nothing was being done. It was not until the old boiler failed completely and operations at the tannery came to a halt that the management's attention was turned to the new boiler at the port. As a result, the accumulated demurrage and other charges that the company paid equalled the cost of the imported boiler! Basically, the company paid more than double for the boiler.

The obvious governance shortfall showed that the importance in practice, given to aspects such as costing, performance evaluation and strategic analysis, was minimal. The company could do better with appropriate techniques and strategies to enhance performance by strengthening decision-making mechanisms required for optimal costing approaches. Management lacked the appropriate skills.

Capacity building

When the tanneries and the other undertakings across the leather industries were established by the government under the supervision of TLAI, it was viewed as a good public policy initiative. The initiative aimed at developing a local leather material-based industry for employment and income creation, foreign exchange generation and the supply of cheap leather products to the domestic market. Overall, however, inefficiency compromised the management of these industries sector-wide.

To ensure that adequate skills exist in the industry, deliberate efforts were made at skill enhancement and technology transfer. Realizing the future need for skills, the government under the auspices of TLAI established the Tanzania Institute of Leather Technology (TILT) to train skilled workers with the assistance of the United Nations Industrial Development Organization (UNIDO). The institute never came into operation, mostly due to the quasi-demise of the Tanzania leather industry (and consequent decline in demand for a sector-trained workforce), as well as lack of funds. At one point, the institute was to be transferred to the Ministry of Industry and Trade, but this was never accomplished. It was instead leased to a private enterprise which utilized the leather production facilities to produce leather products whilst other infrastructure and training facilities remained idle.

The ill-fated TILT represents another governance failure at the sectoral level and adds to the vicious circle faced by the leather industry in Tanzania. The revival of the industry requires trained skilled workers; thus, TILT still has an important role to play in ensuring available and adequate skilled personnel for improved quality of hides and skins production and processing, as the industry slowly moves toward its past glory.

Environmental protection

To improve tannery effluent treatment and waste management capabilities, an environmentally friendly effluent treatment plant (ETP) was introduced to four tanneries in Tanzania under equipment assistance from UNIDO.

Although the ETP equipment arrived at Morogoro Tanneries "in due time," it was rendered inoperable since the basic tannery equipment for the plant had not yet been procured. At Mwanza Tannery, ETP equipment was delivered but was not installed on a timely basis because of difficulties attributed to the inability of adapting the civil works. Apparently, the UNIDO-provided aerators needed modification and the expected results required further improvements. At Tanzania Tanneries Moshi, the process of installing the new equipment was in order but the aeration system clogged rapidly due to the usage of an inappropriate type of diffuser.

The three cases represent a governance challenge. Contrary to the good intentions of obtaining "good results in rehabilitating tanneries and establishing effluent treatment plants," UNIDO. (1997, p. 60) via equipment valued at USD 389,365, absolutely no development results could be accounted for. The big picture is embedded in the unattained waste management objective of recovering untanned waste, which was a major concern because of its environmental impact. Indeed, failure in governance is obvious despite "the tanneries having become sensitive to environmental issues" UNIDO. (1997, p. 45) and embracing ETP measures. Thus, the non-functional effluent treatment equipment at three tanneries represents a failure in governance, despite the touted sensitivity to environmental issues to protect the environment, as well as a waste of resources.

The end – market environment

Following economic liberalization, the leather sector fared the worst, contrary to expectations. As imports became readily available, local production could not compete effectively in the domestic market. Cheap and second-hand imported shoes were able to meet domestic demand with limited buying power. The leather industry in Kenya, where scale economies are far greater, took advantage of minimal barriers to trade between Kenya and Tanzania and supplied leather products at low costs. Likewise, Tanzania hides and skins found a new home close by in Kenya. Kenya's competitive advantage enabled it to import raw hides and skins from Tanzania for re-exporting at a higher price as well as processing and exporting value-added leather goods. Consequently, there was no incentive (if any existed it was consistently declining) for value-added processing throughout the Tanzanian leather value chain. The market environment turned out not to be conducive to production, as the Tanzanian leather lost the competitive edge it had earlier.

Costs along the Tanzania leather industry value chain have been a characteristic feature. From the very beginning, the chain was dotted with costly aspects from slaughterhouses to the collection network, electric power and transportation etc.

compared to the country's neighbours. Tanzania's value chain, topped at 18% value added tax (VAT), is relatively uncompetitive. For example, the estimated per square foot cost of leather for tanning in Tanzania is about 60% more compared to peer countries Zambia and Kenya (UNIDO, 2007).

Demands of the economic environment extending from competition, technological changes, skills and quality of service no longer distinguishes between public and private entities. Respect is commanded not because of ownership origin but because of how one leverages performance to earn the trust of the public (Mwapachu, 2013).

Observations, insights and lessons

Governance failure in the leather sector resulted in a massive waste of resources across the sector and by extension across the economy. Although it was macroeconomic policies that set the ball rolling toward its ultimate deterioration, the overall sector's and the leather industry's abysmal performance following liberalization and subsequent privatization to entities has been contrary to expectation, but given the circumstances was no surprise. What in the end was the quasi-demise of one of the economic sectors with the greatest potential also represented the dearth of the leather value chain's multiplier effect and contribution to other sectors across the economy. The examples offered justify the argument that failure in governance was the major culprit.

As the government seeks to revitalize the industry as enshrined in the Tanzania Leather Sector Strategy (2016–2020) and other policy pronouncements, it will be important to give special prominence to various aspects of governance alongside technical and economic attributes. It is time to move away from the lip service it has given the sector for too long. In his presidential inaugural address to Parliament, former President Kikwete promised to take deliberate measures to improve the livestock sector by changing herders to modern livestock keepers by doing away with archaic ways of livestock husbandry (URT, 2015). The national livestock policy (2006) espoused,

> By the year 2025, there should be a participatory livestock sector which to a large extent shall be commercially run, modern and sustainable, using improved and highly productive livestock to ensure food security, improved income for the household and the nation, while conserving the environment.

Giving priority to human resource and skill development for the sector is of utmost importance. Its neglect as revealed, for example, by the leasing of the Leather Technology Institute to an ill-suited private entrepreneur indicated not only a lack of commitment to the sector but also both lack of foresight and sheer absence of adherence to ethics. Indeed, one of the major problems confronting the leather industry now and in the future, and a necessary attribute in its revival, is the shortage of skilled workers. The workforce required to undertake proper livestock husbandry and perform tannery shop floor-level operations to be able to maintain the desired quality deem necessary the requisite training and skills. Non-availability of trained workers is thus a major obstacle, which is bound to affect productivity and overall competitiveness across the sector. There is thus a need to co-ordinate efforts between the government, various industry players as well as education and training institutions, to ensure the facilitation of capacity building for a trained and skilled workforce across industry segments. The adoption of modern management systems would enable organizations across the sector to improve their innovative capacity and flexibility so that they can continually change and increase performance.

Recent pastoralist versus farmer conflicts across the country are in some fashion an indirect result of the neglect of the sector. There has been an increase in the production of livestock and livestock products, and this is expected to continue into the future. The upsurge, however, obscures the fact that increased supply in absence of optimally planned outlet leads to a drain in resources as well. There is clearly a need to promote the development of livestock production and make good use of the meagre resources.

Revisiting the privatization process and measures taken at the time indicates the first failure in governance. The policy did not leave room for streamlining the sector following the government's apparent abdication. TLAI was still viable, and its role could have remained that of being the fulcrum to organize the industry (public and private) rather than that of a holding company as it was. Its role would be applicable to the functioning of plants be they private or public and provide some form of assurance to potential investors or joint venture partners, as well as providing a sense of direction where we can confidently say, the Tanzania Investment Center (TIC) has failed.

Failings of the privatization process itself are evidenced by the non-existent leather production facilities across the value chain. There is nothing to show of the USD 40 million World Bank loan–funded investment in the defunct Morogoro Industrial estate. The industrial estate, among other things, aimed at building synergy across the leather industry value chain. Its failure had multiplier effects that were felt across the economy. The fact that the majority of the privatized entities are not operational or are operating way below capacity is indicative of the inability to meet aspirations espoused under envisaged privatization efforts. Much of the tanning capacity, for instance, was not re-activated following privatization despite the fact that one of the preconditions for sale was outright recommissioning and development. Consequently, more than 60% of the tanning capacity remains dormant. This is an enormous cost to the economy in terms of multiplier effects, lower export earnings generation, job creation and tax revenue, among others.

Privatization was also thought of as a means to inject much-needed impetus for private sector growth in Tanzania. Indeed, private players have strived to invigorate the sector especially as far as export opportunities are concerned. Notwithstanding the constraints they face, it should be remembered that private sector players respond positively to incentives, hence the need to put forth such measures to reap the most from such efforts across the industry. Emphasis on value addition undertakings and embracement of quality are attributes that the private sector can well articulate to other stakeholders via joint private public undertakings.

A purposeful effort at revitalizing the sector should go beyond addressing the quality of hides and skins. It should encompass all governance aspects, from the adequate planning of actions along the hides and skins value chain, i.e. animal husbandry, disease control, slaughtering, preservation, storage, grading and pricing, laws and regulations, to addressing bottlenecks and potential challenges across the sector.

Tanzania, with its enormous potential to become the main exporter of leather products, has not been able to tap into the potential. The lack of and inadequate value addition investments across the leather industry has resulted in Tanzania's inability to tap massive foreign exchange earnings. Consequently, 90% of export value accounted in the sector are from raw hides and skin; a wasted opportunity and, overall, wasted resources across the sector indeed.

Governance by way of enforcement of laws and regulations across the industry for quality, alongside enhancement of value addition and capacity building as well as effective sector coordination, are some of the key issues that arose from lessons learned from the massive waste of resources across this every important sector of the economy.

Tanzania Ports Authority – waste at the economic gateway

Tanzania Ports Authority (TPA) was established by the Ports Act No. 17 of 2004, as a landlord Port Authority to take over the functions and responsibilities of the then Tanzania Harbours Authority (THA), whose operations ceased with effect from April 2005. The TPA, a public entity, came into being in alignment with the government decision to liberalize and involve the private sector in the operations and development of Tanzania's ports industry.

The mandate and major responsibilities of TPA as provided in the Act are to develop, manage and promote the port sector in Tanzania. The major role of TPA is to enhance the advantages of the geographical position of Tanzania's maritime resources by fulfilling the following functions:

1 Promoting effective management and operations of sea and inland waterways ports;
2 Provision of services in relation to loading and unloading of cargo and passenger services;
3 Developing, promoting and managing port infrastructure and superstructure; and
4 Maintaining port safety and security and entering into contractual obligations with private entities for the provision of port services.

Given Tanzania's geographical location, TPA ports have a naturally endowed competitive advantage. They serve hinterland countries including Zambia, Democratic Republic of Congo (DRC), Rwanda, Burundi, Malawi, Uganda and Zimbabwe.

Recent decades, marked with growth in GDP, population and trade across the region, have contributed enormously to the developments of the regional ports. Overall, the hinterland comprises a total population of over 230 million and a GDP of about USD 142 billion as well as generating 22 million tons of seaborne traffic per annum (TPA, 2014).

Ports constitute an important gateway for developing countries where more than 80% of trade is waterborne (Kessides, 2004). Excessive costs and inefficiencies tend to hinder trade and economic development. Ports are larger assets and tend to exhibit increasing returns to density and increasing returns to scale. They are viewed as natural monopolies, justifying the government's involvement in both provision of optimal investments and overseeing operations.

There is a strong relationship between trade facilitation, trade flows and GDP per capita. To that effect, Wilson, Mann, and Otsuki (2003) identify port efficiency alongside customs environment, regulatory environment and the extent of e-business usage as pertinent factors. Indeed, enhanced port efficiency has a large effect on trade. This is evidenced for instance in Londono-Kent and Kent's comparative analysis of an efficient port (Cartegna, Colombia) and an inefficient port (Puerto Santo Torinas de Castilla, Guatemala) with respect to berthing and cargo dwell times to derive inefficiency costs. The inefficient port was found to have a 49% penalty in costs.

It is important to note also that, in TPA's operating environment, dramatic changes have taken place in a relatively short period. These changes can be seen to trickle across the economy, maritime transport and industrial organization of the transportation industry. The regional economy has seen a boost in seaborne trade as a result of growth, thus highlighting the growing importance of logistics, which translates to an increased role for gateways and as a consequence the role played by organizations such as the TPA.

In recent years, maritime transportation has gone through transformations that witnessed increases in ships' sizes, as well as containerization and transhipment, emerging as dominant forces. Similarly, as far as the industrial organization of the transportation industry is concerned, there has been increased cooperative endeavours including strategic alliances, mergers and acquisitions, and vertical integration and the emergence, growth and development of dry ports and inland terminals, as well as control of intermodal and logistic cycles. Such transformations and massive changes have been affecting the port industry in general. Indeed, port operations have become more capital intensive, labour saving and space consuming. Meanwhile, in the port market, more competition has emerged between ports, as has continued lower tariffs and lower port times, as well as the potential risk of overcapacity (Lam, 2006).

It is undeniable that there exist dynamic relationships that link ports, hinterlands and national economies. First, port concentration is an outcome of investment in port facilities and in related transport infrastructures. Second, the competitive position of a port is critical to its commercial survival; and third (in the specific case), there is a substantial degree of continuity between the past and present in terms of factors, processes and interrelationships (Hoyle & Charlier, 1995). Indeed, ports are just but one important node in the international logistics chain.

The need to continuously strengthen respective ports' hub positions necessitates the forging of links with their hinterland and remains in line with global trends to minimize the risk of being sidelined (Yap & Lam, 2006).

Given what has been transpiring across the industry, one can see how prepared or otherwise TPA is by looking at its corporate strategic plans, i.e. how it addresses identified challenges and past shortcomings as well as how it has aligned itself with the changes taking place in the sub-sector and the economy in the region as a whole.

TPA strategic plan

The future of ports development in Tanzania is articulated in the publicly available TPA 20-years Ports Master Plan (PMP) covering the period 2009 through 2028. The PMP is the roadmap for transforming the country's gateways into modern world-class ports, providing efficient and cost-effective services.

To operationalize the PMP is the TPA's strategic plan, whose highlight, thrust and focus is to optimize the implementation of the Master Plan through numerous actions, including:

i   Increasing the capacity of the port of Dar es Salaam. This entails the modernization of berths 1–7, construction of berths 12, 13 and 14 and development of a new oil terminal and tank farm;
ii Developing new Bagamoyo and Mwambani-Tanga ports to cater to expected traffic increase that in the near future can no longer be accommodated within the existing port footprint;
iii Constructing new port facilities at Mtwara to cater to the oil and gas industry, cement factory and the Mtwara Development corridor;
iv Enhancing the role of smaller coastal ports in supporting local trade by constructing new jetties and rehabilitating existing jetties;
v   Unlocking the potentials of lake ports as gateways to the rapidly growing transit traffic, particularly to and from Uganda, Burundi, Malawi, Zambia, Mozambique and DR Congo; and
vi Computerizing port activities by using modern information and communications technology (ICT) solutions.

The plan is also cognizant of resource mobilization challenges and limitations. It thus zeros in on a few areas it considers to be of high priority. Mostly these are areas whose implementation is expected to unleash operational efficiency and consequent revenue growth. Within the priority areas are the plan-identified critical projects to be undertaken over the plan period.

The plans identified and the priorities notwithstanding, TPA has had a long record of having fallen short in various governance aspects. In addition to management, documented flaws and resource waste worsened as revealed by the gaping hole between potential and actual delivery in this economic jewel – the economic gateway to east, central and southern Africa.

To get the plan going, the TPA plan first identifies the challenges toward the attainment of set objectives and planned targets, shown in Table 5.3.

What has been revealed by TPA's strategic plan is the inability to address the challenges, which culminated in resource waste and failings of the economic gateway mandated to TPA for its management. Governance flaws at the economic gateway were seen in numerous areas:

- Non-attainment of key performance indicators, specifically unrealistic capital development budget and inadequate implementation of earmarked projects;
- Lack of strategic focus across the organization;
- Management framework shortfalls;
- Unrealistic and sub-optimal target setting; and
- Apparent failure in identifying and managing risk.

Non-attainment of key performance indicators

Non-attainment of key performance indicators (KPIs) has been a characteristic feature dogging TPA, it is cited repeatedly in the CAG annual reports as one of the major shortcomings. No follow-through on addressing the identified shortfalls seems to have been taken. The CAG's review of PMP implementation indicated that most of the KPIs were not attained. Non-attainment of KPIs impairs TPA's ability to meet set objectives as identified in the PMP.

The saying "What gets measured, gets done" remains true from a governance perspective, in that KPIs focus employees' attention on the tasks and processes that

Table 5.3 Challenges facing TPA

• Unattractive project packaging for private sector involvement	• Inadequate application of ICT solutions in port operations
• Frequent change of management and Board of Directors	• The newly introduced PPP Act 2010 and its Regulations 2011 could not be effective due to absence of respective PPP operational manual
• Existing infrastructure doesn't cope with changes in shipping technology (shallow berths and entrance channel)	• Lack of the government sovereign guarantee to the prospective private investors in port projects was also a setback
• Inadequate workforce for implementation of capital projects	• Deteriorating marine services on lake ports
• Deteriorating marine services on lake ports	• Inadequate inland transport connectivity (roads and rails)
• Existence of several unstaffed ports	• Inadequate workforce for implementation of capital projects
• Absence of large and functional inland ICDs/CFSs (Inland Container Depots/Container Freight Stations)	

Source: TPA Annual Reports (several)

executives deem most critical to the success of the business. KPIs represent the all-powerful levers that the leadership can pull to direct the organization in new and different directions. As change agents, KPIs can drive unmatched developments or plunge the organization into chaos and confusion. KPIs should, as accurately as possible, translate the strategy, goals and objectives into concrete actions.

How we define effective KPIs is one of the most common questions posed about performance in an organization. The response to the question is pertinent and important, since the KPIs cut across all levels, governing how the Board of Directors, the management and the employees all play their parts. This is how one needs to approach TPA's measurement of its KPIs.

It is unfortunate for TPA that most of the KPIs it sets often fell short of expectation. This in some fashion is an indication of governance, operational as well as logistical inefficiency, which in turn have massive negative impacts. Logistical inefficiency at a port has especially been found to have tremendous impact, as shown for example by Radelet and Sachs (1998) in that shipping costs can negatively impact economic growth by a half percentage. In that regard, transport costs for intra-African trade are more than twice the costs in other main regions of the developing world. They further found that more than 50% of the costs are attributed to infrastructure.

Like any other port sub-sector, TPA's KPIs incorporated and measured service quality from average ship turnaround time, ship service quality index, road service quality index, rail service quality index, average barge waiting time and barge service quality index, among other things, which reflect target setting optimality or otherwise. Looking at the attributes from TPA's performance review, it is no wonder that sub-optimal or unrealistic target setting has been levelled against it.

Sub-optimal targets at TPA

Organizations rely on objectives, which need to be translated into detailed actions by management. Under management by objectives, the creation of meaning and the means to fulfil targets is an important dimension to consider. That also goes for organizational context and obstacles. Premised on the objectives and subsequent actions, it is important that management recognizes and acts to improve overall corporate performance.

The Surface and Marine Transport Regulatory Authority (SUMATRA) Act (2001) requires the regulatory authority to establish standards and monitor the performance of regulated goods and services. It thus developed port performance benchmarks, for instance, to serve as measures and standards of port services in the country.

According to SUMATRA, the adopted indicators and benchmarks characterize legal obligations and international best practices to be adhered to and take into account UNCTAD proposals and comparisons to the peer ports of Beira (Mozambique), Walvis Bay (Namibia) and Mombasa (Kenya). The established indicators are categorized into four groups: physical indicators – measuring how much cargo is moved past the port and how fast ships are serviced and cargo is transferred to other modes of transport; factor productivity indicators – providing information on labour and capita productivity; economic indicators – providing a picture of port finances and the charges to users; and safety indicators – reflecting the state of port safety.

In total, 24 performance benchmarks were developed to facilitate general understanding of port performance trends, to be used to signal the need for timely actions. Of the indicators, 12 provide yardsticks for determining good or bad performance to scientifically assess port management capabilities. The 12 benchmarks include ship turn-round time; waiting rate; berth occupancy; working time over time at berth; dwell time (containerized cargo); gang productivity (tons/gang-shift); ship productivity (tons/ship-day); moves/hour (net SSG); yard density; TEUs per hectare; compliance with ISPS code requirements; and compliance with OSHA requirements (SUMATRA, 2014).

The summary provided in Table 5.4 indicates how far TPA is from the benchmarks set by the regulator and embraced by TPA itself. From a governance and efficiency perspective, is this just a matter of 'in the land of the blind, the one-eyed man is king,' in which case, the Dar port is doing just fine by the regulator's standards?

It is important to be cognizant of the dramatic changes that have occurred in a relatively short period within TPA's operating environment. The remarkable changes that have taken place can be seen in terms of the economy, maritime transport and organization of the transportation industry. Globally, there has been an increase in seaborne trade and thus the growing importance of logistics. In the same time, maritime transport has registered increases in ships' size and enhanced specialization, containerization and transhipment. In the industrial organization of the transportation industry, there has been increased cooperation across the board, i.e. strategic alliances; vertical integration; emergence, growth and development of dry ports and inland container terminals as well as control of intermodal and logistic cycles and logistics outsourcing.

These changes affect the port sub-sector and influence operations. Consequently, port operations have become more capital intensive, labour saving and space consuming. Likewise, there is more competition between ports, lower

Table 5.4 National benchmark vs TPA dar performance

	Benchmark	Dar Port
Ship turn-round time	3–5 days	6.5
Waiting rate	Less than 1	
Berth occupancy	Less than 60%–70%	65%
Working time over time at berth	Closer to 1	
Dwell time (containerized cargo)	Imports 7 days	7
	Exports 4 days	4
Gang productivity (tons/gang-shift)	400–500 tons	416
Ship productivity (tons/ship-day)	4500; 3600; 1500	2486
Moves/hour (net SSG)	25	25.1
Yard density	Below 65%	
TEUs per hectare	1500	

Source: Several SUMATRA and TPA reports

110 *Corporate waste cases analysis*

tariffs and lower port times (pressures from liners), potential risk of overcapacity as well as decreases in producer's (terminal operator) surpluses.

The abovementioned notwithstanding, what we see in the case of TPA could be considered an unrealistic capital development budget and inadequacy in project implementation. To a certain extent, the situation indicates, among other things, a historical lack of strategic focus on the part of TPA.

Unrealistic capital development budget and inadequate projects implementation

Setting of unrealistic capital development budgets has been a characteristic feature at TPA. According to the CAG report, the TPA's long-term plan, the PMP, which basically formulates the authority's strategic objectives, is reflected in respective and rather ambitious annual development budgets as well as the five-year corporate strategic plan (CAG, 2016).

Interestingly, we note that 85% of financial resource requirements are to be sourced from external sources via the PPP procurement approach. All these have been formulated without taking into consideration challenges in the solicitation of external financing and the level of expertise needed to implement the respective strategic objectives for each goal identified in the Master Plan. It all boils down to the conclusion that this is an unrealistic allocation criterion based on ambitious capital development plans which may not come to fruition. The CAG thus recommends the establishment of a resource mobilization strategy (RMS) to place emphasis on diversifying the lender base (CAG, 2016) and finding innovative ways to mobilize resources.

Another characteristic feature at TPA has been inadequate implementation of projects earmarked under the PMP. The authority begun to implement PMP earmarked projects in 2010. The PMP is the roadmap for transforming the country's ports into world-class modern ports for the provision of efficient and cost-effective services. A review of progress made toward the implementation of projects under the PMP reveals that as a result of numerous challenges, most of the projects were either behind schedule, suspended or put on hold. This in itself holds TPA back from attaining its set objectives.

Lack of strategic focus

Strategic focus areas address one or more delivery targets, which should at any cost be clear to all stakeholders. This is because what is expected from the stakeholders is support in the attainment of delivery targets. Subsequently, the targets are measured and re-evaluated on an ongoing basis. At a certain level, TPA suffered from a lack of strategic focus.

In the absence of a coherent strategy, an organization does not have identifiable business objectives, i.e. it lacks the focus needed to achieve corporate goals and develop plans that will move it forward. Lack of clear objectives means that the particular organization does not have a specific set of tasks it is competent in and has no vision for the future. Objectives are meant to develop long-term growth and productivity plans that are essential for the organization's sustained success.

In alignment with TPA's vision and mission, the strategic plan focuses on the transformation into state-of-the-art ports, by placing emphasis on improving port productivity, enhancing operational efficiency and reducing operational costs. The plan runs parallel with Tanzania's second five-year development plan (2016/17 to 2020/21), to align the sub-sectors' goals to national objectives (TPA, 2014).

Business decisions aimed at maximizing opportunities such as the ones earmarked under the TPA plan are in fact a set of interrelated decisions. These decisions are sequential and in line with the basic purpose of the strategy, which is to ensure, as far as possible, that the aims are attained. As opportunities emerge, they require timely and appropriate strategic response. Indeed, for strategic focus, the TPA plan should have undertaken a competitive analysis, evaluating its attractiveness against competitor locations in the region, from a potential investor's perspective. This is over and above other analyses and benchmarking of best practices specifically to assess the respective competitive position to enable it to come up with a course of action for the near, medium and long term. Thus, the sub-sectors' representative identified projects should have been compiled based on real investment opportunity based on existing potential. A matrix combining both qualitative and economic results would reveal the port's competitive position and thus utilize the results to come up with potential impact for the national and regional economy.

A case in point representing the lack of strategic focus is the construction of the fuel storage system to improve its fuel storage management. TPA had planned to have the project implemented by 2015. Due to failure in the procurement processes, the USD 20 million project failed to materialize. The procurement processes proceeded without undertaking a feasibility study. That being the case, the process had to be curtailed to allow for the feasibility study to be undertaken before proceeding. There is thus going to be a delay in the attainment of the set milestones as well as the desired objectives.

Yet another case is that of the incomplete development of a berth designated for the very important fish terminal. TPA's corporate strategic plan provides the landmark berth for fish terminal since 2014 at an estimated cost of USD 21 million. The project is still pending as a result of ongoing dialogues with key stakeholders, who were overlooked prior to the procurement process. Again, it is about shortcomings in governance.

Management framework shortfalls

Desired management frameworks are designed to reduce performance inconsistency and support a seamless flow from strategy to delivery. Such a framework should prescribe strong leadership, proper resourcing, documented business processes, unambiguous accountability and consistent analysis of work improvement.

With changes that have taken place across the economy and the sub-sector itself, there is need for the structure to be reviewed to align with the current need and the authority's future aspirations. The existing TPA structure was last reviewed in 2008 (TPA, 2014). If anything, the structure should facilitate smooth and efficient operations and contribute toward growth of the economy.

In effect, among the structure-related challenges highlighted in the TPA's plan are frequent change of management and Board of Directors; inadequate application of ICT solutions in port operations; inadequate workforce for implementing capital projects; and unattractive project packaging for private sector involvement.

Between June 2013 and December 2015, the Director General position changed hands three times, each removed or sacked for reasons related to non-performance. At the same time over a period of less than four years, the policy-making body, the TPA Board of Directors, was re-organized five different times, in all cases being accused of some form of incompetence or failure to exercise oversight and consequently responsible for TPA's resource waste and massive losses. One of the sources of the resource haemorrhage and waste was the oil flow meter issue.

To monitor and control revenue from oil consignments entering the country, TPA installed flow meters at Tanga and Dar es Salaam Ports, only to be stopped by the Chief Executive Officer of the Weights and Measures Agency (WMA). The WMA is mandated to provide protection to consumers in relation to legal metrological control which includes legal control of measuring instruments, metrological supervision and metrological expertise in trade, health, safety and environment. Among the major reasons brought forth for the stopping usage of flow meters was inaccuracy. This led the TPA to revert to the manual system for measuring fuel volumes. Unfortunately, manual dipping stick measuring is prone to errors and has had a negative impact on the accuracy of revenue collection. The use of flow meters would have assured both TPA's and TRA's revenue and taxes respectively based on correct measurements of the fuel consignments.

All of these, according to the CAG report (CAG, 2016), may have led to a serious shortcoming. The apparent lack of oversight function by TPA (a management framework flaw) has basically put the interests of the government in jeopardy, as revealed at the Tanzania International Container Terminal Services (TICTS). Apparently, TPA does not have in place the means to monitor the total number of containers handled at TICTS. Uncharacteristically, the TPA relied solely on the information it gets from TICTS and without reconciling what is given with the actual number of containers handled by TICTS, it takes it as fact. Under the contract, TICTS pays TPA wharfage charge per container handled. It is this inability to manage the flow of containers at TICTS that renders the government revenue at stake.

What the CAG report revealed are systemic failures of the TPA management framework. How can the management explain results of the revenue audit of revenue at TPA, which revealed that out of 1253 vessels which docked at Dar es Salaam Port during the year, 145 vessels were missing in the revenue system? Of the 145 vessels, management could only provide an explanation and supporting documentation for 60 vessels. The inability to provide documentation raises doubt and leads to the conclusion of either an inherent systemic failure or simply misappropriation. The argument is further testified by the apparent variance involving 1742 cargo leads between records in TPA system against those recorded in TRA system (CAG, 2016).

Most of the identified structural shortcomings relate to shortfalls in the management framework. They range from weaknesses in controls, e.g. controls related to release of vessels, collection of port dues and receipt of goods at the port, to weaknesses in record keeping and inadequate storage charge computation. Some of these are items that were identified in previous years and incorporated in past CAG reports as areas to be addressed at once.

To enhance operational efficiency at the economic gateway, what is required at TPA is the optimization of port structure. Port authorities are globally set up as entities operating independent of government authorities. In processes embracing PPP, some element of privatization or delivery of public service by private service providers is involved. To get to that stage necessitates assessing the strategic tasks and defining which elements are handed over to the private sector and which are kept in the hands of public authorities.

Failure in identification of and managing risk

Port risk management entails the process of understanding, evaluating and addressing risk to maximize the chances of safely attaining objectives. As such, risk in port operations requires identifying and managing risk as important attributes in maintaining secure and resourceful operations. Having been in existence for quite a while, TPA has a wealth of experience in providing operational expertise to different scales of port operations. TPA's marine experts, port management experts and auditors should be able to identify and provide for total risk assessment solutions tailored to TPA needs.

TPA annual report's assessment of its risk management priorities places emphasis on overall financial risk management. It focuses on things like "unpredictable financial markets" and aims at minimizing potential effects on the TPA's financial performance. Consequently, and throughout the years, TPA's identified specific risk management policies include only risk elements associated with financial resources viz. liquidity, credit and financial risk.

It is obvious that TPA either missed out in the identification or prioritization of risk. One would have expected TPA's categories, such as port marine safety, port health checks and regulatory compliance checks covering both shore side and afloat safety, would be high on the risk identification and priority list.

Moreover, as far as ports are concerned, accidents and incidents can significantly affect operations leading to service delays, damage to people, property or the environment and even port closure. One would expect TPA to have high on the agenda an assessment of risk to navigation, operations and the environment and to develop safety management systems and management control. Indeed, port operations-related risks such as aids to navigation review; marine safety management systems; mooring studies; navigational risk assessments (NRA); port marine risk management; port safety health etc. should feature high on the TPA's risk management plan.

There are certain elements more specific to risk management planning that are unique to organizations such as TPA. To ensure risks are allocated to parties best suited to address them, they should be addressed in a project's development phase, including:

- a structured risk management framework to identify and manage risks;
- transparency in key decision processes; and
- identifying project objectives not aligned with the risk management plan.

A good example and case in point here is the inadequate management of Dar es Salaam Port Dockyard, which was identified earlier in the 2011 CAG reports. The tell-tale sign was the failure to see the inadequacy and obsolescence of a dry dock facility (built in the 1950s) as a risk element and how it adversely impacts TPA's operational efficiency. As a result, TPA had to incur massive maintenance and repair costs of its marine crafts at Mombasa Port.

The inability to undertake preventive maintenance due to the absence of a dockyard in port operations prevents some ships from docking at Dar es Salaam Port and results in the loss of revenue to TPA. A modern dockyard to facilitate optimal operations and safety, as one of the appropriate risk management tools alongside availability of marine crafts would further enhance port operational efficiency. The dockyard remains in the plans but is not implemented, thus increasing the port's risk level.

Quantifying the waste

With its natural endowment and enviable locational advantages, Tanzania has incurred irrecoverable real and potential losses because of the numerous governance and management challenges that have besieged TPA over the years. Independently, in 2013 the World Bank presented an estimate of the costs to both domestic and international stakeholders arising from the inefficiencies at the TPA. Significant among the costs were the following:

- US $252 million – the losses incurred by shippers and shipping companies in total annual anchorage costs, as a result of long delays;
- US $1759 million – the total welfare loss to the Tanzanian economy as a result of the port's inefficiency (i.e. potential additional revenues);
- US $830 million – the total welfare loss to the economies of neighbouring countries that use the port of Dar es Salaam; and
- US $157 million – lost revenues for government agencies such as Tanzania Ports Authority and the Tanzania Revenue Authority.

In addition to the above highlighted losses, the World Bank conducted a survey of 100 mid-sized local business, in collaboration with Klynveld Peat Marwick Goerdeler (KPMG) that revealed that 62% of respondents reported that the port's ineffectiveness harmed their businesses slightly, while 20% reported that it harmed them extremely.

These are just a few estimates of some of the financial wastes associated with ineffective governance and poor oversight of what may presently be considered as the country's largest potential source of foreign exchange and a significant contributor to government revenues. There are still a number of other indirect losses that need to be added, including those associated with the country's cost of doing business, its ranking in attractiveness to foreign investment, as well as the welfare of hundreds, if not thousands, of big and small regional businesses that have varying degrees of dependence on import-export operations.

Observations, insights and lessons

Focus on the economic gateway – the ports sub-sector – is important in all efforts aimed at boosting Tanzania's and the region's trade. Every stakeholder expects nothing short of greater operational efficiency at the economic gateway. Obviously, governance flaws notwithstanding, a lot remains to be done for the sub-sector to be able to play its expected role in the economy, now and in the future. The current state of inefficiency in the sub-sector poses massive constraints on trade and limitations to the envisaged economic expansion by not only Tanzania but also its landlocked neighbours in the region. Addressing governance shortfalls head on will help with the inefficiencies in the port sub-sector to ensure that Tanzania as the gateway and its constituent landlocked neighbours make the most of the benefits of trade through enhanced connectivity. The economy stands to benefit from a more efficient port sub-sector.

The port sub-sector's sustainability hinges on having enough transactions to create economies of scale, satisfactory returns on investments and competitiveness. There are several ways that inefficiency in the sub-sector can be seen but more straightforward are the delays, including those faced by shipping companies (the time of anchorage) and dwell time (time it takes to unload and clear). Likewise, delays may be an indirect result of the fees imposed upon users.

The importance of the port sub-sector notwithstanding, one asks oneself why the inefficiency has endured so long, if not an indication of governance shortfalls. It is argued in some quarters that there are parties that stand to gain significantly from the inefficiency. The gain is from: (a) the distorted port incentive structure and (b) the prevalence of corrupt practices across the value chain.

It is a known fact, for instance, that the storage tariff structure does not encourage importers to remove their merchandise from port premises in a timely manner. An authoritative study (World Bank, 2013) argues that this is the case, because when dwell time exceeds the free storage period of seven days, each additional day of storage represents a direct additional profit for them. Moreover, rent-seeking behaviour has been encouraged through the use of discretionary rules applied at will across the sub-sector.

Having recognized what has befallen the sub-sector, numerous efforts are underway for its revamp. The US $565 million Dar es Salaam Maritime Gateway

Project, for example, entails the mobilization of financial support to facilitate capital developments to enhance Dar es Salaam Port's spatial efficiency and operational effectiveness. The overall objective of the World Bank–led co-operative endeavour is to support the TPA in the attainment of the government's set objectives for the maritime sub-sector. These were specifically brought forth under the Big Results Now (BRN) Initiative and as part of Tanzania's Development Vision 2025, where it is planned to raise the port's capacity from around 15 million tons in 2014 to 28 million tons by 2020 (World Bank, 2013).

Dar es Salaam Port, once one of the most effective ports in sub-Saharan Africa and currently the second largest in the East Africa region, saw its performance slip over time. From ships having to wait to dock and transit cargo delays to not being able to accommodate larger ships, the port's constraints become a major problem. All can be traced to governance shortfall.

TPA's strategic plan may be over-ambitious, given the much-needed technical expertise and resource use intensity as well as the obvious miss-out on a lot of KPIs. From a governance perspective there are however, several lessons to derive from. It is these lessons that need be taken to heart.

Obvious flaws were seen in terms of inadequate coordination and communication between TPA and other stakeholders. The consequent delay in implementation of capital development projects have had impacts on TPA's attainment of intended objectives in a timely fashion thus escalating its poor operational performance. The Fish Market and other such projects delays may lead to increased costs and undermine stakeholders' confidence, whilst exacerbating resource waste.

Competitive positioning and benchmarking allows the identification of global best practices in port environment and gauge performance in an objective manner. Sub-sector performance indicators are productivity metrics that allow making comparisons on quantifiable performance gaps, to be able to identify areas for improvement and standards, expeditiously. Dar es Salaam port's constraints are a problem for Tanzania because demand for imports is set to rise dramatically as the population, currently about 51 million people, continues to grow. Its population will double every 25 years if the current rate of growth continues.

Given that the port and shipping industry is one of the most capital-intensive sectors requiring well thought capital allocation decisions, TPA's governance failure have added to overall cost and waste of resources. Governance structures should be able to direct strategic investment decisions' and evaluation of the trade-off between current resource expenditure and expected benefits, in the near and long-term.

It is important to bear in mind that in terms of economic cost/benefit analysis, typical infrastructure development projects would be rejected if public decision makers based respective decisions only on the expected financial return of the project without taking into account externalities such as employment generation, environmental effects etc. As such addition of 'social valuation' would provide for better appreciation by public authorities of other decision criteria over and above financial return on investment. The same goes for risk analyses.

In the final analysis the TPA story, is a story of failure in governance at the economic gateway. The consequent effect is in the failure of Tanzania to take advantage and making effective use of endowed resources for its economic wellbeing. With proper strategy and foresight, proper leadership and optimal resources, TPA can return to lost glory and be able to play its rightful part in national and regional development endeavours. It is only hoped therefore that the governance changes, at the Board of Directors and Management levels, following the entry of the Fifth Phase government in October 2015, will relegate the historical failures and challenges to the archives and usher in a new era of effective governance, better delivery and a real contribution by TPA to the national coffers that is in line with stakeholder expectations.

Notes

1 *Daily News Online*, April 29, 2012.
2 The merger between the South African Airways and Air Tanzania Corporation that resulted in the formation of 'Air Tanzania Company Ltd' has collapsed. Minister for Infrastructure Development, Basil Mramba, told the National Assembly that the two parties were negotiating on how to end the deal without hurting one another. In 2002 South African Airways (SAA) paid $20 million for a 49% stake in ATC. It was expected that half of the $20 million, would go into the 49% shareholding, and the rest would be directed toward the capital and training account earmarked for capitalisation. Before privatisation, ATC owned one passenger aircraft, a Boeing 737-200. Some have accused SAA of failing to meet part of the management agreement. Tanzania Civil Aviation Authority Director-General, Margaret Munyagi, was quoted in the East African as saying that Air Tanzania was in a "worse state than before it was taken over by SAA". SAA in turn accused Tanzania's government of not "being serious" in failing to release about $30 million needed to implement Air Tanzania's business strategy to reverse continued losses.
(Tanzanian Affairs May 1, 2006. https://www.tzaffairs.org/2006/05/air-tanzania-co-ltd-collapses/)
3 The COSO ERM framework provides a common lexicon of terminology, and provides clear direction and guidance for implementing enterprise risk management. The framework requires that organizations examine their complete portfolio of risks, consider how those individual risks interrelate, and that management develops an appropriate risk mitigation approach to address these risks in a manner that is consistent with their long term strategy and overall risk appetite.
(https://www.ucop.edu/enterprise-risk-management/procedures/what-is-erm.html)
4 According to these procedures, the technical unit within the company is required to carry out an investigation of the quality and information of the plane before entering into any lease agreement. On the other hand, TCAA also is required to investigate and inspect the plane to ensure that it complies with international civil aviation standards before registering the respective plane in the country.
(CAG, 2016)
5 The CAG report noted that, both the ATCL technical unit and TCAA conducted their investigations between the 14th and 22nd of January 2008 when the lease contract had been signed. The result of the inspection showed that the plane did not meet the required standards, hence TCAA instructed the lessor to rectify the noted weaknesses

before handing over the aircraft to ATCL. In addition, I noted that Attorney General Chambers on October 8, 2007, advised the company through letter No. JC/I.30/308/3, but these were not taken into consideration when entering into the lease agreement.

6 IATA Clearing House – enables the world's airlines and airline-associated companies "suppliers" to settle their Passenger, Cargo, UATP and Miscellaneous/Non-Transportation billings by applying the principles of set-off/netting thus reducing cost, risk and increasing speed.
7 Of which 71% were in the technical department; many did not have the requisite skills.
8 Controller and Auditor General (CAG) Report – Public Authorities (PA) and Other Bodies (OBs) 2010/2011.
9 Failure to conduct a feasibility study before implementing the TTMS project is the issue. TCRA entered into an agreement with Société Générale de Surveillance to undertake a Telecommunication Traffic Monitoring System project under a build, operate and transfer arrangement. The contract agreement described the investment cost of the project and indicated that feasibility and environmental studies were part of the project costs with a budget of USD 100,000.
10 The CAG report (2016) noted that TRA was not effectively using the module to establish tax revenue due from transaction costs being charged by mobile operators.
11 "Tanzania Suspends Telecoms Chief Over Revenue Loss." Retrieved from https://af.reuters.com/article/tanzaniaNews/idAFL5N17T5UL
12 Tanzania Electric Supply Limited (TANESCO) Website.
13 Tanzania has outlined its medium-term objective of becoming a middle-income country by 2025. Access to affordable and reliable electricity is vital for Tanzania's attainment of its socio-economic goals. With only 36% of households currently having electricity, the World Bank is supporting the government through a programme aimed at expanding access to affordable, reliable and modern energy and ensuring operational and financial sustainability of the sector. "Increasing Electricity Access in Tanzania to Reduce Poverty." www.worldbank.org/en/results/2016/12/06/increasing-electricity-access-in-tanzania-to-reduce-poverty
14 The rationale for the arrangement is said to be to limit financial closure delays, thus committing Songas owners to the project. The allowance for funds utilized during construction were capitalized at project end and included in the capacity charge. In efforts to limit the capacity charge, the government and TANESCO in 2003 effected a US $103 million buy-down.
15 It is noted in some circles that, in absence of competitive bidding, it is difficult to evaluate the direct impact of the investment climate on the bid.

Bibliography

Barnes, F. (2000, Spring–Summer). Good Business Sense Is the Key to Confronting ISO 9000. *Review of Business*, 11. *Academic OneFile*, Retrieved April 19, 2017 from http://go.galegroup.com/ps/anonymous?id=GALE%7CA73182519&sid=googleScholar&v=2.1&it=r&linkaccess=abs&issn=00346454&p=AONE&sw=w.

CAG (2009). *The annual general report of the controller and auditor general on the audit of public authorities and other bodies for the financial year 2007/2008*. Dar es Salaam: Office of the Controller and Auditor General, National Audit Office.

CAG (2016). *The annual general report of the controller and auditor general on the audit of public authorities and other bodies for the financial year 2014/2015*. Dar es Salaam: Office of the Controller and Auditor General, National Audit Office.

CGAP (2014). *Infographic: Tanzania's mobile money revolution*. Retrieved December 12, 2017, from www.cgap.org/data/infographic-tanzanias-mobile-money-revolution

CISCO (2010). *Cisco visual networking index: Forecast and methodology, 2011–2016.* Cisco Public White paper. Retrieved from https://ec.europa.eu/digital-single-market/en/news/cisco-visual-networking-index-forecast-and-methodology-2011%E2%80%932016

Collings, A. (20160. Tanzania: New system to monitor mobile cash will provide higher revenues for the government. *TheNerve.* Retrieved December 31, 2016, from http://thenerveafrica.com/8860/tanzania-new-system-to-monitor-mobile-cash-will-provide-higher-revenues-for-the-government/

Delmon, J. (2011). *Public-private partnership projects in infrastructure.* New York, NY: Cambridge University Press.

Ericsson Mobility Report (2013). Retrieved from http://www.ericsson.com/res/docs/2013/ericsson-mobility-report-june-2013.pdf

Erixon, F. (2005). *Aid and development. Will it work this time?* London: International Policy Network.

Ghanadan, R., & Eberhard, A. (2007). *Electricity utility management contracts in Africa: Lessons and experience from the TANESCO-NET group solutions management contract in Tanzania.* MIR Working Paper, Management Programme in Infrastructure Reform and Regulation, Graduate School of Business, University of Cape Town.

Global Voice Group (2014). *Inauguration of the telecommunications traffic monitoring system in Tanzania.* Retrieved September 18, 2017, from www.sgs.com/en/news/2014/03/inauguration-of-the-telecommunications-traffic-monitoring-system-in-tanzania

Harper, P. (2015). *Public-private partnerships and the financial cost to governments: Case study on the power sector in Tanzania.* Retrieved November 22, 2015, from http://jubileedebt.org.uk/wp-content/uploads/2015/09/Tanzania-case-study_06.15.pdf

Hendricks, K. & Singhal, V. (2001). Firm characteristics, total quality management, and financial performance. *Journal of Operations Management* 19 (2001) 269–285.

Hoyle, B., & Charlier, J. (1995, June). Inter-port competition in developing countries: An East African case study. *Journal of Transport Geography, 3*(2), 87–103.

IFAC (2013). *International framework: Good governance in the public sector, international federation of accountants – IFAC/The chartered institute of finance & accountancy – CIFPA ITU, 2014.* ITU Measuring the Information Society Report 2013. ITU, 2013. ITU 2013: ICT Facts and Figures.

Jabbar, M. A., Kiruthu, S., Gebremedhin, B., & Ehui, S. (2002). *Essential actions to meet quality requirements of hides, skins and semi-processed leather from Africa.* A Report Prepared for The Common Fund for Commodities Amsterdam, The Netherlands.

Kapika, J., & Eberhart, A. (2013). Power sector reforms and regulation in Africa. Chapter 2, *Tanzania: Learning the hard way HSRC Press.* South Africa. Retrieved January 27, 2015, from www.gsb.uct.ac.za/files/Tanzania.pdf

Keeler, R. (2010a). Tanzania: Electricity in the grip of graft. *Ratio Magazine.* Retrieved August 1, 2015, from www.wap.ratio-magazine.com/inner.php?id=2560

Keeler, R. (2010b). *Tanzania: Learning the hard way.* Retrieved September 18, 2015, from www.gsb.uct.ac.za/files/Tanzania.pdf

Kessides, I. (2004). *Reforming infrastructure – privatization, regulation and competition.* Washington, DC; New York, NY: World Bank; Oxford University Press.

Mader, K. (2012). *Corporate social responsibility in Tanzania: An overview.* Retrieved September 11, 2016, from https://csroverviewtanzania.files.wordpress.com/2012/08/csr-overview-tanzania3.pdf

Mazzucato, M. (2015). *Building the entrepreneurial state: A new framework for envisioning and evaluating a mission-oriented public sector.* The Levy Economics Institute of Bard College Working Paper No. 824.

McKinsey Global Institute, 2013. "*Disruptive technologies: Advances that will transform life, business, and the global economy.*" Accessed September 18, 2017. Retrieved from: https://www.mckinsey.com/business-functions/digital-mckinsey/our-insights/disruptive-technologies.

Mhina, A. (2000). Good governance and development in Tanzania: Some ethical issues. *Journal of Social Philosophy, 31*(4), 429–438.

Msekwa, P. (2016). Ethics is the heart of leadership: Why Minister Kitwanga's sacking was a big, good lesson. *The Daily News*, Tanzania; June 2, 2016.

Mwakyembe Report (2008). *Report of the select committee formed by the Parliament of the United Republic of Tanzania on 13th November 2007 to investigate the tendering process for emergency power supply which awarded the tender to Richmond Development Corporation LLC of Houston. Texas in 2006.* Retrieved June 8, 2014, from www.governanceknowledge.org/pro/Lists/Calendar/Attachments/7/Session4-Tanzania_Select-Cttee_H-Mwakyembe_Richmond_ExecSummary_Eng_Feb08.doc

Mwapachu, J. V. (1983). *Management of public enterprises in developing countries: The Tanzania experience.* New Delhi, Bombay, Kolkata: Oxford, IBH Publishing Co.

Mwapachu, J. V. (2005). *Confronting new realities: Reflections on Tanzania's radical transformation.* Dar es Salaam: E&D Ltd.

Mwapachu, J. V. (2013). *Parastatals: Architecture of corporate governance.* Tanzania: The Citizen.

Nyang'oro, J. (2016). *Escrow: Politics and energy in Tanzania.* Trenton, NJ: Africa World Press.

Pyramid Research. (2013, February). Quarterly mobile data forecast, as quoted In *Background Strategic plan for the Union for 2016–2019.* Geneva, Switzerland: International Telecommunication Union (ITU).

Radelet, S., & Sachs, J. (1998). *Shipping costs, manufactured exports, and economic growth.* Retrieved January 22, 2015, from http://lnweb90.worldbank.org/eca/transport.nsf/3b8b3d27260832ec852569fa0059675f/bae7ab18a78a8ba985256b040057e4fa/$FILE/shipcost.pdf

Seddon, J. (2000). The "quality" you can't feel. *The Observer.*

Sheth, J. F. Allvine, C. U., & Dixit, A. (2007). The rise and fall of the major airlines from 1985 to 2004. In Allvine, Fred C.; Uslay, Can; Dixit, Ashutosh; and Sheth, Jagdish N., *Deregulation and competition: Lessons from the airline industry.* Thousand Oaks, CA: Response Books – Sage Publications Inc.

SUMATRA (2009). *Surface and Marine Transport Regulatory Authority (SUMATRA) Port performance indicators and benchmarks.* Accessed October 4, 2017. Retrieved from: https://www.sumatra.go.tz/index.php/publications-statistics/performance-indicators-and-benchmarks.

SUMATRA (2014). *Surface and Marine Transport Regulatory Authority (SUMATRA) Annual Report 2014/2015.* Accessed August 28, 2017. Retrieved from: https://www.sumatra.go.tz/index.php/.../222-annual-reports-and-accounts-2014-2015.

TCAA (2011). *Tanzania Civil Aviation Authority, air operators market share 2009–2011.* Retrieved from http://tcaa.go.tz/files/Air%20Operators%20-%20Market%20Share%202009-2011%20-%202.pdf.

TCRA (2014). *Tanzania Communication Regulatory Authority (TCRA) annual report accounts for the year ended 30th June 2014.* Accessed on August 2, 2017. Retrieved from: https://www.tcra.go.tz/index.php/publication-and-statistics/reports.

TechMoran (2014). *Tanzania's new traffic monitoring system to generate over TZS 20 Billion annually.* Retrieved July 17, 2017, from https://techmoran.com/tanzanias-new-traffic-monitoring-system-to-generate-over-tzs-20-bilion-annually/

TPA (2014). *Tanzania Ports Authority (TPA) annual report & accounts for the year ended 30th June, 2014.* Accessed on October 19, 2017. Retrieved from: https://www.ports.go.tz/index.php/en/publications/reports-annual-reports-and-accounting/275-annual-report-for-the-year-ended-june-2014

UNIDO (1997). Regional Africa Leather and Footwear Industry Scheme Report of the program evaluation: Quality Assurance and Evaluation Branch General Management. p. 60

UNIDO (2007, May 20–23). *United Nations industrial development organization – present and future role of Africa in the world of leather and derived products industry and trade.* Sixteenth Session of the Leather and Leather Products Industry Panel. Gramado, Brazil: UNIDO.

URT (2010). *National Public Private Partnership (PPP) Policy.* Dar es Salaam: Prime Minister's Office.

URT (2016). *Tanzania leather sector development strategy.* The International Trade Centre (ITC). Retrieved June 7, 2017, from http://unossc1.undp.org/sscexpo/content/ssc/library/solutions/partners/expo/2016/GSSD%20Expo%20Dubai%202016%20PPT/Day%202_November%201/SF%204_Room%20D_ITC/Value%20chain%20roadmaps/Tanzania/Tanzania%20Leather%20Sector%20Development%20Strategy.pdf

van Niekerk, S., & Hall, D. (2013). *Overview of energy in Africa.* Public Services International Research Unit (PSIRU-PSI Africa). Retrieved from www.psiru.org

Wilson, J. S., Mann, C., & Otsuki, T. (2003). Trade facilitation and economic development: A new approach to quantifying the impact. *World Bank Economic Review, 17*, 367–389.

World Bank (1988). *Parastatals in Tanzania: Towards a reform program.* Report No. TA 7100-TA. Country VI Department, Africa region.

World Bank (1990). *Project performance audit report: Morogoro Industrial Complex Project report.* Report No. 8836. Morogoro industrial Complex Project (Loans 1386/1385T-TA).

World Bank (2006). *Project performance audit report – Morogoro Industrial Complex Project.* Report No. 8836. Operations Evaluation Department, World Bank.

World Bank (2008). *Implementation completion and results report (IDA-33000 IDA-3300A).* Public Sector Reform Project. Public Sector Reform and Capacity Building (AFTPR); Eastern Africa Country Cluster 1; Africa Region.

World Bank (2011). *Power tariffs – Caught between cost recovery and affordability.* The World Bank Africa Region Sustainable Development Unit.

World Bank (2013). *Tanzania economic update: Opening the gates – how the port of Dar es Salaam can transform Tanzania* (3rd ed.). The World Bank Poverty Reduction and Economic Management Unit Africa Region; Issue 3. http://www.worldbank.org/tanzania/economicupdate

Yap, W., & Lam, J. (2006). Competition dynamics between container ports in East Asia. *Transportation Research Part A: Policy and Practice*, 40(1), 35–51.

6 Reflections and recommendations

Corporate governance remains one of the significant determinants of an enterprise's long-term success and sustainability. This view is premised on the fact that good corporate governance practices dictate and influence an enterprise's culture and values, and in the process provide a solid platform for ethical conduct at all governance levels in the enterprise. Good corporate governance is evidenced by conduct that applies certain core principles in an enterprise. These include the principles of accountability, responsibility, transparency and respect for the interest of all stakeholders. Almost certainly, an enterprise that applies these core principles in its day-to-day operations has a good chance of outperforming competitors and attracting investors.

Value creation, which is the basis of economic activities undertaken by corporate bodies, is in the long-term interest of all stakeholders and is largely dependent on a high degree of ethical conduct, which includes compliance to principles of good governance, not only in letter but also in spirit. Corporate governance thus goes beyond seeing that the business is run in a proper manner (Tricker, 2015), and has been observed, activated, and fortified around the world, in numerous forms, such as the revered corporate governance scorecard (Saldana, 2000). The embracement of good governance has been further facilitated, for example, by the leverage of CSR initiatives, if sprouted in such values as ethical and caring relationships. Much as such values take time to mature, they are not hard to grow at all. If anything, values can also be learned (Williams, 1995, cited in Holbeche, 2006, p. 175). Moreover, organizational ethical behaviour can be attained through, among others, planning of ethics, building an understanding and embracement of ethical behaviours.

Good corporate governance is about ethical conduct in business, which again traverses beyond the realm of law (Bhasin, 2005). In effect, it has evolved to become principle based, rather than being based solely on rules and regulations (OECD, 2004). In other words, corporate governance structured as a set of guidelines for strategic conduct of organizational members is more proactive and applicable rather than reactive, i.e. rather than a set of laws, rules and policies to prevent deviant behaviours. Indeed, corporate governance is a way of life and not a set of rules (Bhasin, 2005), and this permeates the social strata, as evidenced in ethical behaviours. Studies have observed that laws are not effective in making organizations behave ethically and sustainably. Some thus recommend that non-legal factors have more determinant power of organizational conduct (Di Lorenzo, 2007, p. 276). We therefore view corporate governance as a framework for sustainable growth at all levels of the organization.

Codes of conduct functioning as boundaries within organizations inform ethics of justice and nurture desired behaviours. These codes of conduct are proactively reflected to stakeholders to help prevent or confront emerging ethical dilemmas that may undermine an organization's corporate governance. There should not be a gap in business ethics performance, i.e. the organization should proactively be a step ahead of the expected norms, beliefs and values in the society, to minimize the potential of unethical behaviours developing (Svensson & Wood, 2004) and becoming entrenched.

Transparency, as a key component of good governance (Bhasin, 2005), should not be law or rule based but rather endeavour to harmonize the interests of stakeholders in public service delivery. State-owned enterprises' (SOEs) performance indicators, as well as ethical standards, are integrated into the governance scorecard whether stated or not. Likewise, ethics indicators are communicated throughout the organization via members at all levels and are in effect via deliberate policy measures. Movement towards an ethical organization that is meaningful and real can be achieved when leaders bring to the fore such measures (Rushton, 2002). SOE leaders are expected not only to appear to make choices that support the organization's values regardless of the associated difficulty (Thomas, Schermerhorn, & Dienhart, 2004), but also to make sure that everyone is aware of the significance at all levels of SOE operations. Leaders are the change agents who leverage ethical standards to reinforce the organization's corporate governance at all times. This is what is premised by the efforts led by the late President of Tanzania, Mwalimu Nyerere, at the outset.

The discussions that ensued in the previous chapters provided a platform to reflect on the continuum; from the evolution of SOEs in Tanzania, through milestones within the four administrations, all the way through to the current environment. From the perspective of governance and ethics, it deduced along the way the massive waste incurred or inflicted by otherwise would-be public service providers. As such, the happenings were not isolated historical incidents over the long haul but rather deliberate policy-based and socially tolerated and sometimes enabled circumstances. The resultant effects, therefore, should not be surprising. Many enablers in the form of abdicating responsibility, enforcement failures, compromisers and advantage takers made the situation worse. The enablers can be seen in the name of leaders, executives, gatekeepers, employees and even consumers.

Chronological perspective

It was under the First-Phase government, President Nyerere's era (1961–85), that SOEs were initiated, and by the time he stepped down from the presidency, he had laid the foundation to enable a systematic break from past policies. With such a foundation, he thought Tanzania had laid a strong ethical base upon which good governance would be built. Without a doubt, Nyerere, "the Father of the Nation," was able to build a national consensus on ethical leadership and oversee its adoption across varied institutional set-ups across the country.

To better understand Nyerere's premises, we may need to begin by asking a couple of questions to get some clarity. For starters, what may have prompted or influenced Mwalimu Nyerere to make the decision to nationalize – the inflexion point of SOEs in Tanzania – beyond ideological leaning? Nyerere's term was characterized by policies that promoted the nationalization of private entities in major sectors of the economy, the formation of new parastatals and an import-substitution industrialization strategy. It should be remembered as well that it was during Nyerere's era following privatization and the emergence of SOEs (following the adoption of the Arusha Declaration) that there emerged the first group of indigenous parastatal executives.

It has been reported that prior to the nationalizations, President Nyerere had undertaken an extensive tour of Tanzania, which assisted him in drawing attention to the widening gap in the standards of living of rural and urban producers (Che-Mponda, 1986). He was, as a result, concerned with political profiteering and was made aware of the rise of new elite groups across the country. He thus decided that it was time to address the issue head on (Dias, 1970). It was around the same time that Nyerere's frame of thought highlighted the importance of ethics and accountability via the Arusha Declaration. By the time he left office, he was sure the measures could have been done better.

President Ali Hassan Mwinyi, Tanzania's second president (1986–1995), began with not only a clear political consensus but also a mandate to begin and implement economic reforms. As such, his presidency represented a fundamental turnaround. His leadership not only ushered in a new free market era but also the embracement of structural and institutional reforms, aimed specifically at reversing the poor economic performance that Tanzania registered over a number of years. As far as SOEs are concerned, this was the period that the privatization process was initiated as part of the institutional and structural reforms packaged and overseen by the Bretton Woods institutions. Ironically, in terms of ethics, it was through these reforms that the leadership code espoused under the Arusha Declaration of 1967 were watered down or abandoned with the adoption of the Zanzibar Resolution of 1991. Indeed, it was during this period that the Parastatal Sector Reform Programme (PSRP) and Privatisation Master Plan were first rolled out.

President Mkapa, the third president (1995–2005), took charge of the reform process from his predecessor, and implemented the privatization process and public sector institutional reform. It was then that a milestone in the governance arena was set. The last nail in the coffin of the leadership code espoused under the Arusha Declaration was put in during this administration, which was marked with massive economic and institutional reforms. One would have thought that if anything, the reform era should have placed emphasis on and incorporated governance reforms as well. Paradoxical as it was, this era is credited with the economic turnaround that Tanzania experienced.

As Shivji (2011) noted, the Arusha Declaration was for all intents and purposes (without saying so) being abandoned with the disposal of the previously revered 'leadership code.'

> The public sector executives of yesteryears became the frontliners to clamor for privatization of the parastatals for they were a burden to the 'poor' Tanzanian taxpayer, they lamented. And, of course, they should be privatized to wazawa, that is, indigenous Tanzanians. Parochial ideologies against which Nyerere had stood steadfast in his attempt to build a nation were making a comeback. Nonetheless, Mwinyi moved with caution, partly because he still worked under the shadow of Mwalimu, and partly because he was still an old guard nationalist. His successor, President Benjamin Mkapa, had no such qualms or constraints leading the neo-liberal counter-revolution that saw the final burial of all vestiges of the Arusha Declaration along with its policy of socialism and self-reliance. Mkapa opened the doors to steroid-liberalisation of the economy, to the pillage of natural resources and to the uninhibited entry of speculative capital. State positions became a means of private accumulation and wealth. Overnight Tanzanian politicians became filthy rich as class polarization deepened. Nyerere watched the beginnings of this development from political sidelines. His last ditch effort to save the state-owned National Bank of Commerce from being decimated and privatized failed miserably.
>
> (Shivji, 2011, p. 9)

It was under President Mkapa's leadership that the legal framework which largely defined Tanzania's governance parameter for the future was first put in motion. Several new acts came into being or in some cases moves toward their review were rolled out. The acts included the 1995 Public Leadership Code of Ethics Act (amended in 2001); the 2001 Public Finance Act; the Prevention of Corruption Act (2002 and amended in 2007); the 2002 Public Service Act; the 2004 Public Procurement Act; the 2006 Anti-Money Laundering Act (amended in 2012); the 2008 Public Audit Act; and the 2010 Elections Expenses Act, to mention but a few (Andreoni, 2017). Ironically, it was the same time that the legalization of the widespread *takrima* (hospitality) practice was formalized (at the political platform level).

Since 2005, Tanzania has registered tremendous economic growth performance which nonetheless could not be matched in terms of governance indicators against which it performed poorly by far, especially in the control of corruption and government effectiveness indicators (Andreoni, 2017). In addition to that, on one hand the rule of law also showed that Tanzania was on a downward trend, while on the other hand regulatory quality seemed to have recovered after initially performing below par.

On the footsteps of his predecessor, the President Jakaya Kikwete phase (2005–2015) started out by addressing issues around ethics and good governance head on and placing them high on its political agenda. When defining the vision and policy of his administration during the opening of the new Parliament on December 30,

2005, President Kikwete underlined two overarching issues. First was the need to increase government revenues with renewed vigour and new zeal, and second was to ensure financial discipline of the highest order possible concerning the use of government resources. He underscored the fact that to deliver successfully on promises made hinged on sound public resources management, which he considered critical for the promotion of socio-economic development. It was reckoned that discipline of the highest order in the management of national resources was deemed necessary. During the address, President Kikwete also highlighted the significance of integrity to public officials. It came as no surprise, therefore, that during his tenure Tanzania embraced the Open Government Partnership (OGP) initiative with the intent to open government business to the masses as a way to improve not only public service delivery, but also government responsiveness, accountability and the building of public trust. It is rather unfortunate that in 2017 Tanzania withdrew its membership from the partnership.

Furthermore, President Kikwete signed integrity pledges[1] for public and private sectors in an effort to combat corruption and cultivate an ethical culture amongst public officials. The pledges were to ensure that the state was free from corruption and to communicate a stern warning to those involved in corrupt practices. All government departments' executives, other public officials and those from the private sector were expected to sign the integrity pledges to signify commitment in efforts to fight corruption in the country. The pledges aimed to improve ethics, transparency and integrity amongst public and private sectors across the economy, as corruption was a serious challenge facing the country despite several earlier initiatives to curb it. He said, "It is a vital measure to ensure Tanzania is free from corruption, this is to show we are serious in curbing corruption in the country and at the same time have zero corruption from grassroots to national level" (CEO Roundtable, 2015). He specifically called upon and urged the private sector to become involved in the fight against corruption. The private sectors' participation, he stressed, would help the nation address the challenge and would acknowledge that corrupt practices do not only take place, are tolerated or flourish in the public sector alone.

In effect, the integrity pledge was part of the government's dozen Big Results Now (BRN) anti-corruption drive objectives. The drive encompassed such approaches as raising awareness, shaming corrupt elements and inculcating the anti-corruption objective in education curricula across the education system.

In 2011, the Government of Tanzania took a step to adopt the Malaysian institutional innovation of the Big Fast Results (BFR) under Performance Management Delivery Unit (PEMANDU). After a series of high-level visits to Malaysia and cabinet discussions, the PEMANDU/BFR approach was approved for adoption in Tanzania. The cabinet resolved that a strong and effective monitoring and evaluation system on implementation of development priorities was the best for Tanzania, hence the Big Result Now (BRN). The system identified six national key result areas (NKRAs) to begin with: agriculture, energy, education, transport, water and resource mobilization.

By the trend of how things were going governance-wise, the beginning of the President Joseph Magufuli's phase signalled nothing short of a game changer. The characteristic and definitive feature of the first two years has been, at face value, the unflinching determination to pursue ethics, integrity and accountability at all levels of leadership including public corporations, thereby in the process disrupting the status quo. Many have compared the administration to that of the founding father, Julius Nyerere, with an additional kick.

From the outset, President Magufuli did not subscribe to business as usual, but rather ushered in dramatic changes through swift action. His hands-on, snap decision-making approach via directives resulted instantly in mixed results and what may appear to be adherence to basics in public corporation governance. For example, in a snap visit to the economic gateway, the Tanzania Ports Authority (TPA), he caused waves by demanding the authority to bring up its performance for the better. Similar approaches have been applied on the Tanzania Revenue Authority (TRA) with the launch of revenue collection enhancement drive and plugging in revenue collection loopholes. Likewise, an audit of the public service payroll ensued and led to the purge of over 19,000 'ghost workers' as well as servants with questionable academic qualifications.[2] It quickly became apparent that the president was in earnest waging war on not only corruption and corrupt tendencies but also irresponsibility in the Tanzanian state and public corporation machinery.

President Magufuli's invoking demand on multinational companies operating in Tanzania to play fair is merited, but to a certain extent has made investors nervous and at times caused second thoughts to prospects of investing in Tanzania. Companies envisaging Tanzania as a potential destination for mineral prospecting and off-shore gas fields, for example, may consider approaching the table differently. In one case, in a highly publicized debacle with a multinational mining company, it become apparent that the era of easy deals was gone. On the other hand, the experience may lead to doubting the word of a government that in effect tore up existing mutually binding contracts! Repeatedly, the new approach seems to have virtually placed the president at the centre of contract negotiations and management, an area that reveals obvious governance shortfalls on the part of public entities.

President Magufuli has concertedly sought to root out corruption and ineptitude while aiming at improving governance and performance. His reformist approach is premised primarily on the need to make the public entities more efficient, upright, transparent and accountable. These indispensable principles are commendable and are likely to permeate through policy-making, institutional reforms and broader decision-making across the public sector. Some results have already been registered in the uncovering of grand corruption in some state corporate bodies and the infusion of greater accountability as far as spending and performance are concerned.

It is evident that from the Mwalimu days, Tanzania has been craving and striving for improvements in governance at all levels and all aspects of life and economy. The envisaged goal of attaining middle-income status by 2025 characterized by a more diversified and productive economy hinges on good governance. Regrettably, governance shortfalls via the pervasiveness of corruption and ineffective anti-corruption strategies have negatively impacted the operating business environment as well as all sectors of the economy. Since poor governance affects the public and the private sector almost equally, efforts should not demarcate the two sectors but rather have in-built mechanisms that will enshrine good governance principles into the way of life of all policy and decision makers in the country.

Contextual reflections

When one reflects on the long journey taken by Tanzania's SOEs on governance (ethics, integrity and accountability inclusive), it is important to take a glance at different related attributes. The CAG's and other publicly available reports, from which the authors gathered most of the information for this work, have formed the basis of the accounts of resource waste from a governance perspective. These encompass a broad range, from claims of shortfalls in regulator monitoring, non-optimal revenue generation, quality and efficiency of service delivery to non-optimal resource use or channelling of the same toward development endeavours. Likewise, issues such as ownership, gatekeepers' performance, regulators and governance mechanisms, nature of investment, etc. require specific attention to be able to bring to the fore Tanzania's context.

Privatization

Tanzania's privatization experience and examination of post-privatization performance renders a verdict that calls for a critical eye. The review by Temu and Due (2000) reveals post-privatization productivity gains and increases in government revenues respectively. In hindsight, however, it can easily be understood why privatization may work (in a limited way), but it is no panacea. As such, it is important not to raise unrealistic expectations with regard to privatization measures. The policy choice for Tanzania has been between maximizing economic efficiency and maximizing revenue via divestiture. In effect, some have taken the view that efficiency maximization is far better that maximizing revenue (Megginson, 2005).

In our view, the best guiding principle for policymakers should have been adopting and sequencing reform efforts such that they garner and maximize support for further reforms, building on recorded success. Controversial privatization efforts, especially in respect of core entities, should have been undertaken after the less controversial privatizations had been considered first and allowed for their respective success to settle in. Indeed, privatizing well is always better than privatizing fast (Megginson, 2005).

That said, there are several critical questions that arise regarding privatization and governance in the Tanzanian context. Were there undertakings that should not have been privatized primarily because the cost-benefit analysis did not work in their favour? The response could be either yes or no. Privatization could result in both quantifiable economic benefits alongside less quantifiable non-economic costs.

Accountable ownership

One of the major governance concerns in Tanzania's context revolves around how best to promote responsible ownership. Generally, this is best related to the agency problem. As La Porta et al. (2000) have alluded to, the agency problem in developing countries has had mostly to do with majority-minority shareholders issues, more than the typical owners-managers challenge. Whether the managers are given enough flexibility to do what is best for the owner (the public), the issue as far as public entities are concerned has been the appearance of the 'not-belonging-to-anybody' syndrome when it comes to ownership (kind of a tragedy of the commons). Surprisingly, for example, following the nationalization and merger of five private milling companies after the Arusha Declaration, the late Sir Andy Chande, then the owner of the largest private milling company in Tanzania, was made the head of the newly created National Milling Corporation (Andreoni, 2017). It is yet to be ascertained as to what Nyerere was driving at with such a move, although it is probable that it was very much helped by Sir Chande's deep sense of nationalism. Yes, the former owner became the agent and remained accountable in both cases; once as an owner and later as an agent. The same could not be said in the ensuing periods and of the different personalities that managed the SOE. In effect, public entities have gone for years without an iota of accountability, integrity or responsibility, despite the existence of acts and requirements to adhere to good governance regulations.

The question that lingers on is, what is it that would make owners responsible and accountable? This applies to both the owners' representatives (the board) and their agents, the management executives. In my opinion, for a long time the boards have but abdicated their fiduciary duties by being conflicted, unaccountable and way beyond irresponsible. Through the years, CAG reports have repeatedly revealed that time and again the boards are guilty of non-adherence to statutory requirements, failure to abide by their own decisions, including failing to set and meet goals, and behaving as everything except responsible managers. It is true that sometimes there is a perception of helplessness at SOE board levels because of direct interference from the shareowner or even political interference from higher-ups, which ends up distorting accountability by empowering the management executives with powers reserved for boards. It may also be regarded as a misunderstanding of who is who, who is to do what and what powers they have, e.g. the appointing authority and reporting process. Most often, the concern therefore is about whether the boards and managements of SOEs looked out for the interests of the shareholders and the public, as much as those of the private sector do to shareholders of their (private) enterprises.

The nature of investments

It is also true that the nature of investments remains a major issue and source of concern around the development impact of corporate governance. The quest to attract foreign direct investments (FDI) at times renders the recipient vulnerable and thus ends up making compromises out of desperation. This lowers the governance threshold. It is notable that data indicate that Tanzania has concentrated FDIs in construction and the extractive sector, where they are attracted by high-level rents (Andreoni, 2017). As such, in the absence of optimal negotiation skills, FDI attraction correlates with desperation on one hand and inability to offer counter-arguments on the other. In the absence of such skills, the threshold is diluted and a precedent set. Since then, such situations in the guise of attracting FDIs became tolerable and acceptable. Greenfield ventures are especially prone to attracting 'middle men' to link the local authorities and potential investors. This is especially so in the absence of regulatory guidelines. At times, the 'facilitators' are extremely proactive in identifying such projects compared to brownfields or mergers and acquisitions. Over and over, unfortunately, the politically leaning job creation argument has been invoked to trump all other arguments.

Within the realm of governance has risen several issues associated with the provision of incentives to attract investments. Tax holidays, regulatory concessions and other tie-ins have been neither technically nor quantifiably justified for both external and internal investors benefitting from such offerings. There are schools of thought that argue that the incentives should be viewed as costs that not only devalue the benefit of new investments, but also undermine the possibilities of providing for alternative social programmes. In other words, the incentives eat away funds that could be allocated to further the provision of public goods such as social and educational programmes. Such circumstances bring about the perception of the necessity of entities striving to influence government decisions.

Gatekeepers for SOEs

Gatekeepers represent an important feature in good governance. They embody individuals, institutions or agencies interposed between playing a watchdog role to minimize agency costs and of executing an oversight function to ensure good performance. In the absence of prudent gate-keeping or where the gatekeepers fail to perform their roles effectively, it is unreasonable to expect SOE managers to behave in a manner consistent with public interests, in lieu of self-interest. Falling under the gatekeeper category are the National Audit Office (NAOT) headed by the Controller and Auditor General (CAG) and the regulators, collectively referred to as independent regulatory agencies (IRAs). NAOT's vision and mission encompassed in provision of efficient services, enhanced accountability and value for money in the use of public resources cannot be reflected better than in the gate-keeping function. NAOT is basically responsible for the oversight of the financial health of public entities comprising of SOEs, government departments, as well as autonomous bodies and authorities.

The Public Audit Act, No. 11 of 2008, outlines constitutional mandates of the office of the CAG. For all intents and purposes, the objective has always been for the CAG to be the eyes and voice of the people. The CAG could have truly been the people's voice, standing up to expose inefficiency, ineptitude and corruption.

It is unfortunate that this is not the case, going by the historical outcomes of CAG's reports.

The CAG's mandate appears sweeping, but its audit findings and recommendations are in most cases not given due credence on a timely basis. At times it appears to be ignored, neglected or used at convenience. Stonewalling, delays and non-responsiveness are the order of the day. Every year, the CAG finds shortcomings, faults, deficiencies and inadequacies and in each of these cases renders professional recommendations for bright spots. We are not sure if new wide-ranging powers for the CAG would be needed, but the importance of the office in promoting and enhancing good governance remains indisputable.

In addition, important for good governance is the Public Procurement Regulatory Authority (PPRA) and the related Public Procurement Appeals Authority. As per the Public Procurement Act (2011), the two were put in place to oversee the "application of fair, competitive, transparent, and non-discriminatory and value for money procurement standards and practices." (PPRA, 2011, p. 21). It is not without flaws, but since its inception and subsequent amendments, the Public Procurement Act (and regulations) has caused improvements in procurement processes and significantly enhanced good governance practices in our SOEs.

Independent regulatory agencies

IRAs represent the other group of gatekeepers that give cause to a major governance question, i.e. as far as their respective mandates are concerned, are they delivering what they are supposed to deliver? The official underlying principle for the IRAs has been multi-pronged, viz. the need to enhance policy credibility through independence from political decision-making and boost decision-making efficiency built by expertise (Majone, 1996, 2001).

The regulatory system strives at supervising and coordinating economic activities in a free market economy environment (market distortions and all). It provides the oversight function by assisting to correct market failures and protecting consumers. To that effect, the Tanzania government via individual acts or the Executive Agencies Act has established several independent regulatory authorities, and each comes into play under separate legislation. The IRAs include the Tanzania Food and Drugs Authority (TFDA), Government Chemist Regulatory Authority (GCRA), Energy and Water Utilities Regulatory Authority (EWURA), Surface and Marine Transport Regulatory Authority (SUMATRA), Occupational Safety and Health Authority (OSHA), Tanzania Communications Regulatory Authority (TCRA), Weights and Measures Agency (WMA) and the Energy and Water Utilities Regulatory Authority (EWURA), to mention but a few.

At the same time, the Executive Agencies Act (No. 30 of 1997) came into being to make provisions to facilitate the establishment and operation of semi-autonomous agencies within the ambit of government ministries for the purpose of providing public services in selected areas in a more efficient and effective manner. The stated objectives include improving the delivery of public services; creating an environment conducive to efficient and effective management; improving the quality of the services hitherto provided by the department concerned; and promoting the potential for the continuous improvement of the services provided.

The success of an executive agency in Tanzania is a function of both its core business and its major client base. In an environment characterized by sporadic monitoring limited to a large extent to two bi-annual reports, many have been left to develop their own operational targets (Caulfield, 2012) which are more for convenience than optimal, cost-effective public service delivery. Much as progress has been made by the executive agencies toward result-oriented management system, the goals cannot be met in isolation. There must be room for appropriate performance measures, accountability systems and systemic reforms (when appropriate), for cost-effective public service delivery.

Similarly, there are multiple roles with potential conflicting objectives that the government plays in SOEs – as regulator, owner, adjudicator and executive. The multiplicity and ambiguity of roles unfortunately has helped the government in using SOEs as agents of political interest rather than public policy. As revealed previously, the provision of grants and bail-outs to poorly performing SOEs, at the cost to the public, have often provided the government misplaced reasons for continued unjustifiable controls (Reddy, 2001). It can be argued that the inefficiencies evidenced in the sustained cases of waste elucidated in the previous chapters may be used as proof that government involvement did not help matters much, as the bleeding of the SOEs was obvious and persistent. Understanding SOEs' governance mechanisms and striving to build systems devoid of conflicting objectives and political interference, amongst other things, remains necessary for the gate-keeping function (World Bank, 2006). It can be further argued that extensive government intervention (coupled with excessive regulations) in the functioning of SOE boards tend to impair their ability to make commercially sound decisions. The Tanzanian narrative reveals that corporate governance challenges in SOEs have a structural dimension.

Governance mechanisms in SOEs

Good corporate governance standards include the existence of processes and structures that define the division of power and clearly establish the mechanisms for ensuring accountability between the Board of Directors, management and shareholders. It is therefore correct to take the view that achievement of accountability, as one of the core principles, is one of the major reasons why corporate governance standards are promoted globally.

In general terms, board accountability is about taking responsibility for all of a company's activities and presenting a fair, balanced and understandable assessment of an organization's position and prospects to all stakeholders. It is generally understood that the first step towards effective accountability is the establishment of clear decision-making and communication channels. However, board effectiveness is constrained by a number of reporting and approval requirements specified by law. These include, for example, reporting directly to the parent ministry for establishment and remuneration matters; obtaining budget and investment approvals from the Treasury; and reporting to and justifying their accounts to the Parliamentary Public Accounts Committee, the Treasury and the CAG.

In the majority of Tanzanian SOEs, boards have very limited or no authority in the appointment of the Chief Executive Officer and at times even of other top managerial positions. In a number of large SOEs, the President appoints the Board Chairperson as well as the CEO. In others, the Board Chairperson is appointed by the President, while other board members and the CEO are appointed by the line Minister with responsibility over the SOE. This practice, which has been ongoing since the nationalization period of 1967, significantly weakens the authority of boards in their exercise of oversight over the SOEs. These practices are contrary to generally accepted standards of good corporate governance which have established that the Board must have responsibility over the appointment of the CEO to ensure effective accountability at two levels: first, of the CEO to the Board; and second, of the Board itself to the shareowners.

When it comes to the remuneration of the SOE management, i.e. functional directors and the Managing Director (MD)/CEO, a lot remains to be resolved. The appreciation of the management team performance by way of delivery of short-term and long-term goals have fallen short. While during the early days of SOE (the Ujamaa years) salaries and benefits were fixed according to the guidelines issued by the now-defunct Standing Committee on Parastatal Organisations (SCOPO), remuneration packages for executives of public corporation bodies in recent years led to one of the corporate governance challenges, namely, relatively excessive executive compensation. The justifications for the out-of-proportion remuneration have been diverse. They ranged from the argument that institutions strive to get on board the best managerial talents in the market, to striving to match the competition, i.e. private sector levels. In absence of a market mechanism, such ad hoc remuneration system at higher levels hampers efforts to pull up the rest, who generally face an ill-remunerated system which in turn might affect performance in the long run.

The responsibilities of the Board of Directors or advisory board (as stipulated under the Executive Agency Act), mostly relate to functional activities pertaining to operations, finances and general management. As evidenced by the numerous cases presented earlier, the mostly managerial functions for the boards provide for little control over governance and strategic aspects, hence the witnessed resource waste. In some cases, this matches the arguments presented by Varma (1997) that SOE boards do not play a meaningful role in strategic decisions. All such decisions are instead handed down by the owner (i.e. the government) through the sector ministry or through directives from the finance ministry.

SOEs poor performance

Governance shortfalls, as discussed in the preceding chapters, go hand in hand with registered performance and consequently resource waste. A look into the causes of poor SOE performance provides a revealing insight. The fact that it is the government as an owner that decreed the SOEs operate at a profit, on a commercial and efficient basis, whilst at the same time provide goods and services sometimes at prices below cost, create jobs, provide markets to SOEs along the value chain, etc., raises questions. The dual-natured objective, i.e. social and commercial, created a platform for political interference in operations which in turn proved detrimental to governance – managerial autonomy, performance and efficiency. Such a syndrome manifested itself in the previously discussed poor investment decision-making, inadequate capitalization and poor reporting system, to mention but a few.

Often, the government either directly or indirectly failed to monitor SOE performance. Similarly, it also failed to act timely on pertinent information pertaining to the respective SOE. As SOE losses accumulated and mounted over time, so did subsidies and direct budget transfers to institutions that were meant to generate a profit. The alarming financial situation of the SOEs was not a one-time event; it was rather an accumulation of unattended issues over time (Nellis, 2005).

What ensued concerning the public entities was a teachable moment, as Tanzania aspires to move toward the middle-income economy status. Having mulled over what it is that Tanzanians of good faith want from a corporate governance perspective, it will not be an over-exaggeration to say that it is has reached a point where they desire, among other things, a reason to believe and have total trust in corporate leaders; to be involved in the creation of a new institutional setting capable of meeting expectations and aspirations; leaders to step up to higher accountability; leaders ready to rebuild trust and directly face the challenges on hand; and leaders ready to pay attention to good governance and to do away with archaic ideas or benefit from the present delicate and fluid accountability structures.

It is not an overstatement, therefore, to say that today we face a dearth of leaders who are ready to be ethically accountable. The kind of leaders we yearn for are the ones ready to go beyond rhetoric to not only embrace but also believe in aspired ethical values into day-to-day modus operandi.

Decades of a leadership guided by greed and self-interest (in place of responsible public interest) have resulted in the massive losses in resources. These have been encountered at a cost, borne by the entire population. It is time that Tanzanians as a people probe their thinking, understand the essence of the public entities and deduce more meaning from ethical perspectives. It is not a misplaced effort to require each and every public entity to develop its own institutional code of ethics (beyond the client service charter), guided by the national code of ethics, so that behavioural expectations are made aware to all stakeholders – employees, clients and the general public.

We should accept as a fact that when it happened, the Zanzibar Resolution not only diluted the leadership code but also changed the institutional landscape in public service delivery and the leaders' overall attitudes. Whether because it was hurriedly concocted, ill-prepared, forced upon or made to impress someone or for any other reason, it marked a turning point in corporate ethics in Tanzania. Is it too late or unjustifiable to review? No. Placing the desired qualities of the leaders required in public service delivery is exactly what is of essence, first and foremost.

Conclusion

What characterized Tanzania's SOEs public service delivery for a long time was a flawed system. Flawed systems are by nature intricate and hard to cure. As we have noted throughout the discussion of the complex situations reflected in the Tanzanian context, flawed systems evolve over extended periods (years, or even decades). People in positions of power make policy and other decisions that create favourable conditions for the emergence of undesirable outcomes, i.e. when leaders' actions (including reactions, interactions and inaction), choices and leadership decisions work to create conditions that incubate governance and/or ethical failure. It is such conditions that guide the behaviour of those operating within the system, in other words, one must simply do what the system dictates.

Furthermore, in settings such as large sector or industry-wide complex systems, it is not a single leader acting alone or a collection of leaders' covert collaborations that leads to the flawed system. In effect, it is the combination of many decisions made by multiple independent leaders and informed by governance systems, including ethics guidelines.

Indeed, it is possible to shape systems and build institutions that produce outcomes that embrace appropriate governance principles and approaches. Without a doubt, there are no quick fixes or one-size-fits-all approaches, and the requisite essential effort is substantial.

As a starting point, it must be recognized that compliance, rules, regulations, guidelines (i.e. *miongozo* and *semina elekezi*) and other formal artifacts of corporate governance are necessary but not sufficient. To make it worse, their imposition can and may have perverse impacts and influence the outcomes that were designed to be avoided. There are numerous reasons behind the situation, but perhaps more than anything the formal mechanisms operate on the premise that we are rational humans who engage in deep deliberative thinking before engaging in wrongdoing.

If anything, it is crucial that environments that embrace transparency are created across organizations and across sectors. By so doing, those who highlight wrongdoing and wasting of resources would be treasured instead of being shunned, seen as abnormal or chastised. Formal systems of compliance, no matter how robust, are generally agreed to have their shortcomings. The best way to compensate for these shortcomings is to enhance an organization's human capital systems. A central component of any organization's human capital system is human capital voice. The human capital should be equipped with not only the requisite skill and confidence to speak up but also the knowledge that their voicing would not be ignored but be listened to and respected, and that people would have their concerns addressed in an appropriate manner.

Building systems that produce ethical outcomes most of all deem necessary strong and committed leadership. Democratic or otherwise, it is those who hold positions of power within a system that in the final analysis influence how the system operates.

Characteristically, it is leaders who fall short in terms of integrity, humility of purpose and courage and who are more likely to preside over a flawed system. Integrity ensures that a leader will display a deep commitment to their organization's purpose and values, in both deeds and words. Humility of purpose remains the mirror on which a leader will view and acknowledge respective fallibility and use the perspective to empower others and to hold them accountable when they fall short. Yes, some will, as expected, fall. Courage on the other hand ensures that a leader will have to make difficult decisions as he/she opts to hold dear and put respective organization's principles on the forefront, ahead of both profit and personal privilege.

Of the many invaluable lessons associated with the experiences shared across the discussions in the foregoing chapters, we have tried to explain failures in governance as far from being straightforward. Much as we understand the desire for simple explanations and justifications, we did not want ours to be a search for scapegoats. Rather, the approach was deliberate in nature, intended to be informed by an intuitive appeal that acknowledges that governance shortfalls (including ethical failures) are nurtured within the flawed systems.

Cases in point: the reform of TANESCO from a governance perspective (as shown in the case) stalled because of deep-seated interests as revealed in the choice of inefficient yet costly solutions, coupled with poor policy choices. If anything, reforms in TANESCO's governance quagmire call for an approach toward a viable solution across the economy. Likewise, at the economic gateway, the TPA, inefficiencies that culminate to resource waste, losses and massive opportunity cost are a revelation of governance shortfalls that do not facilitate enhancing revenues from trade flows. Failure to address technical skills shortfalls that would enable to tap onto the potential that abounds in the leather sectors is a serious governance shortfall that magnified across the leather sector is a constraint in the envisaged industrialization endeavour.

Regulators sleeping at the wheel represented in TCRA's ineptitude revealed what is lacking in the gatekeeper's governance role. A complete and transparent regulatory system is a *sine qua non* in the telecom regulatory environment, with the requisite powers, staffing requirements and funding sources. In absence of such a regulatory regime, anticipated efficiency gains across the sector may not be attained. The nature of the telecom industry demands in independent regulatory regime to facilitate a competitive and level playing field.

Along the same lines, politics of national sentiments should not be allowed to interfere in governance reform at ATCL. Indeed, governments across the world historically established national airlines for no reason other than prestige. Very few have been profitable, and many depend on substantial government subsidies to continue. From a governance perspective, the ATCL case is irreversible. No Band-Aid solution from a governance perspective would work. If anything, starting afresh with a clean slate is possibly the most viable proposition.

Many established approaches to leadership and governance in Tanzania are not well suited to the uncertain, ambiguous and sometimes changing contexts. Contexts that organizations and society now face justify the argument that there is no one-size-fits-all approach to leadership and governance. It is possible, nonetheless, to navigate the volatile and complex terrain and benefit from outcomes valuable to all stakeholders and society in general.

The list of offered way outs and potential solutions is not exhaustive. Indeed, it takes a whole lot more to build and sustain any good governance system. Nonetheless, there are two things of which one can be sure it will take: significant effort and time.

Some, like Shivji (2011), assert that Tanzania's prospects for becoming a prosperous nation cannot be attained unless the country revives the values and principles of the Arusha Declaration and emphasizes adherence to leadership ethics and the promotion of human equality. The incorporation of some of the broad values in the perspectives elucidated in Tanzania's Development Vision 2025 is a hopeful indication of their appreciation.

Recommendations

It is only hoped that the changes embraced following the entry of the Fifth Phase government in 2015 will relegate the historical failures and challenges to the archives and usher in a new era of effective governance, better delivery and optimal contribution in line with stakeholder expectations.

So what needs to be done now and on the way forward? To respond to that question, one needs to look at governance from the perspective of different levels: public enterprise level, leadership level, industry/sectoral level, and societal level etc. We will restrict ourselves to the two levels of public enterprise and industry.

At the public enterprise level, we need to ensure that the leadership, i.e. the executive (CEO/MDs/management) and the Board of Directors, place an ethical management framework with the right encouragement features that reward right behaviour alongside ones that not only expose but also sanction inappropriate behaviour. At that level, the Board of Directors needs to have mechanisms that inspire the management (CEO and other executives) to inculcate respective institutional culture that ensures appropriate remuneration to ethos builders beyond the attainment of performance goals. Such incentives should be aimed at promoting long-term accountabilities, combining self-interest with collective interests.

At the industry level, good governance includes placing emphasis on the collective development efforts of the industry itself. Timely and appropriate research should help to identify within the industry/sector the systemic sources of unethical behaviour. With the identification, appropriate governance metrics can then be adopted to provide continuous monitoring and strive to always raise standards.

The attainment of long-term objectives can be realized by gradually doing away with the pre-occupation for short-term gains only. Raising standards would build sustainable best practices that become part and parcel of an industry's culture.

Although self-regulation has not been the norm in Tanzania, it is a viable proposition to be taken into consideration. Self-policing efforts to deter unethical behaviour would specifically shift leaders from being inactive bystanders to dynamic proponents of ethical culture. An ethical culture that needs to be built is one under which everyone comprehends the impact of such decisions on stakeholders (employees, customers, suppliers, the community, the environment). The system to be enforced must ensure that leaders are conversant with the integrity of ethical decision-making, not only to build organizational authenticity but also to ensure value creation for positive benefits to accrue across the society.

It is important to be cognizant of the fact that ethical behaviour and integrity are embedded in the organizational culture. This in turn helps to shape an employee's behaviour. Often we choose to explain organizational culture as the shared values, practices, behaviour standards and assumptions that guide how people work and interact at the workplace. In our opinion, this debatable view is among the simplest ways to internalize and experience a set of shared values.

We strongly believe that the key factors in building organizational integrity in our public may entail several measures and include the government or appointing authority taking appropriate measures, once aware of misconduct by its respective appointees and employees, to be able to freely, without fear of retaliation, bring to the fore misconduct. Likewise, it is equally important to ensure respectful treatment of employees by respective senior supervisors whilst holding all employees accountable, per laid-down regulations. All these should help build high levels of trust among co-workers. It is important to realize as well that ethical behaviour and integrity are not instituted through controls.

Efforts to advance compliance to corporate ethics need to include not only socialization of the leadership, but also support mechanisms and strategies. This also extends to measures that speak to conflict between public and private morals, as well as social obligations. Whereas the introduction of ethics officers in several countries (e.g. Uganda and local governments in the UK) is not new, having ethics officers, or something along that line, tends to focus more on investigation and compliance, rather than support mechanisms to build capacity or to develop and enhance a culture.

The design and implementation of such a code of ethics deems necessary the involvement of all stakeholders partly to earn a buy-in and partly to address their concerns. By so doing, all stakeholders would be able to identify key ethical concerns and dilemmas faced every day and possibly to suggest solutions.

Strategies should be incorporated to integrate questions of ethics in the training of public servants, political appointees and elected politicians as well as inculcating ethics in education, from elementary schools all the way to the institutions of higher learning. Obviously, ethical issues and emphasis placed on each group may vary, and training should be tailored to respective needs; there is no easy way out of the conflicts between public and private morality. Appropriate training in professional ethos (Rohr, 1998; Lewis & Gilman, 2005) is one way to challenge the institutionalization of corruption across the board in organizations, as attempts are made to create a balance between competing and contradicting moral requirements.

In the final analysis, the question of unethical choices and corrupt behaviour are often more than tangled with fair distribution of resources. As such, ethics and accountability at a crossroads are at the core of corporate governance and envelope varied issues. These range from public servants training to stakeholder education as well as the understanding of rights and obligations across the board.

Training in public service ethics would be of help to public service professionals, who deal with ethical dilemmas on a daily basis. Nonetheless, merely adhering to professional codes of conduct does not prevent corrupt tendencies from permeating different levels and sectors of society. It is important therefore to educate all stakeholders on the root of and risk associated with public morality. Citizens must recognize that their respective personal rights and obligations as political and moral actors necessitate rights to claim just, corruption-free governance (Helsten & Larbi, 2006). Therefore, civic ethics education across the board, alongside training in professional ethics, should ensure a wider diffusion across society. Once values and ethics are internalized by stakeholders, from public servants to ordinary citizens and leaders all over via civic education, it would be easier to build a base across the broader civil society.

Good governance and culture

It is important to realize that corporate governance is beyond rules and regulations, systems and processes; it is also about culture. At the crux of good governance are efforts to build a culture of integrity. This is basically about people carrying out ethics into organizations to shape organizational culture. It goes without saying, therefore, that if there is integrity at the top of the organization, it should filter down. Ethics practiced at the individual and micro level will influence corporate governance. Indeed, the tone is set at the top.

Employees that are motivated by strong moral values and ethics at the institutional level are less likely to behave unethically and opportunistically. The resultant effect would be enhanced productivity and well-being. The greatest challenge is not so much in finding what is right, but in consistently doing what is right, and buying into the principle that good ethics is good business across the board.

Challenges in governance and managing risks

Boards of Directors at SOEs have the responsibility to manage institutional risk by adding value in different ways toward the attainment of set objectives. It is the Board of Directors that has the ultimate responsibility for the organization's performance. In other words, it is fully accountable and must act in the best interests of the stakeholders. Unfortunately, often the governance structure, i.e. appointments and hence accountability, renders such a process ineffective.

The key mandated roles encompass the development and oversight of institutional strategy as well as monitoring its implementation by the management. It is not surprising that Boards of Directors do not have the power to appoint and remove senior management, especially the Chief Executive! The appointment of the Chief Executive most of the time rests with the responsible line Minister or the President. Consequently, the perception is that they are accountable to the respective appointing authority and nobody else. Much as the process may necessitate calls for the involvement of and dialogue with government, the ultimate responsibility must reside with the board; but it does not. Scuffles between the Boards of Directors and the executive have been common as a result and negatively impact decision-making and subsequently operations. It is undisputed that SOE boards have not been granted full responsibility and the authority required for providing strategic guidance and overseeing management and its accountability. Moreover, the boards view their duties encroached from higher up (central government) and from below (management executives). In some instances, government perception is that SOEs are extensions of the executive arm and hence have the right to intervene whenever and wherever, thus allowing for the circumvention of the Boards of Directors.

Along the same lines are the appointments of board members themselves. Although there have been some improvements in recent years by way of transparency, the boards of SOEs have failed to be composed in such a manner as to promote objective and independent judgement. This could be fulfilled if the appointment is undertaken based on professional merits alone, i.e. board nominations should be based on an apparent, contestable and merit-based process. In absence of such measures, nominations will fail to adhere to best practices applicable to the sector.

The appointment and removal of the corporate Chief Executive Officer should be a key role for an SOE Board of Directors. If CEOs feel that they "owe their jobs" to the executive powers in government or the ownership function, it is then virtually impossible for the SOE boards to exercise their monitoring function and assume full responsibility for corporate performance. Moreover, and surprisingly, it is evident, as revealed recently following President Magufuli's purge of public boards, that some directors are there to add value and augment performance, but they do not know where and how value is added. They consequently are not aware of what and where the institution is exposed to in terms of strategic risk. That being the case, the most significant risks faced may be the least understood by the Boards of Directors.

Until the directors understand how and where value is added, where risk exposure is critical and what policies need to be in place to manage those risks, institutional waste of resources will continue across industries and sectors. Decisions about risks at strategic levels cannot and should not be delegated. They should be taken as the foremost responsibility of each member of the Board of Directors. Such decisions are fundamentally part of the board's responsibility for formulating strategy, providing the lead that the respective institution needs to attain objectives.

Board training in corporate governance is especially important to expand the pool of persons with the right training and temperament, and thus qualified to serve on such public boards. It goes beyond the customary leaning on only strong financial as well as management skills of potential board directors, to include strong ethics and integrity culture. It is imperative that board members are knowledgeable of the attributes and their subsequent evolving role via the institution, across the economy.

Reflections and recommendations 141

It is important that public boards are inculcated with the understanding that:

a   good corporate governance should be integrated with the strategy and not viewed as simply a compliance obligation;
b   while legislation and agency rule-making are important to establish the basic tenets of corporate governance, corporate governance issues are best solved through collaboration; and
c   transparency is a critical component of good governance because a well-governed organization should ensure that it has appropriate disclosure policies and practices, at appropriate levels of transparency.

While the principles of good governance may be, in essence, the same for all corporate bodies, there is great scope for creativity and innovation in applying such principles to the specific circumstances facing individual institutions. The challenge is thus, to find the path and solutions that fit its circumstances.

The commitment of the leadership is a *sine qua non* of any sustained programme of improvement in an individual institution's governance. The institution must have a board that reflects the championing of strong internal good corporate governance. To that effect and to be fully successful, the board must be able to effectively communicate to stakeholders the unshakeable commitment to the goals of corporate governance. Board credibility is essential.

The board must inculcate rewards, comprehensive efforts and a virtuous circle of adoption of better practices, always. Experiences have demonstrated the positive contribution good governance has had to operational performance. Moreover, the use of appropriate managerial tools will enhance performance. It is a fact that even motivated executives and board directors must go through a learning curve of sorts, to identify enlightening measures and utilize them effectively. Indeed, the good corporate governance journey is never a destination.

It is important to underline that the society's expectations of public organizations, and the respective Boards of Directors, change. Events of recent years have resulted in corporate governance acquiring new dimensions and expecting more stringent measures from Boards of Directors. Growing scrutiny of directors' behaviours and concerns about business ethics, stewardship and ethical behaviour is not an accident when minimization of resource waste gains prominence. It is indeed a new day as far as Tanzania's corporate governance is concerned. There is hope for the better.

Notes

1   Kikwete signs three integrity pledges – "President Jakaya Kikwete has signed three integrity pledges for public and private sectors in an effort to combat corruption and cultivate an ethical culture amongst public officials." Retrieved from https://ceo-roundtable.co.tz/in-the-news/kikwete-signs-three-integrity-pledges/.
2   "Number of Phantom Workers Reaches 19,700." *The Citizen*, Feb 8, 2017.www.thecitizen.co.tz/News/Number-of-phantom-workers-reaches-19-700/1840340-3804574-g8rkbfz/index.html

Bibliography

Andreoni, A. (2017). *Anti-Corruption in Tanzania: A political settlements analysis*. Anti-Corruption Evidence (ACE)- Making Anti-Corruption Real. SOAS; Working paper 1.
Bank of Tanzania. (2008). *Guideline of boards of directors of banks and financial institutions in Tanzania*. Dar es Salaam & Tanzania: Government Printers.
Banks, E. (2004). *Corporate governance: Financial responsibility, controls and ethics*. London: Palgrave Macmillan.
Bhasin, M. (2005). 'Dharma' in corporate governance: Transparency the biggest challenge in Asian countries. *EBS Review, 2*(20), 99–109.
Caulfield, T. (2012). Should we call it fraud? *The Hastings Center Report 42*: 49.
CCA. (2008). Citizens' circle of accountability. *The issue of public accountability: A summary for citizens*. Retrieved January 25, 2016, from www.accountabilitycircle.org/
CEO Roundtable (2015). *Kikwete signs three integrity pledges*. Retrieved June 6, 2016, from https://ceo-roundtable.co.tz/in-the-news/kikwete-signs-three-integrity-pledges/
Che-Mponda, A. (1986). Aspects of Nyerere's economic thought – a study in the dynamics of African leaders' aspirations in directing their countries' economic growth after independence. *African Study Monographs, 6*, 45–55.
Dias, C. (1970). Tanzanian nationalizations: 1967–1970. *Cornell International Law Journal, 4*(1), Article 4. http://scholarship.law.cornell.edu/cilj/vol4/iss1/4
Di Lorenzo, V. (2007). Business ethics: Law as a determinant of business conduct. *Journal of Business Ethics, 71*(3), 275–299.
Dobel, P. J. (1990). Integrity in the public sector. *Public Administration Review, 50*(3), 354–366.
Helsten, S., & Larbi, G. (2006). Public good or private good? The paradox of public and private ethics in the context of developing countries. *Public Administration and Development, 26*, 135–145.
Holbeche, L. (2006). *Understanding change: Theory, implementation and success*. Burlington, MA: Butterworth, Heinemann.
Kassala, C. D. N. (2002, January 29). *From corruption of good governance to good governance of corruption in Tanzania*. Presented at the Debate on Corruption in Tanzania, Karimjee Grounds, Dar es Salaam.
Kato, T., & Long, C. (2006, December). CEO turnover, firm performance, and enterprise reform in China: Evidence from micro data. *Journal of Comparative Economics, 34*(4), 796–817.
Kinana, A. (2011, March 4). *Keynote address to the "Legacy of Julius Nyerere: Economies, Politics and Solidarities in Tanzania and Beyond"*. Conference; Carleton University, Canada.
Kiondo, A. (1993). *Political implications of Tanzania's economic reforms: 1982–1992*. Paper presented at a conference on the road to a market-based economy in Tanzania, Dar es Salaam.
La Porta, R., Lopez-de-Silanes, F., Shleifer, A., & Vishny, R. (2000). Investor protection and corporate governance. *Journal of Financial Economics, 58*, 3–28.
Lewis, C., & Gilman, S. (2005). *The ethics challenge in public service: A problem solving guide*. San Francisco, CA: Jossey-Bass.
Majone, G. (1996). *Regulating Europe*. London: Routledge.
Majone, G. (2001). Non-majoritarian institutions and the limits of democratic governance: A political transaction-cost approach. *Journal of Institutional and Theoretical Economics, 157*(1), 57–78.
Mazzucato, M. (2014). *The entrepreneurial state: Debunking public vs private sector myths*. London, New York & New Delhi: Anthem Press.
Mazzucato, M. (2015). *Building the entrepreneurial state: A new framework for envisioning and evaluating a mission-oriented public sector*. The Levy Economics Institute of Bard College Working Paper No. 824.

McDougle, M. (2006). *Understanding and maintaining ethical values in the public sector through an integrated approach to leadership*. San Diego, CA: University of San Diego.

Megginson, W. (2005). *The financial economics of privatization* (1st ed.). New York, NY: Oxford University Press.

Mgonja, B., & Dossa, A. (2015). Exploring the link between governance and institutions: Theoretical and empirical evidence from Tanzania. *Humanities and Social Sciences Letters, 3*(1), 37–54.

Msekwa. (2016, May 12). Ethics is the heart of leadership: Appreciating President Magufuli's refreshing stance on leadership ethics. *The Daily News*, Tanzania.

Mwapachu, J. V. (2005). *Confronting new realities: Reflections on Tanzania's radical transformation*. Dar es Salaam: E & D Ltd.

Mwapachu, J. V. (2013). *Parastatals: Architecture of corporate governance*. Tanzania: The Citizen.

Nellis, J. (2005). *The evolution of enterprise reform in Africa: From state-owned enterprises to private participation in infrastructure – and back?* Washington, DC: Center for Global Development.

PPRA (2011). Public Procurement Act No. 7 of 2011. United Republic of Tanzania. Government Printer, Dar es Salaam.

Reddy, Y. (2001). *The first principles of corporate governance in public enterprises in India: The Yaga Report*. Standing Conference on Public Enterprises and Yaga Consulting.

Rohr, J. (1998). *Public service, ethics and constitutional practice*. Lawrence: University of Kansas Press.

Rushton, K. (2002). Business ethics: A sustainable approach. *Business Ethics: A European Review, 11*(2), 137–139.

Saldana, C. (2000). *A scorecard for tracking market-preferred corporate governance reforms in East Asian corporate sectors*. Working paper, The Institute of Corporate Directors, Makati City.

Shivji, I. (2011). *Nyerere, nationalism and Pan-Africanism*. Retrieved September 18, 2015, from www.pambazuka.org/printpdf/69968

Shleifer, A., & Vishny, R. W. (1997). A survey of corporate governance. *Journal of Finance, 52*(2), 737–783.

Svensson, G., & Wood, G. (2004). Codes of ethics best practice in the Swedish public sector: A PUBSEC-scale. *International Journal of Public Sector Management, 17*(2), 178–195.

Thomas, T., Schermerhorn, J., & Dienhart, J. (2004). Strategic leadership of ethical behavior in business. *Academy of Management Executives, 18*(2), 56–66.

Tricker, R. (2015). *Corporate governance: Principles, policies, and practices* (3rd ed.). New York, NY: Oxford University Press.

Varma, J. R. (1997). Corporate governance in India: Disciplining the dominant shareholder. *Management Review, 9*(4), 5–18.

Williams, R. (1995). *The sociology of culture*. Chicago, IL: University of Chicago Press.

World Bank (2006). *Held by visible hand: The challenge of SOE corporate governance for emerging markets*. World Bank Corporate Governance. Retrieved July 17, 2017 from http://documents.worldbank.org/curated/en/396071468158997475/pdf/377110Corporate0Governance0SOEs01PUBLIC1.pdf

Index

Note: page numbers in **bold** indicate a table.

accountability 1, 7, 8; concept and theory behind 19; definition of 18; relationship to ethics in governance 19–22; *see also* ethics; public life
agricultural sector in Tanzania 45, 48, 126
Air Tanzania Corporation Limited (ATCL) 4, 66–75, **70**, **71**
Airtime (Automated) Revenue Monitoring Solution (ARMS) 80–81, 84
Arusha Declaration 1, 3–4, 6; abandonment of 26, 124, 125; economic impacts of 45–48, 50, 59, 129; era of 31; ethics and accountability 34; implementation of 48; and the Leadership Code of Ethics 32; and the national vision 34, 41, 137; and the Zanzibar Resolution 9–11; *see also* Public Leadership Code of Ethics (PLCE)

Big Fast Results (BFR) 126
Big Results Now (BRN) Initiative 116, 126
business ethics and corporate responsibility 7–8

Commission for Human Rights and Good Governance (CHRAGG) 31, 33
corporate environment in Tanzania 6–7
corporate failures in Tanzania 11–12
corporate governance in Tanzania 1–3, 8–9; and accountability 15; and the Arusha Declaration *see* Arusha Declaration; and economic management 12–13; history of 6; and Tanzania's Development Vision 2025 *see* Tanzania's Development Vision 2025; and the Zanzibar Resolution *see* Zanzibar Resolution
corporate social responsibility (CSR) 56–57, 122

corruption 11, 40, 41; confronting of 7; control of 22; deterrents to 38; and the disintegration of the social fabric 10; fight against 54; financial 26; and fraud in the public sector 53; limits on 32; as a symptom 25; *see also* National Anti-Corruption Strategy Action Plan

Dar es Salaam Maritime Gateway 115–116
Dar es Salaam gas-to-power plant 90
Dar es Salaam Port 106, 112, 114, 116

Energy and Water Regulatory Authority (EWURA) 92–93, 131
ethics 15; absence of adherence to 102; and accountability *see* accountability; and the Arusha Declaration *see* Arusha Declaration; corporate 124; ethics code 35–30; erosion of 39; definition of 16–17; of justice 123; and good governance 125, 128; guidelines 135; and human equality 137; need for 17–18; planning of 122; and privatization 40–41; public sector code of 30; Tanzania's code of 31–33; and Tanzania's future 41–42; *see also* business ethics and corporate responsibility

First Five Year Development Plan (FYDP) 46; *see also* second five-year development plan
Fifth Phase government 117, 137
First Phase government *see* Nyerere, Mwalimu Julius
foreign direct investments (FDI) 98, 129, 130

Index

governance *see* corporate governance in Tanzania

Independent Power Producers (IPPs) 88, 89, 92–93; entry into Tanzania 90–91; and TANESCO 95
Independent Power Tanzania Limited (IPTL) 88–89, 90–91, 93, 95
independent regulatory agencies (IRAs) 131–132

Kenya 48, 101, 102, 108
key performance indicators (KPIs) 107, 108, 116
Kikwete, Jakaya Mrisho 54, 77, 102, 125–126

leather industry in Tanzania *see* Morogoro Tanneries; Tanzania Leather Associated Industry (TLAI); *see also* Parastatal sector
livestock and livestock products in Tanzania 96, 98, 102–103

Magufuli, John Pombe 7, 36, 41, 85, 126–127, 140
Mkapa, Benjamin 39, 51, 124, 125
morality: and the free market 7; private 25, 138; public 26, 138, 139
Morogoro Industrial Complex Project 98
Morogoro Tanneries 91, 97, 101
Moshi Tanneries 100, 101
Mwalimu *see* Nyerere, Julius Kambarage
Mwanza Tannery 101
Mwinyi, Ali Hassan 124, 135

National Anti-Corruption Strategy Action Plan (NACSAP) 31, 33, 40–41
National Audit Office (NAOT) 130
National Development Corporation (NDC) 45–46
National Price Commission 49
Nolan principles 21, 31
Nyerere, Julius Kambarage (known as Mwalimu) 31, 34, 39, 45, 49, 53; adoption of Ujamaa 97; era of 123–125, 127, 129

Open Government Partnership (OGP) 53, 126

Parliamentary Parastatal Organisation Accounts Committee (POAC) 58
Parastatal sector, parastatals 1, 4, 10, 124; diminishing role of 12; evolution of 44–47; governance of 35–36, 39, 50–53; leather 97–98; non-performance of 40, 50, 53; oversight of 58; reforms 59–60; role in Tanzania 47–49; *see also* Parastatal Sector Reform Programme (PSRP)
Parastatal Sector Reform Programme (PSRP) 49, 69, 124
Performance Management Delivery Unit (PEMANDU) 116
port and shipping industry *see* shippers and shipping industry
Prevention and Combating of Corruption Bureau (PCCB) 30–31
Price Control Act 49–50
Public Audit Act 54, 125
Public Ethics Commission 54
Public Leadership Code of Ethics (PLCE) Act 1, 6, 21, 31, 32, 33, 54
public life, principles of 21, **22**, 31
Public Private Partnership (PPP) 81, 85, 88, 92, 110, 113; absence of risk mitigation strategies 96; lack of guidelines regarding 95; policy 93, PPP Act of 2010 **107**
Public Procurement Act 131
Public Procurement Appeals Authority 131
Public Procurement Regulatory Authority (PPRA) 81, 131
public sector governance 23–25; *see also* accountability; ethics
'public sector' institutions *see* Parastatal sector
Privatisation Master Plan 124

resource mobilization strategy (RMS) 110
Richmond Development 91–92, 95
risk mitigation strategies 96

second five-year development plan 111
shippers and shipping industry **107**, 108, 114, 115, 116
Songo Songo natural gas reserves 90–91
state-owned enterprises (SOEs) 4, 6, 23, 25, 32; case studies of 66; demise of 59; emergence of 124; gatekeepers for 130; governance 128, 131; management 129; performance of 123

Tanganyika African National Union (TANU) 9, 31, 35
Tanzania Communications Regulatory Authority (TCRA) 4, 66, 75–87, 118, 131

Tanzania's Development Vision 2025 (TDV 2025) 10–11, 34, 41, 61, 102
Tanzania Electric Supply Company (TANESCO) 4, 49, 94–95; and EWURA 92; import of generators 93–94; and IPPs 90–91; management 94; and PPP policy 93; regulatory governance 91–92; rental of emergency power plants 91–92; wastefulness of 66–67, 87–89
Tanzania Harbours Authority (THA) 49, 104
Tanzania Leather Associated Industry (TLAI) 4, 66, 96–97, 100–104; hides and skins 99–100; and the leather industry 97–99; market environment 101–102; operations management 99–101
Tanzania Leather Sector Strategy 98, 102
Tanzania Ports Authority (TPA) 104–106, 115–117; budgets 110; challenges facing **107**; failure managing risk 113–114; financial waste 114; failure managing risk 113–114, 115; lack of strategic focus 110–111; management framework shortfalls 111–113; non-attainment of key performance indicators 107–108; sub-optimal targets at 108–110, **109**; strategic plan 106–107
Tanzania Revenue Authority (TRA) 113, 127
Telecommunication Traffic Monitoring System (TTMS) 78–79, 85, 86; and ARMS 80–81, 84; Fraud Management System 82; implementation of 77, 81; and mobile money banking 83

Ujamaa era 4, 35, 37, 133; *see also* Arusha Declaration
Ujamaa villages 46–47

Villagisation Programme 47; *see also* Ujamaa villages

World Bank 18, 22, 114–115, 116; and leather parastatals 97, 98, 103

Zambia 102, 104, 114
Zanzibar Electricity Corporation (ZECO) 87
Zanzibar Resolution 4, 9–10, 34, 39, 124, 134